International Trade in the 1970s

International Trade in the 1970s

The US, the EC and the Growing Pressure of Protectionism

Giuseppe La Barca

BLOOMSBURY
LONDON • NEW DELHI • NEW YORK • SYDNEY

Bloomsbury Academic
An imprint of Bloomsbury Publishing Plc

50 Bedford Square	175 Fifth Avenue
London	New York
WC1B 3DP	NY 10010
UK	USA

www.bloomsbury.com

First published 2013

British Library Cataloguing-in-Publication Data
A catalogue record for this book is available from the British Library.

ISBN: HB: 978–1–4411–4784–4

Typeset by Fakenham Prepress Solutions, Fakenham, Norfolk NR21 8NN
Printed and bound in Great Britain

Contents

Acknowledgements vii

List of Tables viii

List of Figures x

Introduction xi

1 Background to the Upheavals and Settlement Attempts of the 1970s 1

An overview of the backdrop to EC and US difficulties in the early 1970s. 1

Trade expansion, trade interventionism and extension of corporations' activities beyond national borders 13

2 Conflict and Cooperation on Trade Issues Between the Transatlantic Partners and the Launching of a New Multilateral Round of Trade Negotiations 26

The background to the Tokyo Round negotiations 26

The undoing of the Bretton Woods regime and its impact on trade relations 34

The Road towards a new round of multilateral trade negotiations in the GATT 46

3 Crisis and Unstable Recovery (October 1973–December 1976) 59

The economic conjuncture and its impact on domestic and international policies in the United States and in the European Community 59

The initial phase of the multilateral trade negotiations 71

Bilateral agreements and disputes in the framework of GATT 84

4 The Slackening of Growth in the EC Countries and the Strengthening of Protectionism on Both Sides of the Atlantic 87

Differences and similarities in the economic trend of the transatlantic economic areas and their impact on the EC and US economic policies 87

Growth and recession in main US and EC industries and measures adopted to support them 90

A comprehensive assessment: to what extent was protectionism on the rise in the years following the first oil crisis and which forms did it take? 104

5 The Last Phase of the Uruguay Round 115
The re-launch of the multilateral negotiations under the Carter administration 116
The final stages of the negotiations 127
Results of the Tokyo Round 130

6 The end of the 1970s and the Dawn of a New Decade: the Second Oil Shock and the Aftermath of the Tokyo Round Negotiations 144
The second oil shock and its impact on the US and EC economies 144
The implementation of the Tokyo Round codes 154
Sectors calling for financial aid and protection from foreign competition 158
Overview of the development in the 1970s from the perspective of the following decade 166

Conclusions 173
Appendix 179
Notes 205
Bibliography 221
Index 229

Acknowledgements

This book is the outcome of a two-year sojourn at the University of Swansea. It could not have been written without the gracious hospitality of this university and the facilities, including the well-stocked library, made available to the writer.

The author wishes to express his gratitude to Professor Maxine Lawson of Palermo University who overviewed the linguistic aspects of this work and to Mr Antonio Di Dio who overviewed the computer files. He also likes to thank two anonymous referees for their kind comments and useful suggestions.

List of Tables

Table 1 Gross National Product, Gross Domestic Product, Exports and Imports of the United States, 1950–80 (Billions of 1972 US dollars) 179
Table 2 Trade Balance and Current Account Balance of the United States, 1950–80 (Millions of US dollars) 180
Table 3 US Exports and Imports by Broad End-Use Class, 1951–80 (Millions of US dollars) 181
Table 4 US Exports and Imports by Areas and Selected Countries of Destination and Origin, 1951–80 (Millions of US dollars) 182
Table 5 US Direct Investments in Foreign Countries by Areas, 1951–80 (Percentage Shares) 183
Table 6 Share and Growth Rate of Canada and Western Europe in US Foreign Direct Investments in Manufacturing (1951–80) 184
Table 7 Foreign Direct Investments in the United States by Main Areas and Industries, 1951–80 (Millions of US dollars) 185
Table 8 Annual Percentage Changes in Productivity and Related Data in the US, 1950–80 186
Table 9 US Federal and Total Government Receipts and Expenditures, 1950–80 (billions of US dollars) 187
Table 10 GDP Growth Rate in the EC Member States, 1960–80 (1975 prices) 188
Table 11 EC Member States Total Exports, 1960–80 (Mill. ECU) 189
Table 12 EC Member States Total Imports, 1960–80 (Mill. ECU) 189
Table 13 EC Member States Exports to the US, 1960–80 (Mill. ECU) 190
Table 14 EC Member States Imports from the US, 1960–80 (Mill. ECU) 190
Table 15 Intra-EC Imports, 1960–80 (Mill. ECU) 191
Table 16 Percentage of Intra-EC Imports over Member States Total Imports, 1960–80 191
Table 17 EC Trends in Trade by Commodity Groups: Exports, 1970–80 (Mill. ECU) (1970–2: EC–6; 1973–80: EC–9) 192
Table 18 EC Trends in Trade by Commodity Groups: Imports, 1970–80 (Mill. ECU) (1970–2: EC–6; 1973–80: EC–9) 192

Table 19 General Government Surplus and Deficit in EC Member States as % of GDP, 1960–80 193
Table 20 Industrial Production in Major Industrial Countries, 1960–80 (1967 = 100) 194
Table 21 Civilian Unemployment Rate in Major Industrial Countries, 1960–80 195
Table 22 Percent Annual Growth Rate in Consumer Prices in Major Industrial Countries 196
Table 23 Percent Annual Growth Rate in Wholesale Prices (Manufactures) in Major Industrial Countries 196
Table 24 Percent Annual growth Rate in Export Prices in Major Industrial Countries (Unit value in US$) 196
Table 25 Increase in Exports of Selected Products: United States and European Community, 1955–80 197

List of Figures

Figure 1 US$ Cents per Unit of Foreign Currency, 1967–84 (Index: March 1973 = 100) 198
Figure 2 Multilateral trade-weighted value of the US dollar, 1967–84 (Index: March 1973 = 100) 198
Figure 3 Unit Labour Costs in Manufacturing, 1960–80 (national currency basis and US dollar basis) Index: 1970 = 100 199–201
Figure 4 US Farm Trade and Income, 1965–80 (US$ Bill.) 202
Figure 5 Degree of Farm Product Self-Sufficiency in the EC, 1973–9 203
Figure 6 Main Exporters of Farm Products, 1971–9 (US$ Mill.) 203
Figure 7 World Export Share of the Main Exporting Countries, 1965–80 204
Figure 8 World Manufactures Export Share of the Main Exporting Countries, 1965–80 204

Introduction

Conventional wisdom relates that the 1970s witnessed a deep transformation of the world economy and that it was a change for the worse. In particular, a socially acceptable price rise rate in a few years turned into inflation which threatened to inflict a severe blow to the stability of many western economies; the world production growth rate declined, at times becoming negative; the rate of trade growth slackened, growth which in the previous two decades had appeared to be the engine of economic expansion. The apparently stable anchor of fixed but modifiable exchange rates established by the Bretton Woods Agreements was abandoned for the uncertain course of floating exchanges. As regards Western Europe, scholars have contended that 1973 marked the end of its golden age.[1]

Overall, the data confirm this pessimistic perspective. Consumer prices and wholesale prices for manufactures from an average below five per cent in the 1961–73 period increased to double figures in the main industrialized countries in 1974 and in 1975, even crossing the 20 per cent threshold in some of them and, with few exceptions like Germany, did not return in the following years to levels preceding the inflationary outburst (Tables 22–23). World commodity output doubled between 1960 and 1973 and its 1963–73 growth rate averaged 6 per cent; in the following seven years the yearly growth rate was halved to 3 per cent.[2] Finally, the volume growth of world exports averaged 8 per cent between 1960 and 1972, sharply declining to 4 per cent in 1973–80.[3]

Common knowledge also claims that the 1970s saw the rise of protectionist tendencies. The report of the General Agreement on Tariffs and Trade on international trade in 1980 made a strong plea for 'arresting protectionism', arguing that the extent of protection was a major cause of the poor performance of the core economies, inhibiting the expansion of their potentially dynamic industries by reducing foreign demand for their products while locking up resources in the protected activities.

Yet, there are factors that, if they do not gainsay the validity of the above assessment, call for a more detailed analysis. For instance, pressures on the dollar date back to the 1960s, well before the abandonment of the Bretton Woods system in the early 1970s. Deficit marked many sectors of the US merchandise trade balance, from consumer goods to motor vehicles long before the oil crisis. The US negative balance with Japan dates back to the mid-1960s. With the relevant exception of the Federal Republic of Germany, the EC member states, including Denmark, Ireland and the UK, mostly had a negative trade balance not only in the 1970s but for most of the previous decade. Calls for protection on both sides of the Atlantic date back to the 1950s and by the early 1960s were legitimized and regulated by the GATT. On the other hand, the 1970s witnessed the apparently successful drive for an ambitious reform of the world trade system, the Tokyo Round, going beyond tariff reduction as in previous GATT rounds and addressing a set of non-tariff barriers of particular concern for the two main parties to the negotiation, i.e. the United States and the European Community (EC).

Indeed, this research focuses on the position and role in shaping the international trade of the 1970s of the two transatlantic blocs: the United States and the EC. The analysis, which is not confined to trade between the two partners, addresses the subject from different angles. The first one concerns the economic dimension of trade, that is, changes in the current account balance, factors that influence it and their impact on the national economy. The second and the third angles focus on the legal and political framework in which trade must be carried out. In the first place, measures taken at national levels, either unilaterally, or in agreement with a foreign counterpart, are examined. And this is where the question of protectionism enters this research. The word 'protectionism' refers to a set of trade-distorting policies shielding domestic firms from foreign competition. If measures in the so-called 'grey area', such as voluntary export restraints (VERs) and orderly marketing agreements (OMAs) are protectionist in nature, also antidumping and countervailing duty proceedings along with licences and product standards could result in unwarranted protection for domestic firms failing to stand up to foreign competition. The users of some of these measures might rejoin that they are the only way to counter trade-distorting practices followed by foreign competitors, often with financial support from their governments. The question is whether there was an upsurge of such measures in the course of the 1970s and, in the affirmative case, the nature of their economic or political causes. The third aspect of the research focuses on the negotiations, the Tokyo Round in particular, that took place in the framework of the GATT to reach a multilateral agreement that was to go beyond tariff concessions and to establish a legal framework offering greater opportunities for efficient exporters while guaranteeing fair play between domestic and foreign competing industries. The goal of this research is not to provide a comprehensive analysis of the Tokyo Round, as this task was already fulfilled a long time ago by Gilbert Winham.[4] The research examines only the stance of the United States and the EC on the main topics of reciprocal interest in the negotiations.

As regards the economic angle of trade, this work tends to suggest that the US and EC positions in international trade were largely determined by factors predating the 1970s. The unrivalled predominance of the US as producer and, therefore, as exporter had been reversed by the 1960s as a result of the rise of the EC member states and Japan. US exports accounted for 29. 4 per cent of world trade in manufactures in 1953, but just exceeded 15 per cent by 1965, while the EC had gained a 34 per cent share, destined to grow further in the following nine years.[5] On the other hand, factors that emerged only in the 1970s, in particular the first and second oil crises, altered the established trade context to the disadvantage of the industrialized nations and triggered recession. For several industries in the US and in Western Europe the contraction of demand engendered by the first oil crisis ushered in a period of prolonged decline even when the economy as a whole was getting back on its feet.

This research will therefore remind the reader that protectionist measures were not the offspring of the 1970s. Arrangements to control inflows of cotton textiles into developed economies were in force in the previous decade with the blessing of the GATT and other industries like steel and man-made textiles were soon subjected to various forms of more or less voluntary export restraints, boiling down to the imposition of quotas. Nevertheless, the aftermath of the first oil crisis witnessed an acceleration of protectionist measures under the strain of growing unemployment. These measures, however, did not concern all sectors of the economy. In the first place, they were, unsurprisingly, directed to buoy up only the growing number of industries in major difficulties and those suffering greater exposition to foreign competition. Secondly, both the American and the EC authorities carefully avoided straightforward unilateral imposition of tariffs and quotas as this was not consistent with the then established GATT rules. Instead, the authorities on both sides of the Atlantic artfully exploited the room for manoeuvre of legitimate remedies to force foreign competitors, allegedly guilty of commercial malpractices, to curb their exports. Therefore, it is arguable that there was no rampant increase in protectionist barriers, rather there was a quietly insidious rise of such barriers which did not run overtly afoul of existing multilateral trade rules.

As regards multilateral negotiations and the establishment of new trade rules, while allowing that the Tokyo Round achieved significant progress wherever the two main actors, the US and the EC, had a common view, this research contends that whenever there was the likelihood of a clash, the parties ended up by simply leaving aside or covering up the contentious issue, as was the case for agriculture, subsidization and countervailing measures. This allowed the parties to the negotiation to maintain their present practices undisturbed. On the other hand, it paved the way to prolonged and acrimonious disputes in the following decade.

In keeping with the above approach this book is divided into six chapters. The first chapter provides an overview of the economic and legal factors in the two previous decades that contributed to the developments of the 1970s. The second chapter deals with the monetary turmoil and reshuffle of the early 1970s and its impact on trade as well as with the negotiations between the EC and the US that led to the launching of a new trade round. The third chapter addresses the impact of the first oil crisis on the economy of the United States and of the EC member states and on their trade and provides an overview of the first stage of the Tokyo Round. The fourth and the fifth chapters focus on the rise of protectionist measures on both sides of the Atlantic and on the final negotiations and results of the GATT multilateral talks. The final chapter considers the impact of the second oil crisis, the aftermath of the Tokyo Round and the position in international trade of the US and the EC at the onset of the new decade.

1

Background to the Upheavals and Settlement Attempts of the 1970s

An overview of the backdrop to EC and US difficulties in the early 1970s

The United States

When in August 1971 the US executive renounced convertibility of the dollar and slapped a 10 per cent tariff surcharge on imports, it justified these measures with the need to stop an accelerating balance of payments deterioration. According to the US administration, this had been caused by erosion of the current account surplus, which, having turned into deficit by 1971, rather than offsetting the capital account deficit, was adding its destabilizing effects to those of the capital movements. Though recognizing that the turnover in the current account was basically due to domestic inflation and the ensuing erosion of American competitiveness, the administration claimed that the efforts to reduce the external deficit had also been hampered by an overvalued dollar and by the discriminatory trade practices of certain states, among which the EC member countries were prominent. According to US Congress, the trade deficit had been present since 1966; it being concealed by what were allegedly incorrect methods that were adopted by the Department of Commerce in assessing exports and imports.[1]

One explanation of the US trade balance difficulties views them as the result of long-term trends in American competitiveness relative to Japan and most Western European countries which had been able to catch-up with the American colossus depriving it of its lead. With the exception of the military and aerospace spheres, the technological supremacy of US industry had petered out in sectors like steelmaking and automobiles and was even declining in some technology-intensive products.

Before examining these strands of thought in greater detail it seems appropriate to examine first the extent and features of the decline in the US trade balance. Actually, as shown by Table 1, from 1950 to 1980, at least in real terms (at 1972 dollars), the US trade balance, comprising both goods and services, never went into the red, although it severely contracted after 1966 to recover strongly following the exchange rate realignments of the early 1970s. Exports and imports, although steadily increasing, continued to represent a modest portion of the Gross Domestic Product (GDP). This, however, does not mean that imports and exports could not have a significant impact on the balance sheet of many industries, some of which were pivotal for the economy of several regions, and, therefore, for the national economy.

On the other hand, the scenario is quite different for the merchandise trade sector. The balance of goods at current prices, positive at the beginning of the 1960s, declined in the course of the decade and after a short recovery in 1970 became negative in the following year (Table 2). Even if it offers no great level of sophistication, Table 3 does provide a clear picture of the trend marking the main trade sectors in the f States. The 'foods, feeds and beverages' class, characterized by a negative trend_in the 1950s, had a positive balance for a great part of the 1960s, to fall once again into the red between 1968 and 1971. However, a very different picture characterized the remaining years of the decade. The 'industrial supplies and materials' class, which already had a negative balance for most of the 1950s, declined during the 1960s, worsening further in the following decade in spite, or perhaps because of, the depreciation of the dollar. The 'consumer goods' class, excluding food and automotive, whose balance was slightly positive until 1957, went into the red from 1958, increasingly worsening in the following two decades. The 'automotive vehicles, parts and engines' class, which for a large part of the 1950s had been one of the most competitive foreign trade sectors, gradually declined during the 1960s, reaching a negative balance in 1968 and was marked by a soaring deficit in the following decade. The only broad class to show a positive trend was that of 'capital goods, except automotive', which almost constantly had a markedly positive balance, often showing a high growth rate.

As shown by Table 4, US trade with Europe was only second to trade with the Americas and had a constantly positive balance. With the brief exception of 1972, the balance of trade with the EC was positive for the United States (Tables 13 and 14). However, West Germany's exports exceeded imports from 1966 onwards and also Italy had a positive balance in the early 1970s. The US merchandise trade balance with France and the UK remained constantly positive. Japanese exports to the United States overtook imports in 1965 and the gap went on widening. The US trade balance with the whole of Asia became negative in 1969 (Table 4).

The trend of the merchandise trade balance appears to reflect the performance of the main sectors of the US economy. As pointed out by Vatter with reference to the 1950s, the American economy had its slow growers and its growth industries.[2] Among the former were sectors that had been the spearhead of the nation's economic development and had reached their maturity before World War Two.

The post-war decline of the steel industry has been prevalently attributed to the progress of US competitors, especially the Japanese, in terms of productivity and average costs. Total factor productivity in the sector rose more slowly than in Japan as well as in the rest of the US economy. Although after the hike of the 1950s, the wage growth rate in the steel industry showed a lower gap with the whole manufacturing sector rate, other input costs increased. Japanese producers were able to find nearer sources of ore supply in Australia and Brazil, thus cutting transport costs relative to those borne by their American competitors in getting raw material to the Midwest steel heartland.[3] The Western European countries too were able to improve their competitiveness in raw material availability thanks to the establishment of the European Coal and Steel Community (ECSC). The US steel industry also failed to keep pace with technical innovation by not installing basic oxygen furnaces in the 1950s and 1960s and by dragging its feet when converting to continuous casting from the 1960s onwards.[4] The failure to stay abreast with technical progress occurred despite the investments carried out in the second half of the 1950s to increase productive capacity, which consequently remained partially unutilized.

The other main industry that showed a declining trend in competitiveness and market share was the automobile industry. In 1950 three-quarters of motor vehicles in the world were produced in the United States, but by 1958 the US share of world production had already dropped to 49 per cent. The first main inroad by foreign firms was carried out by Volkswagen, a standard bearer of the West German industrial regeneration in the aftermath of World War Two. The sale of Volkswagen Beetles in the US reached one million by 1955. From 1959 the American car industry counterattacked with its own compact model, but only with partial success as Volkswagen's share of the US market continued to rise, which suggests that relative quality and price competitiveness of American cars was already slipping.[5] Also the textile industry, in particular the clothing sector, showed a declining trend. The industry, which in the 1930s had had a strong productivity advantage over its main European competitors, Germany, Italy and the UK, started to lose ground in the 1950s, although not against European firms but against Japan and other Asian producers.

At the other end of the spectrum, there was quite a heterogeneous group of fast growing industries, whose main common feature was their high-tech content. Taking 1946–9 as base, the index number for electric and gas utilities production in 1960 was 287 and 289 respectively. The index number for electrical machinery was 285 and that for industrial chemicals was 320, while the index for aircraft and other equipment reached 368.[6] As expected, these were the sectors in which the United States established its export supremacy. Yet, during the 1950s and the first half of the following decade exports of high and medium research-intensive products showed a higher growth rate in Western Europe and in the Community member states in particular than in the United States. Nevertheless, the dynamic of these export groups in the second half of the 1960s showed a recovery in the United States compared to its EC trading partners (Table 25).

Maddison's estimates show that, in 1985 US relative prices, GDP per man hour in the United States started from a very high base, $11.39 in 1950 but grew by only 75 per cent in 23 years reaching $19.92 in 1973. The score for its main West European trade competitors was quite different. In 1985 US relative prices, Germany almost doubled productivity per man hour between 1950 and 1960 ($3.40 and $6.62) and repeated the exploit between 1960 and 1973 ($6.62 and $12.83). Italy started from a very low base in 1950 ($3.52) and made substantial gains in the following ten years (57 per cent) but more than doubled its productivity between 1960 and 1973 ($5.52 and $12.82). The same can be said for France's progress during this period ($4.58, $7.17 and $14). The progress of the UK was certainly slower than that of its EC counterparts, but it was faster than the USA's ($6.49, $8.65 and $13.41).[7]

Certainly Maddison's data cover too long a period to provide a causal explanation of the circumscribed events of the early 1970s addressed by this research. As the crisis of the dollar occurred between 1971 and 1973, the question is whether there were factors that specifically affected the US external competitiveness from the second half of the 1960s. According to the Economic Report of the President, between 1966 and 1973 US productivity underwent a significant slowdown which did not pick up in the following years. Productivity growth in the private sector averaged 3.3 per cent per year between 1948 and 1966, but between 1966 and 1973 it was only 2.1 per cent per year, below the long-term trend. The decline was prevalently attributed to slower growth in capital formation per worker, a larger proportion of less experienced workers and the changing industrial composition of labour input, as well as to slower technical progress and, in a subsequent phase, higher energy prices.[8] It must be noted, however, that, as often happens, the scenario is different if one focuses on the non-farm business sector and selects periods that do not exactly coincide with those selected in the Report. After the peak of the late 1940s, productivity in the sector grew by a yearly average of 1.7 per cent from 1951 to 1960, rising to a 2.3 per cent average in the following decade (Table 8). But in the first five years productivity growth averaged 3.2 per cent, subsequently slackening to 1.5 per cent. From 1971 to 1973 the growth rate averaged 3.2 per cent and plummeted in the following years. It must also be noted that the decline of US dominance in industrial trade occurred long before the beginning of the 1970s. In 1953, 29 per cent of global manufactured exports came from the United States but by 1959 the US share was down to 18.7 per cent; in 1962 it was 17.6 per cent and by 1965 it was 15.8 per cent, remaining constant in the following five years. During the whole of the 1970s it stabilized at just over 13 per cent.[9]

Certainly, lower productivity contributed to the gap between West European GDP growth rate and US GDP growth rate in both the 1950s and 1960s, but for most of the 1970s the United States managed to achieve a GDP growth rate not lower than the EC average though its productivity growth was declining. The productivity slowdown was one of the main causes of the increase in unit labour costs hampering the competitiveness of US products in the international market, but it was not the only variable in the equation. Productivity gains and losses can be offset by rises and falls in wages. This did not apply to the US during much of the 1950s, but in the early 1960s compensation in the private business sector rose proportionally to gains in productivity resulting in extremely moderate increases in labour costs, which constitute the main component of production costs. However, despite the productivity slowdown in the non-farm business sector, hourly wages rose faster in the second half of the 1960s than in previous years, thus causing the unit labour cost to rise more than proportionally (Table 8 and Figure 3.) Comparison with unit labour costs in West European countries does not offer a univocal explanation of the alleged loss of international competitiveness of US products. The upward slope of unit labour costs in Figure 3 (both in national currency and US dollar basis) indicates that in the EC member states as in the United States nominal compensation rose faster than output per hour. On the other hand, labour costs converted into US dollars showed greater fluctuations along the upward trend than their counterparts in national currency. The index number for Germany was almost constantly below

100 for much of the 1960s but soared in the last years of the decade when the Deutschmark revalued against the dollar. In contrast, the index number for France and the UK approached and even exceeded 100 for most of the 1960s but went down when the two countries devalued their currency, in November 1967 and in August 1969 respectively. The unit labour cost in Italy started from a low base and remained well below 100 until 1968 when it rose by over 15 per cent both in national currency and in dollars. Correspondingly, the export unit values in manufacturing in the European nations, denominated in US dollars and taking 1970 as a base, demonstrate that exchange rate movements were at play along with other factors in determining each country's competitiveness.[10] The index of West Germany's relative export prices slightly declined until 1969 when the Federal Republic allowed a revaluation of the Deutschmark. The index for France and the UK showed significant variations in the years immediately preceding and following the devaluation of their currencies. The US relative prices started to go up from 1965, reaching a peak in 1970, but went down after the 1971 realignment. Japan's unit labour costs and relative prices in US dollars started to move significantly upwards after the 1971 realignment. All in all, it is arguable that a plurality of factors was at play before the US balance of payments reached breaking point in 1971, and this cannot be limited to productivity gaps. It is, therefore, necessary to consider in greater detail the evolution of the economy and the economic policy choices in the transatlantic area and their impact on the balance of payments of the countries involved; this would help explain the origin of the early 1970s currency and trade upheavals and, even more importantly, the response of the governments concerned.

In the United States after years of slack growth, the gross domestic product started to rise vigorously in 1962, reaching for five years levels which were not below those of the West European partners (Table 1). On 26 February 1964 President Johnson signed into law the Revenue Act of 1964 which reduced taxes for individuals by about 20 per cent over 1964 and 1965. To this Keynesian fiscal stimulus was added a set of measures declaredly aimed at waging war on poverty. Although the monetary authorities adopted corrective measures by increasing the discount rate in November 1964 and December 1965, the US GDP rose by 5.4 per cent, 6 per cent and 6.1 per cent in 1964, 1965 and 1966 respectively. In the same years investments grew by 6.4 per cent, 13 per cent and 10.2 per cent. The unemployment rate went down from 5.2 per cent in 1964 to 3.8 per cent two years later.

Problems started when military engagement in Vietnam became irreversible and costly, and the executive failed to foresee its impact on the budget.[11] In

1966 the economy began overheating as it was approaching the full extent of its productive capacity. Wages were increasing and prices accelerated: the Consumer Price Index (CPI) rose by 2.9 per cent, the Wholesale Price Index (WPI) by 3.2 per cent and the implicit price index by 3.2 per cent. The positive merchandise trade balance, which was already lower in 1965, declined further by 23 per cent (Table 2). The decline was the result of a steady growth rate for exports and an acceleration of imports and concerned particularly those sectors in which the United States had long been a net importer: 'industrial supplies and materials' and 'consumer goods'. That decline was therefore easily explainable in terms of macroeconomic theory: expansion of demand brought about an increase in imports, not matched by exports. On the other hand, the Johnson administration failed to use the fiscal instrument to deflate the economy, as the tax increase proposed by the government for the 1968 fiscal year turned out to be too little, too late. The monetary authorities reacted by raising the discount rate and reining in the growth of money supply, which led to a widespread rise in interest rates. Yet, the overheating did not abate. After slowing down in 1967 the US GDP grew by 4.6 per cent the following year, while the implicit price deflator jumped to 4.7 per cent.

The incoming Republican administration tried to curb inflation without causing a recession and increasing unemployment. Disinflation was to be accomplished primarily through monetary policy. Restraint marked fiscal policy too and a $9.9 billion surplus was achieved in 1969 (Table 9). The GDP growth rate slowed down to 2.8 per cent, but prices and the cost of labour continued to rise. December 1969 was the last month of the positive cycle that characterized the whole decade. In 1970, for the first time in 12 years, the GDP growth rate was negative (−0.2 per cent), while the implicit price deflator grew to 5.4 per cent. It was the first evidence of the phenomenon known as stagflation that characterized the decade in the US and in Europe. The slight recession that lasted until November 1970 was accompanied by persistent financial difficulties afflicting many leading corporations. In September many brokerage houses were facing bankruptcy and Congress had to pass the Securities Investor Protection Act to protect customers against losses caused by their failure. To avoid the looming crisis, the Federal Reserve opened the discount window by pumping liquidity into the economy. The executive adopted an expansionary fiscal policy turning the fiscal surplus of the previous year into a $10.6 billion deficit. In 1971 the GDP started to grow again at a 3.3 per cent rate but the implicit price deflator rate did not descend below 5 per cent and for the first time the merchandise trade balance was negative. The same applied to the current account balance, reversing an 11-year trend (Table 2). Yet, the trade and current account balances were far from being the main cause of the balance of payments deficit. They only failed to offset the impact of long-term capital movements, contrary to what macroeconomic theory would usually expect, and in the final years the prospective of their decline stimulated a short-term capital outflow. All this engendered a surge in foreign reserves, mostly denominated in dollars, which the United States' most successful trading partners had to accept often unwillingly but sometimes willingly because it was the price to pay to defend their undervalued exchange rates.

The European Community and its member states

The decline of the United States was mirrored by the ascent of most countries on the other side of the Atlantic, the EC member states in particular. Yet, their economic performance in the second half of the 1960s had lost some of the lustre of the 1950s and the first part of the decade. West Germany went through a brief recession in 1967. The following year saw the 1968 French social crisis, followed a year later by a devaluation of the French franc. Italy had left behind the economic miracle years to enter on a much more uncertain course.

The EC members prevalently had a negative trade balance. The decisive exception was West Germany, whose export surge was among the main engines of the economic miracle of the Federal Republic. By the mid 1950s merchandise trade accounted for about 20 per cent of Gross National Product (GNP) and continued to rise. The West German share of international trade in goods rose from less than 4 per cent in 1950 to 12 per cent twenty years later. The Deutschmark (DM) exchange rate was fixed by the 1948 currency reform but was devalued a year later. A fixed parity of DM 4.20 to the US dollar stimulated German exports in the 1960s, supported by a significant increase in world trade, lower transport costs, high demand for capital goods in which West Germany specialized, a very elastic labour supply and a relatively low average rate of inflation.[12] At the same time the exchange rate established in 1949 constrained foreign competition in the domestic market. The ability to expand of German industries that enjoyed constantly growing demand, such as mechanical engineering, motor vehicles, electrical and chemical engineering, enabled them to successfully compete with the United States in the European and world market and to conquer a growing share of the American market. From 1966 onwards West Germany's trade balance with its transatlantic partner registered, with few exceptions, a surplus (Tables 4, 13 and 14). The positive performance of the trade balance, despite the weakness of the service sector, entailed a balance of payments surplus and with it upwards pressure on the DM from the mid-1950s onwards. In 1961 the Deutschmark was revalued by 5 per cent to 4 DM to the US dollar but remained undervalued as German prices rose by less than those of other major trading countries. Thus, current surpluses continued during the 1960s and the level of reserves nearly doubled between 1960 and 1970.[13] The continued inflow of capital was bound to cause inflationary pressures, but this was an unacceptable prospective for a country that for historical reasons had entrusted its central bank with the task of preserving monetary stability and to this end had legally sanctioned its independence from the executive. The alternative would have been to allow the Deutschmark to revalue but such a choice would have hindered exports, which by themselves accounted for a large part of GDP, without considering their multiplier effect on the whole economy. To square the circle, the Bundesbank resorted to restrictive monetary measures to sterilize the inflow of foreign funds, thus keeping bank liquidity in line with a moderate rate of inflation. This monetary policy was not without difficulties. Indeed, the attempt to reduce money supply increased interest rates, which in turn induced further inflows of foreign funds. Restrictive monetary measures could only be effective as long as the higher interest rates they generated remained below those of other major countries, which was not always the case. Things were made more difficult by the attraction of portfolio investments for the German market, viewed as a hedge against inflation, and because of the likelihood of a revaluation in the near future; to prevent this happening a series of administrative control measures had to be adopted.[14] The foregoing meant that German foreign reserves went on rising along with exports. In 1969 the Deutschmark was revalued by 9.3 per cent, but this did not reverse the trend.

Overall in the 1960s France's economy was characterized by a steadily high growth rate (5.5 per cent on average) paralleled by a smooth performance of the foreign sector, marked by virtually unchanged relative export prices, stable export shares and a smooth rise in imports. This trend was not altered by the social unrest of 1968 which brought about a 5 per cent increase in unit labour costs as a year later the franc was devalued, restoring cost and price competitiveness. As labour costs fell slightly in the following years, employers' profits rose allowing higher investments and thereby a higher level of growth. In short, like the 1958 precedent, the 1969 devaluation was an aggressive one aimed not only at closing the price gap developed in the preceding years, but also at anticipating future inflation. However, whereas the 1958 devaluation was particularly directed at boosting exports, the 1968 devaluation was prevalently aimed at reconstituting French firms' profit margin and allowing an investment boom that would mark the French economy in the following years.[15]

Italy's 'miracle' lasted till the beginning of the 1960s but after the overheating of the economy in 1963 restrictive measures ushered in a slowdown. Despite favourable productivity and unit labour cost trends, profit shares in industry already started to decline in the early 1960s entailing a contraction in investment. Although recovering in the second half of the decade, they could not regain their 1950s level. On the other hand, compensation of employees remained flat for much of the decade and this helped preserve the competitiveness of the Italian manufacturing industry for much of the period (Figure 3). Exports, whose performance boosted the Italian GDP in the second part of the decade, increased due to high foreign demand and to a slow-growing domestic demand that, in turn, curbed imports. However, at the end of the decade and at the outset of the 1970s the acceleration of inflation largely consequent upon the 'Hot Autumn' of 1969 worsened the Italian products' competitiveness causing imports to rise and export shares and export profitability to fall.[16]

In the 1960s the United Kingdom, the main prospective new member of the EC, continued to fall behind the six EC members in many respects. During the decade its GDP on average grew by 3.1 per cent annually, but the growth rate averaging 3.7 per cent in the first five years fell to 2.5 per cent in the following (Table 10). Likewise, the UK's industrial production grew less fast than its continental counterparts'. Nevertheless, at least in retrospect, its record was far from negative. The main problem was the stop-go sequel triggered by the repeated crises of an overvalued pound.[17] British governments alternated between expansionary monetary and fiscal policies designed to maintain full employment and encourage growth, and austerity programmes aimed at counteracting deterioration in the current account, decline in international reserves and speculation against the pound. The Labour government, formed in October 1964, inherited a strained current account balance from its conservative predecessor which quite soon turned into an exchange crisis. The government decided not to resort to devaluation and preferred to stem the growing flow of imports by applying a 15 per cent surcharge duty on imports, coupled with export rebates. The surcharge was reduced to 10 per cent in the spring of 1965. Two other exchange crises followed in July 1965 and July 1966 and by this time a massive austerity programme had been instituted and external assistance was provided by the Federal Reserve (FED) and other central banks. As the tight fiscal and monetary policies were relaxed in view of declining output and rising unemployment in early 1967, the balance of payments deteriorated and a speculative attack on sterling was launched in November, which finally led to the decision to devalue the currency by 14.3 per cent to US$2.40. The devaluation marked the effective end of sterling's role as a reserve currency, thus leaving the dollar in the frontline against speculative attacks. The benefit of the devaluation was far from impressive. The current account turned into surplus but the trade account remained negative and pressure against the pound did not disappear. Although unemployment remained low, the GDP went significantly up only in 1968 to decline the following year, while inflation jumped to 4.8 per cent in 1968, 5.2 per cent in 1979 and 6.4 per cent in 1970.

Trade among the EC members soared during the 1960s. Intra-EC imports grew by over 320 per cent between 1960 and 1970, while total imports grew by less than 200 per cent and the share of the former swelled from 34.3 per cent to 48.7 per cent (Tables 12, 15 and 16). The question of whether the establishment of a customs union and the abolition of tariffs among the six founders of the Community was trade-creating or trade-diverting has been widely debated. A trade creation effect occurs if the removal of trade barriers between customs union's members results in concentration of production in lower-cost producers and in increased exports to other members of the union. But, if with the establishment of the customs union a member country switches from low-cost external sources of supply to high-cost sources within the union, the latter has diverting effects.[18] Overall the available evidence points to an affirmative answer. Apart from agriculture, for which it is incontrovertible that the establishment of a common policy engendered a barrier to foreign imports, relevant examples of trade diversion could be found in the industrial sector too. Certainly the establishment of the customs union coincided with the Kennedy Round negotiations and their massive curb of tariff barriers. Yet, industries outside the EC tariff wall had to compete with opponents able to offer their products at zero duties in the growing market of the Community. This was the case of the British automotive industry which found itself more and more excluded from the market of the six EC members, once a secure outlet, and later was not able to recover lost ground.[19]

For Britain the effects of exclusion from the expanding European economic market were made more acute by the changing economic trend of British trade. In 1955, 39.8 per cent of the United Kingdom's imports came from Commonwealth members and 40.6 per cent of its exports were directed to those countries. Imports from and exports to the six countries that would form the EC accounted respectively for 12.6 per cent and 14.1 per cent; those from and to the European Free Trade Association (EFTA) countries for 11.5 per cent and 11.8 per cent. Imports from and exports to the United States amounted to 10.9 per cent and 6.6 respectively. By 1972 the Commonwealth's share of imports and exports had more than halved. The share of imports from the EC doubled, while the share of exports to the Six increased by 62 per cent. EFTA's share substantially increased while that of the United States remained almost unvaried.[20] Thus, the EC had become Britain's largest market in a period, however, during which Britain's share of exports to major industrial countries had fallen from almost 21 per cent in 1955 to less than 12 per cent. Full integration into the Common Market was, therefore, seen as an occasion that, as had happened for the six member states, would force numerous sectors of British industry to compete and raise efficiency and reduce costs. This would also provide new opportunities for industries like computers, chemicals, automobiles and textile machineries which were believed to enjoy a competitive edge. Besides, there was the perceived risk that British industry could find itself squeezed between US transnational corporations and firms within the EC once the interpenetration of capital in the Common Market permitted the latter to reach the size of their American competitors. The only rational solution, therefore, was to participate in the interpenetration of capital within an enlarged European Economic Community.[21] On 10 May 1967 the British government formulated an official application for accession to the Community, soon followed by the applications of Denmark, Ireland and Norway. In September the EC Commission addressed a preliminary opinion to the Council which stressed that the accession of the four applicants, whose political and economic structures were very close to those of the EC member states, would strengthen the Community. It underlined, however, that applicants had to accept the basic principles of the common policies implemented by the Community, its customs tariffs in their entirety and EC contractual obligations towards third countries. Progress towards an agreement proved difficult and long. It was only on 30 June 1970 that the negotiations were officially opened and were completed in nineteen months. In January 1973 Denmark, Ireland and the UK formally joined the EC, while Norway opted to stay out. The Accession treaties provided that tariffs on trade with the EC were to be abolished in five equal stages beginning on 1 April 1973 and ending in July 1977, and that the acceding countries' tariffs on imports from the rest of the world were to be brought in line with the common external tariff over the same period. The Common Agricultural Policy (CAP) system, based on domestic intervention prices and minimum import prices and levies for major products, would be extended to the three new members. The new members would accede to the association and preferential trading agreements between the Community and the Mediterranean countries. As regards Britain in particular, a guaranteed but diminishing market at guaranteed prices was ensured for New Zealand butter and cheese during the transition period, while the Commonwealth sugar agreement was to remain in force until 1974, to be replaced subsequently by special arrangements within the framework of association or trading agreements with the enlarged Community. Independent Commonwealth countries in Africa and the Caribbean might choose between association under a renewed Yaoundé Convention or a more limited form of association like that already enjoyed by Kenya, Uganda and Tanzania under the Arusha Convention or a straightforward trade agreement.

The main British difference with the Community of the Six lay in agricultural policy since the United Kingdom's support system was based on deficiency payments rather than domestic support prices and non-tariff barriers to foreign farm products which imposed a burden on the budget but did not affect consumer prices. However, food policy in the UK had already undergone substantial changes that made accession to the CAP easier. The Conservatives, back in office in 1970, contemplated replacing the existing deficiency payment regime, considered too heavy a charge on the budget, with a minimum import price regime, implemented through import levies, despite the foreseeable hike in the cost of living. Developing a pattern already partially implemented by the Labour government, the Tory executive extended the levy system to beef and veal and to dairy products other than butter, revised minimum import prices and levies for cereals and introduced duties on imports of mutton except from the Irish Republic. In short, to participate in the common external tariff and the CAP, the three new members had to undergo on average slight reductions in their tariffs on manufactured goods, while accepting higher and more cumbersome trade barriers in the agricultural sector.

Trade expansion, trade interventionism and extension of corporations' activities beyond national borders

It is uncontroversial knowledge that the 1960s marked the heyday of trade expansion. World trade grew at an average of over 8 per cent yearly, well above the remarkable GDP growth rate. Various factors contributed to create a favourable environment. The trend can be represented as an upward curve with a 0.08 parameter. Yet, like most models, a curve, however accurately drawn it may be, implies the existence of scattered points above and below the slope, some of which strongly diverge from it. The curve represents the internationalization of the economy brought about by the removal of obstacles to trade expansion, which, however, always has a national origin. Ricardo's paradox pre-supposed that factor optimization led to trade between England and Portugal and, since Ricardo developed his theory before the advent of global warming, wine was provided by Portugal while clothes were traded by cold, rainy England. Trade balances reflect each country's exports to and imports from the rest of the world. In a global economy, on the other hand, economic subjects extend their production activity beyond national borders. The setting up of branches and subsidiaries in foreign countries is bound to alter the original production pattern and to accelerate the catching-up process. On the other hand, governments may implement policies that either stem competition from foreign producers or strengthen the competitive edge of domestic producers beyond the advantage provided by existent factor endowment, thus impinging directly or indirectly on the course made possible by the curtailment of duty and monetary restraints. Both trends were well established in the 1960s.

Protection and subsidization in industry and agriculture

From 1962, the year in which the Trade Expansion Act triumphantly sailed through Congress leading to the Kennedy Round of Trade negotiations, to the end of 1970 the number of US industrial imports subject to restrictions, including voluntary restraints, rose from seven to 67.[22] Obviously restrictions concentrated in the sectors most affected by import competition from Europe and even more by a growing number of developing countries, prominent among which was Japan. Growing imports in basic industrial sectors, such as textiles and steel, though reflecting the shift in comparative advantage towards higher-technology and capital-intensive industries and services, were perceived as a threat to the survival of industries with a high concentration of employees. A similar trend towards protection of the weakest import competing sectors can be found in the Western European countries, although, due to a time lag in the aging of industries, the sectors concerned did not always coincide during the decade. The two trade areas soon converged in devising import restraints on cotton textiles, that is the sector most threatened by low-cost import from developing countries.

Despite the structural and technological decline of a great part of their traditional textile industry, the EC member states were initially able to keep imports from non-European countries at a low level (5 per cent of domestic consumption) because of their tariff barriers and quantitative restrictions. The United Kingdom industry was not less hampered than its continental partners by a legacy of outdated equipment and an aging labour force. However, in contrast with the EC member states, the UK, although able to severely restrict imports from Japan, had to maintain an open door for imports from Commonwealth countries, which benefited from a zero tariff and unlimited access. Only in 1959 were inter-industry agreements signed with Hong Kong, limiting cotton exports from the colony. By 1960 import of cotton textiles constituted 35 per cent of United Kingdom domestic consumption.[23] The US cotton textile industry, although maintaining after World War Two a productivity level higher than that of its Western European competitors, was hindered by governmental policy. Low depreciation allowance for taxation purposes discouraged modernization of productive plants and a two-tier system of raw cotton pricing, under which US manufacturers had to pay up to 25 per cent more for raw cotton than their foreign competitors, placed them at severe disadvantage. As early as 1955 the Eisenhower administration had signed a bilateral agreement with Japan, then the main exporter, under which the latter agreed to restrict the volume of exports to the United States for various cotton textile products. Quite soon, however, the decline in Japanese exports was offset by the inflow of cotton textiles from Hong Kong. In 1961 the Kennedy administration sought a multilateral agreement under GATT aegis, in which the European industry was requested to take part in and share the burden of textile imports. A short-term arrangement entered into force in October 1961 for a period of 12 months and on expiring was replaced by the Long Term Arrangement Regarding International Trade in Cotton Textiles (LTA) for an initial period of five years, subsequently extended for two further three-year periods. The parties to the Arrangement were divided basically into two groups. Group I included the industrialized countries, among which the United States, the United Kingdom and the EC member states, that is the importing countries. Group II included 14 developing countries. Japan and Poland were treated separately. Some important net-exporting countries, such as China and most East European countries did not accede.

The LTA provided for the progressive relaxation of the quota restrictions that existed at the time the arrangement was signed and established strict rules for new restraints that could be initiated by importing countries. In particular, any new action had be justified on the basis of proved disruption within the cotton textile market of the importing country and had to be preceded by consultations between the importing and exporting country. However, the

LTA also envisaged the possibility of mutually acceptable bilateral agreements regulating the import of a wide range of cotton textiles as long as they were not inconsistent with the basic aim of the Arrangement, that is, the orderly expansion of cotton textile trade. Bilateral agreements, whose lifespan varied from one to five years, were thus the alternative usually followed by the parties to the Arrangement. Therefore, the LTA functioned as an umbrella to a wide set of bilateral agreements, whose consistency with the general principles of the GATT is rather doubtful. Certainly, the importing country had to meet some of the demands of the exporter, at least not curtailing the inflow of its products. However, the 'mutually acceptable' agreements quite often turned out to be a 'shot-gun' wedding as the alternative could involve the unilateral imposition of import quotas by the importing country.[24] The United States was the main user of LTA provisions and by 1971 concluded bilateral agreements with 27 members of the Arrangement, while unilaterally restricting imports from eight other non-participating countries. Three stages can be distinguished with regard to the participation of the EC member states to the Arrangement. In the first phase, which spans the period between 1962–7, the member states gradually dismantled their pre-existent quota restrictions, which were individually administered, more strictly by Germany and France and relatively more liberally by Italy and the Benelux countries. In 1967–8 each of the EC member states signed a series of bilateral agreements. Finally, the European Economic Community as such concluded a series of bilateral agreements with seven developing countries which replaced the bilateral agreements signed with individual member states as well as the individual quotas still in place.

Overall the Arrangement secured the steady increase of cotton textile trade, showing a growth rate of about 85 per cent between 1961 and 1970, while curbing import competition particularly from developing countries. Indeed, throughout the period the most important single component was intra-Group I trade. On the other hand, Group II countries were able to increase their relative share of the Group I market and managed to achieve a dominant position in the supply of certain clothes and yarn. Quite soon, however, the cotton textile industry was subjected to the fierce competition of man-made fibres. In particular the share of synthetic fibres in world production grew from 5 per cent in 1961 to over 23 per cent in 1970. By 1969 clothing imports manufactured from synthetic fibres constituted 35 per cent of all imports from industrialized countries. Clothing manufactured from man-made fibres, including cellulose fibres, formed 46 per cent of their imports. The bulk of trade in man-made fibre textiles was concentrated among the Western European countries, which were net-exporters but also large importers. The United States' imports came from Western Europe but especially from Japan and three emerging Asian countries – Hong Kong, Taiwan and South Korea. The US industry thus started to claim protective measures covering man-made fibres and eventually a replacement of the Cotton Textile Arrangement and found a sympathetic ear both from Congress and the executive. The Nixon administration persuaded the principal Asian suppliers to voluntarily restrict exports of wool and man-made fibre textiles to the US, but there was also the possibility of analogous requests for Western European producers, and to mollify the Europeans, therefore, in October 1969 the US increased to 85 per cent ad valorem the duty imposed on certain fabrics affecting an estimated $15 million worth of Community export trade per year. In December 1973, 50 countries signed the Multifibre Arrangement (MFA), which covered cotton, wool and man-made textiles.[25] The new agreement, which came into force on 1 January 1974 and was valid for four years, recognized the need for industrialized countries to protect their textile industries while acknowledging the importance of the textile sector for the economic progress of the developing world. Overall, the arrangement was free-trade oriented providing that new restrictions should be permitted only in case of market disruption to be determined according to a detailed list of criteria and that bilateral agreements between importing and exporting countries should include base levels and future growth rates.[26]

In the other main declining sector, steel, after a peak in imports in 1968, the United States negotiated a series of VER agreements with Japanese and EC member states industries. The VERs, which covered the years 1969–71, were not intergovernmental agreements but were signed with steel industry organizations which undertook to limit their exports to the US until 1971 and to maintain the same product mix and geographic distribution pattern as prevailed in 1968. In May 1972, Japanese and EC producers, as well as the British, considered it prudent to renew their VERs for three further years, and with some additional provisions, in particular a reduction of the annual growth rate of shipment from 5 per cent to 2.5 per cent and firm assurances on maintenance of the mix of products exported.

However, the main examples of resistance to prevailing liberalization trends were to be found in agriculture, particularly in the EC's (CAP – which turned out to be a stumbling block to the successful completion of the Kennedy Round. The protectionist features of the CAP were partially the result of the weakness of the sector in most areas of Western Europe, but other factors were at play too, notably the efforts of some member states to secure favourable outlets to their increasingly productive farm sector. Farming in the EC could be divided into three sectors: 'competitive agriculture', composed of profitable farms (usually of more than 100 acres), which with intensive farming methods could provide sufficiently high income to producers at prices not far removed, for instance, from those guaranteed to American farmers. At the other end of the spectrum there was the so-called 'social agriculture' composed of farms too small to be modernized and able to survive only through subsidies. The term 'social agriculture' highlighted the fact that the protection of these farmers was not justified by economic reasons but by the need not to affect the social equilibrium of the countries or the regions in which they lived. In the middle of the spectrum there was the potentially 'viable agriculture' consisting of farms that could be made to pay by means of an adequate modernization policy.[27] Overpopulated and overexploited regions included Hesse, Baden-Wurttemberg and Bavaria together with Sardinia and Southern Italy. The most prosperous areas which enjoyed the highest potential for further expansion were to be found in the Paris region, Upper Normandy, Picardy, Belgium and the Netherlands. France and the Netherlands aimed at securing an outlet in the re-emerging industrial heartlands of Western Germany. The latter, however, was politically committed to guarantee to its farmers an income level fairly comparable to that of workers in the industrial sector. The Agriculture Act of 8 July 1955 provided for the guarantee of a reasonable standard of living for the agricultural population along with increased productivity, price stability and regular food supply.

When the common price for grain in the EC was laboriously agreed in 1964, Germany had to accept a curtailment of the high price previously guaranteed to its growers but the established price, whose adoption was postponed until 1 June 1967, was somewhat higher than the price prevailing in France which was close to the world market price due to the devaluation of 1959.[28] The result, therefore, was a mixed blessing for French farmers, as they obtained higher proceeds from their sales within the Community, but, in the absence of corrective mechanisms, would be made uncompetitive vis-à-vis producers outside the EC. The logic that informed the grain agreement extended to price fixing for the whole range of produce covered by the CAP. In short, the domestic price system in the Community allowed marginal producers to survive but principally benefited big, competitive producers guaranteeing higher prices than those warranted by the market, whatever the supply. In turn, this mechanism fostered an unprecedented production growth not so much through effective modernization of the farms, but through the widespread use of more chemicals together with the introduction of higher yield seed, brought about by technical progress.

The preservation of the system was obviously conditional on barriers that could only allow foreign products to fill the gap between EC demand and domestic supply. The mechanisms of the CAP varied for different products but essentially relied on the administration of three prices. The 'target price' represented the desired price in the EC, agreed yearly by the Council of Agricultural Ministers. The 'threshold price' was the minimum for imports and was set below the target price to reflect some notional cost of transport from ports of entry to national markets. The difference between the CIF (cost, insurance, freight) and the threshold price was bridged by a variable levy, calculated on a daily basis. This levy, therefore, contrary to import duties, constantly varied according to world prices and never allowed import prices to fall below the supported price of EC products, thus guaranteeing Community preference. Finally, every year the Council established the 'intervention price', which was the minimum price that the Community guaranteed to domestic producers. It established a floor to the Community market, as intervention agencies had to buy in at that price any product supplied by farmers on condition that required minimum quality standards were met. The mechanism ensured a welfare increase for EC farmers as they could place more produce in the EC market at higher prices to the detriment both of domestic consumers and of foreign competitors facing high and flexible barriers to their exports to the Community. There was no burden on the Community budget as long as domestic demand was large enough to absorb domestic supply. However, when the Community reached self-sufficiency, the EC budget was bound to face soaring expenditure in the farm sector as intervention agencies had to buy farm products at fixed minimum prices (intervention prices) and had to dispose of them at a loss. Sometimes agricultural commodities were resold when there was less pressure on the market; alternatively they were distributed as grants or at subsidized rates to disadvantaged people within the Community or as development aid to foreign countries. A more sophisticated way of disposing of farm products (known as restitution payments) was to sell them abroad at subsidized prices, thus allowing EC producers to effectively compete on the international market despite higher domestic prices.

Domestic and export subsidies as well as import quotas were also present within the US farm regime. Since the New Deal Agricultural Adjustment Act, the US had adopted a price support system based on non-recourse loans – giving farmers the option of either paying the loan back at concessional interest rates or defaulting and forfeiting the produce pledged as commodity – along with forms of direct payments and bolstered by production limits on a voluntary basis. Import quotas, due to a waiver granted by the GATT members in 1955, were applied on quite a few products including dairy products, flax, peanuts and peanut oil, increasing price and marketable production for American farmers. Since 1964 quotas could be imposed on fresh, chilled or frozen meat when estimated imports exceeded trigger levels based on the relationship between imports and domestic production. In addition to direct price and income support, US farmers benefited from other measures such as processing, marketing and consumer aid. The United States also implemented a series of programmes to boost farm exports. Export payments, either in cash or in kind, helped exporters to sell US agricultural products at world prices when US prices were higher, and to counter the effects of competitors' export subsidies. Export credit and credit guarantee programmes assisted foreign buyers with liquidity constraints and balance of payments problems in purchasing US agricultural products. However, in the 1950s the Republican administration adopted a more flexible support price, while curbing the various crop limitation schemes inherited from the previous executives. Also, the Democratic administrations of the 1960s kept loan rates at world market equilibrium and income support was mainly achieved through direct payments to producers who participated in authorized production control programmes.[29]

After the decline of the 1950s, the US farm trade balance, with the only exception of 1962, was increasingly positive and agricultural exports accounted for a growing share of gross farm income. In his special message to Congress to obtain authority for a new round of multilateral talks, President Kennedy stressed the importance of securing and enlarging access to the EC farm product market 'as our agricultural trade with that area is four to one in our favor'.[30] However, the United States' hopes were not met by the results of the Kennedy Round. The EC did not concede any ground on the liberalization of its CAP, whose regime, moreover, was not fully implemented during most of the round. Tariff reductions on dutiable imports of non-tropical products other than cereals, meat and dairy products averaged 22 per cent, a substantial cut but somewhat lower than the cuts agreed on non-primary products.[31] However, the products that were most relevant for the US market in the EC were left outside. World grains trade was regulated by an arrangement signed in September 1967 with no provision for access market sharing, while no progress was realized in the beef and dairy products sectors.

Multinational corporations

On the other side of the spectrum the beginning of the second half of the twentieth century witnessed the rise of multinational corporations (MNCs), American ones in particular. Whereas in agriculture and textiles the state played an active role in supporting and protecting the national industry against foreign competitors, the MNC phenomenon meant the expansion of the company abroad. However, expansion was not synonymous with transfer, as actually the parent company, that is, the managerial centre remained in the home country while establishing affiliates in foreign countries. No doubt multilateral corporations had been in operation long before World War Two. Leaving aside the long history of the trading companies, suffice it to mention for the manufacturing sector those American firms, like Levis and Smith & Wesson, which set up branches in the UK in the late nineteenth century. What was remarkable, however, was the speed that marked the rise of the multinational corporation era led by the United States. Between 1950 and 1970 US foreign direct investments (FDIs) skyrocketed by over 540 per cent, and the lion's share was secured by Western Europe. Until the 1960s FDIs in the United States, originating from both Canada and Western Europe, accounted for only one third of outward US direct investments. However, the inflow of FDIs, in particular from Europe, accelerated in the 1970s (Table 7). It was only at the end of the 1970s that Japanese investments in the US reached any statistical significance.

Several theories have been advanced to explain the reasons for the spread of multinational corporations. The 'product cycle' theory argues that defensive reasons, that is, the need to protect their place in the market, explain the MNC. Firms sell their products abroad first through export. When their exporting ability is threatened they establish foreign subsidiaries with lower costs and better market access in order to retain their advantage. When the advantage is finally lost the firm may move on to new products or try to modify those already marketed.[32] The 'monopoly' theory of foreign investment contends that firms expand abroad to exploit the monopoly power they possess through factors like control of technology, managerial skills and access to capital.[33] Likewise, the 'oligopoly' theory argues that firms engaged in oligopolistic competition move abroad to exploit their technical and financial advantages as part of their overall competitive strategy. Thus, some firms may move aggressively to exploit a new foreign market hoping to gain a permanent advantage over their competitors, while other firms react defensively to prevent their competitors from gaining a survival threatening advantage.[34] The 'internalization' (or transaction cost) theory explains the option for direct investments and the establishment of affiliates over exports and licensing by the fact that the cost of internal flows of factor services and goods is sometimes lower than the cost of organizing markets, that is, when internal transaction costs are lower than external transaction costs. This can apply when markets become less-than-optimal allocators of resources as they fail to capture externalities in market prices.[35] The 'eclectic' theory of multinational activity implies that location specific advantages and ownership specific advantages are at work at the same time. International production is therefore attributable to the firm's monopolistic advantage and its ability to internalize it as well as to the presence in one or more foreign countries of specific advantages that could bring unique benefits to the firm.[36]

The 'eclectic' theory seems to offer the best explanation of the explosion of American FDIs in Western Europe and in the European Community in particular since the late 1950s. In 1951 US FDIs to Europe accounted for a poor 15.3 per cent of the total amount, while Canada accounted for over 30 per cent and Latin America and the Caribbean for 38 per cent (see Table 5). Fifteen years later the Canadian share was unchanged, the share of Western Europe had jumped to 31.6 per cent and the Rest of the World's share was 38.5 per cent. In 1970 the share of Western Europe reached 33.5 per cent, while Canada's was below 28 per cent. The phenomenon is more evident if we concentrate on FDIs in manufacturing, that is, the sector in which Western Europe was a valid option (Table 6). In 1951 US foreign direct investments to Canada made up 46.2 per cent of $4,348 million and FDI to Europe covered 24.7 per cent. Seven years later US FDIs in Canada accounted for 48 per cent of $8,673 million, while those directed to Europe amounted to 28.6 per cent of the total. In 1965 American FDIs in Canada had fallen to 35.5 per cent of $19,339 million, while Europe's share had risen to 39.3 per cent. Fifteen years later the shares of Canada and Europe were respectively 21 per cent and 50.7 per cent of $89,290 million FDIs. In short, in just 20 years Western Europe managed to secure the lion's share of a fast growing flow of US foreign investments and was able to increase it in the following years.

Scholars of transatlantic economic relations in the 20 years following World War Two point to the exceptional opportunities offered by the West European market, especially the EC member states in the late 1950s and early 1960s.[37] The economic recovery of Western Europe was certainly of relevance, but it represented only a backdrop to the process. Progress in currency convertibility was a further factor. In December 1958, most Western European countries adopted non-resident current account convertibility. Article XIV of the International

Monetary Fund (IMF) Charter allowed member countries to maintain, if authorized by the Fund, exchange controls on current payments. In February 1961 nine European countries that had hitherto availed themselves of Article XIV (Belgium, France, Germany, Ireland, Italy, Luxembourg, Sweden, the Netherlands and the United Kingdom) agreed not to appeal any longer to the article protection. It must be noted, however, that convertibility concerned only current payments and did not extend to capital account transactions. The main attraction for American investments, acting both as an incentive and as a threat, was the establishment of the European Economic Community in 1958 and the prospect of a common external tariff ten years later. Steps were soon taken by the EC member states to implement Article 67 of the Rome Treaty establishing the EC which called for the abolition of restrictions on movements of capital belonging to residents to the extent necessary for the proper functioning of the Common Market. Further steps were adopted to enact Articles 52–8 of the Treaty, extending the right of establishment in each country to residents of other member countries and harmonizing the national requirements for establishing a business. On the other hand, American enterprises had to take into account the approach of a customs union between the six EC member states to be established by July 1968, which would abolish tariff barriers within the EC while raising a common tariff against foreign products, which could be higher than that imposed by some European trading partners like Germany. They had, therefore, to create a foothold inside a market of potentially great expansion so as to avoid being left out in the cold. It must be said, however, that the opportunities offered by the establishment and consolidation of the EC cannot be viewed as the sole relevant factor in attracting American investments to Western Europe at least in the 1970s. Indeed, during this decade not only did FDIs from the United States – which are only part of the capital needed to create and expand a subsidiary – not decline but their inflow accelerated (Table 6). In 1971 American FDIs in Europe were almost 15 times as high as 20 years earlier; in 1980 they were over 42 times as much. During the same periods US investments abroad had grown respectively by 690 per cent and by 1,950 per cent. There was, therefore, an accelerating expansion of American FDIs and a growing concentration of such investments towards Western Europe, which tended more and more to coincide with the EC member states.

US economists debated whether foreign investments created new opportunities for American exports or displaced them. The supporters of the former thesis contended that in the first place FDIs displaced competitive foreign exports, in particular in the product cycle model case. According to this perspective, the only real choice for American firms was between establishing a foreign subsidiary in order either to create a foothold in a foreign market or to exploit the cost advantages of a foreign country or allowing the establishment by a competitor of an export displacing facility. Thus American exports and investments were not viewed as opposed but as complementary to each other. Those criticizing foreign investments stressed that even if for an American company the net return of an investment abroad were higher than the combined return from a comparable investment in the US, the latter would have a more beneficial effect. It stimulated technological change and other so-called externalities, whereas foreign direct investments transferred to the recipient country abroad not only resources but also improved technology and technical skills.[38] Dunning's research illustrated that, at least with reference to the 1954–64 period, those European countries that most improved their competitive position in the export of research-intensive products relative to the US attracted the greatest share of American FDIs. Moreover, the increase in US investments to Western Europe was in general concentrated in those industries that recorded the most impressive increase in exports.[39] In other words, US MNCs helped to close the technological gap between the US and the Western European countries, in particular the EC member states, and boost their exports in a phase in which exports from the United States were slowing down.

Thus in the 1950s and 1960s some West European countries such as Belgium and the Netherlands were keen to attract American investments by offering subsidies and tax incentives. Others, with very few and non-lasting exceptions, refrained from hindering them, aware that a more restrictive policy than their partners only helped their competitors at their own expense. On the other hand, prominent politicians and political writers on both sides of the Atlantic quite often regarded with suspicion the spread of US multinational corporations in Europe. Servan Schreiber's argument that, in the absence of offsetting policies directed at enhancing the competitiveness of domestic firms in the EC, the settlement of American subsidiaries would be the Trojan horse for economic colonization was echoed, for different reasons, in the United States by Kennedy's statement that the outflow of capital abroad might weaken the American economy.[40] Defending his proposal for a new foreign trade programme, Kennedy contended that 'the European Common Market has attracted American capital, partly because American businessmen fear that they will be unable to compete in the growing European market unless they build plants behind the common tariff wall' and it was, therefore, necessary to 'negotiate down the barrier to trade between the two great continental markets so that the exports of our industry and agriculture can have full opportunity to compete in Europe'.[41]

Those who looked favourably on the role of the multinational corporations in the American economy contended that they had overall a positive impact on the US balance of payments. This was because the long-term capital outflow, which quite often was only the trigger of a much larger total investment, was more than offset by their return, which improved the current account balance. This argument is undoubtedly borne out by data on investments in the oil and mineral sectors. It is open to dispute with regard to FDIs in manufacturing, where the assessment of earnings is subject to accounting manipulation and the repatriation of revenue can be delayed and even indefinitely postponed. Indeed, in the early 1960s foreign subsidiaries' undistributed income had become the target of the US Revenue. Subpart F of the Revenue Act of 1962 taxed US shareholders on the income of controlled foreign corporations in the fiscal year in which income accrued to the subsidiary, considering it for fiscal purposes as distributed dividend. This system, however, made the US parent company's fiscal burden heavier, without providing any fiscal incentive to exports from the US. On the contrary, from an export incentive angle the US tax system, relying heavily on income and corporation taxes, put American firms at a disadvantage in relation to companies in the EC prevalently subjected to indirect taxes, because, according to GATT Article XVI the deduction of the latter was not considered a subsidy, whereas no equivalent benefit was provided for direct taxation. When the US trade balance went into the red ten years later this apparent disparity made the US executive and Congress think of tax stimuli that could directly benefit American exporting companies without extending to their foreign affiliates. On the other hand, the very structure of the MNCs destined them to be staunch supporters of free trade. As transnational corporations were engaged in intra-firm trade, they had a natural interest in reducing national tariffs and other trade barriers to the intra-firm flow of goods and services as they acted as an additional tax on internal transfers. And yet, as we shall see in the final chapter of this book, the allegiance of the multinationals to the principle of free-trade started to fade when, in the declining economic environment of the 1970s, many MNCs began to feel the bite of foreign competition on the parent company's market.

2

Conflict and Cooperation on Trade Issues Between the Transatlantic Partners and the Launching of a New Multilateral Round of Trade Negotiations

The background to the Tokyo Round negotiations

The legacy of the Kennedy Round

The overall conclusion of the Kennedy Round on 30 June 1967 meant significant progress in the reduction of trade barriers between the transatlantic partners. The average tariff reduction was 36–9 per cent and about two-thirds of tariff cuts were 50 per cent or more.[1] Yet, in the first place, the tariff reductions were not homogeneous, nor were their benefits evenly distributed between the two partners. As expected, greater cuts were agreed in those sectors characterized by dynamic technology where the main trading partners' industries were more eager to compete and less affected by import competition. Sectors like steel and particularly textiles did not see equivalent progress. In agriculture, where the formation of the CAP was to establish a strongly protected market for EC farmers, substantial reductions were made on a wide range of products, which, however, were far from accounting for the bulk of trade between the Community and the United States. Limited and unstable progress was achieved for the grain market, while no effective agreement could be reached for dairy and meat. The balance for tariff binding on industrial products was probably weighted in favour of the United States. According to the Economic and Social Committee of the EC both the arithmetic average and weighted average of the EC were lower than those of the US: respectively 6.9 per cent and 6.4 per cent versus 11.1 per cent and 7.3 per cent. Secondly, less than 7 per cent of EC customs tariffs exceeded the 12 per cent rate, whereas in the United States and in Japan almost one-third of them exceeded that threshold.[2] In this context, the

EC also argued that the linear cut system prevalently adopted in the Kennedy Round made the problem of tariff disparities worse since an equal reduction on either side would leave the protective effect of the high tariff substantially untouched while considerably reducing that of the lower tariff. For instance, a curtailment of a tariff rate from 80 to 40 had a much lower impact than a reduction from 30 to15.[3]

At the outset of the Kennedy Round the parties agreed that non-tariff barriers to trade should be included in the negotiations, but no real progress was made and quite soon the attempt was abandoned. Indeed, not only were non-tariff barriers difficult to assess but their international regulation was harder to achieve than tariff cuts. Unlike tariffs, approaches to the reduction of non-tariff barriers were difficult to embody in the delegation of negotiating authority, as in most cases they had their roots in domestic concerns only indirectly related to foreign trade and were subject to domestic laws. Only two agreements were signed: an antidumping code and an engagement to eliminate the American Selling Price (ASP) system in the US along with equally discriminatory measures in the EC. The ASP system was essentially a device by which the value of imports for tariff purposes was set by the price of like or similar American products instead of the actual price of the foreign product, which was the basis of tariff valuation for most other imports. The system applied, although not exclusively, to benzenoid chemical imports. The only equivalent non-tariff barriers that the US managed to find in the EC were discriminatory road taxes in West Germany, France and Italy which penalized high-powered, mostly American, cars. The agreement reached at the end of the round envisaged the elimination of the ASP regime in exchange for tariff concessions on chemicals by the EC. The US Congress did not ratify the agreement and refused to repeal the ASP legislation and the Community put on hold its tariff concessions.

Also the consistency of US law with the Kennedy Round 'Agreement on the Implementation of Article VI' was open to dispute. Although in signing the antidumping code the executive claimed that nothing in its provisions ran counter to existing US law, many in Congress and the US Tariff Commission argued that there were several inconsistencies between the two rules. In particular, while the code provided that an injury determination could be made only if the dumped imports were demonstrably the principal cause of material industry, the US administrative practice identified material injury with any injury that was more than 'de minimis'. Also the parameters set by the Kennedy Round Agreement to determine regional industries affected by the influx of dumped products were viewed as much more restrictive than those applied by the US.

Thus, Public Law 90–634 implementing the Kennedy Round antidumping code in the United States allowed its application but only to the extent that it did not conflict with existing US law and did not infringe on US practice based on such law.

Soon after the conclusion of the Kennedy Round, in November 1967 the GATT Contracting Parties agreed to draw up a list of non-tariff and para-tariff measures by April 1968, which was to be submitted to the newly established Committee on Industrial Products.[4]

In short, the future round of multilateral negotiations was expected to fulfil three tasks: to further cut tariff rates among GATT parties and above all to harmonize the level of tariff concessions; to work out appropriate procedures to cope with problems caused by a set of non-tariff barriers, which in a first stage were to be identified and subject to comparative scrutiny; to reform agricultural trade, achieving at the same time greater stability in the market. The viewpoints of the United States and of its transatlantic trading partners on how to achieve these goals were not necessarily close on all fronts.

The proposals for a Trade Act and the uneasy coexistence of free and fair trade in the US

Criticizing the proposals aimed at imposing selective tariff barriers on products entering the UK, Sir T. H. Farrer pointed out in 1885 that 'the programme of the Fair Trade League is not definite in particulars, but its principal features are as follows: .... Import duties to be levied upon the manufactures of foreign countries which now impose prohibitory or protective duties on our manufacturers; such duties are to be removed in the case of any nation which will agree to take manufactures free'.[5]

Applied to the twentieth century experience, the foregoing suggests two observations. First, fair trade as an alternative to free trade was not an economic policy approach born in the US in post World War Two as a result of the declining competitiveness of the American industry. In other words, nothing new under the sun. Secondly, in the economy of the last century where the support available to foreign industries was not limited to protective tariffs, fair-trade measures could have wider reasons and take wider forms than in the nineteenth century. On the other hand, the absence of a precise gauge like tariffs allowed the complaining country much greater discretion in deciding where the unfairness lay.

The pursuit of fair trade became one of the main planks of the economic policy of the Kennedy administration when it became evident that trading partners and competitors were closing the gap with the United States. Fair trade was viewed from different angles. In the first place there were the hindrances raised by the prospective importing country either through tariff or non-tariff barriers. But there was also the threat to the domestic industry brought about by exports boosted by the exporting competitor through a set of measures directly or indirectly aimed at fostering the export sector. It was the import competing sector of the American industry that was most successful in capturing the ear of the executive and Congress. There is nothing surprising in this. Certainly, as Table 1 shows, imports were a small fraction of the domestic and national product but this does not imply that the weight in the national economy of the output of the import-competing industries was comparably small. Secondly, the contribution to employment of the import-competing industries could be somewhat greater than their contribution to GDP, as quite often these industries, just because they were traditional, absorbed a greater portion of the working population than those active in more advanced sectors. Besides, the import competing industries were often the hub of the economy of several regions and their difficulties had, therefore, a negative multiplier effect. Examples could be found in the textile industry and later in the steel and automotive sectors.

These multifaceted problems were not less pressing when in November 1969 the Nixon administration submitted its trade bill to the US Congress.[6] The bill proposed a set of measures under the banner of free trade but not without giving due consideration to fair trade appeals and to the need to support those sectors of the US economy in difficulty because of trade competition, whether fair or unfair.

Nixon urged the renewal until June 1973 of the presidential authority of reducing US tariffs, an authority which had expired in 1967, just after the completion of the Tokyo Round. However, the president made it clear that the authority was not designed for major tariff negotiations – that is, in view of multilateral negotiations which were not foreseen in the short-run – but for minor adjustments, which, for instance, could be linked to the adoption of an escape clause or to changes in statutory classification. The president also called for a statement of congressional intent to assist the executive in future negotiations to obtain reciprocal lowering of non-tariff barriers, but Nixon was careful not to arouse lawmakers' sensitivity, pointing out that he was not looking for a blank check, but pledging rather to maintain close consultation with Congress. As a first step Nixon suggested the elimination of the ASP, which at that time was the main irritant in the relations with trading partners and in particular with the EC.

To strengthen the defence of US exports against unfair foreign treatment Nixon urged the modification of section 252 of the 1962 Trade Expansion Act, which authorized the imposition of duties or other import restrictions on the products of every country placing unjustifiable restrictions on US agricultural products. The authority was to be expanded by covering unfair actions against all US products and by taking action against foreign subsidized competition affecting American exports in third markets.

Finally, the president called for the amendment of the Trade Expansion Act of 1962 to enhance governmental assistance to industries, firms and workers affected by a surge in imports. The amendments concerned both the escape clause to industries and the adjustment assistance to individual firms and groups of workers. The so-called 'escape clause' is the possibility of temporarily suspending tariff concessions on imports that, as a result of changed circumstances, are causing or threatening to cause serious injury to domestic producers. In the GATT the escape clause is regulated under Article XIX which allows the imposition of higher tariffs only when the injury is the result of the concession sought to be suspended, of unforeseen developments and of increased quantities of imports. Domestic laws providing for the escape clause had to be consistent with the GATT provisions. The trade bill submitted by the administration wanted to 'liberalize' the 1962 Trade Expansion Act's provisions which were accused of being too stringent and technical, making it impossible for seven years to justify any recommendation for relief. Thus, according to Nixon's recommendation, relief should be available whenever increased imports were the 'primary cause' rather than the 'major cause' of actual or potential serious injury and was no longer to be related to a prior tariff reduction. The first amendment meant that the impact of imports would no longer have to be larger than that of all other causes combined, but only the largest single cause. The second provision was probably inconsistent with the requirements of GATT Article XIX which referred to 'obligations incurred by a contracting party under this Agreement, including tariff concessions'. Also the existing adjustment assistance provisions were 'liberalized' to allow individual firms and workers to receive loans, technical aid, tax relief, relocation and training when increased imports were found to be a 'substantial' rather than a 'primary' cause of actual or potential injury. This expanded the government's room for manoeuvre to keep afloat domestic industries affected by fair import competition through tariff barriers and domestic subsidies, temporary though they may have been.

If the administration's trade bill, in spite of its free-trade claims, contained some overtures to protectionist feelings, it risked becoming an example of a congressional-type sorcerer's apprentice when it started its journey through Congress. The president was initially opposed to all kinds of import quotas, but later could not resist pressure from industrialists affected by foreign competition, particularly in the southern textile industry, and their supporters in Congress. When the administration's bill went to the House of Representatives' Ways and Means Committee, its Chairman, Wilbur D. Mills proposed establishing import quotas for textiles and footwear. The administration, which in 1969 had unsuccessfully tried to negotiate textile agreements with Japan and the EC, endorsed Mills's provision with regard to the former item but opposed its extension to footwear. The Committee not only upheld the extension proposed by its Chairman, but introduced a provision requesting the president, unless he found it contrary to national interest to do so, to impose import quotas on other commodities when the US Tariff Commission found that domestic producers were seriously injured by imports according to specific standards, often based on arithmetical parameters. Analogous provisions were adopted by the Senate's Finance Committee, which, however, suggested qualitative, more flexible standards. Both the Senate and the House of Representatives granted presidential authority to eliminate ASP treatment on chemicals, but not on rubber-soled footwear, the other major commodity affected.

The administration strongly opposed the changes made by House and Senate Committees to the bill it had forwarded. The president threatened to veto mandatory quota legislation on products other than textiles, arguing that the modified bill would set off a trade war and that if quotas could save some jobs 'they cost more jobs in the export that would be denied us'.[7] In a final attempt to save its modified version of the trade bill the Finance Committee attached it to a bill on social security examined by the Senate during the same legislation. However, at the end of December 1970 the Senate returned the bill to the Committee with instructions to delete all but the social security provisions. This meant the death of the bill in both its modified and original versions. Thus, the moderate and, on the whole, free-trade oriented government proposal was dragged down by the attempts made by several economic groups and their supporters in Congress to secure a more protected environment for American industries, which finally prevented its enactment. Organized labour was particularly active in promoting a protectionist approach to foreign trade. As Bergsten noted, by the end of the 1960s the US unions' attitude reflected that of their members. Having achieved sufficient income levels, they had become more interested in avoiding shifts of geographic location and kind of work, a threat increasingly caused by the steady advance of foreign competition and by the factors of production mobility that was one of the main features of US multinational corporations. Besides, organized labour was at that time under-represented in the high technology industries which often had a great interest in liberalizing world trade, whereas it was over-represented in non-technology intensive industries which were increasingly threatened by foreign competitors and were therefore eager for governmental protection.[8]

Also, the circles that promoted greater participation of the United States in international trade, rather than a defensive attitude, argued that the international rules of the game should be changed and that the needed amendments implied the dismissal of protectionist or interventionist practices of the main US partners. In May 1970 the president appointed a Commission on International Trade and Investments under the chairmanship of Albert Williams, Chief Executive Officer (CEO) of International Business Machines (IBM). The Commission submitted its report in July 1971 recommending a programme of immediate and longer-term measures, domestic and foreign, to be undertaken concurrently in the areas of trade, monetary policy and investment.[9] As regards international trade policies, the Williams Commission called for the prompt start of multilateral negotiations for the elimination of barriers to trade and capital movements within 25 years. The prospective multilateral negotiations had to pay particular attention to hindrances and distortions to trade in agriculture, implying in particular a thorough revision of the EC CAP, to preferential arrangements, to the progressive elimination of all tariffs and quantitative restrictions and to the reduction of non-tariff barriers, including a code on government procurement practices and the dismantlement of export subsidies.

On the other side of the Atlantic the perceived rise of protectionist attitudes in the United States was worrying the Community member states and Brussels. As far back as January 1971, the EC commissioner for External Relations and Trade, Ralf Dahrendorf, warned the European Parliament that the proposals discussed in the US Congress would automatically trigger quantitative restrictions that were bound to affect all Community exports. However, at that time the commissioner argued that a new worldwide round of multilateral negotiations 'would not promise much' and favoured instead bilateral talks between the concerned trading partners.[10]

The undoing of the Bretton Woods regime and its impact on trade relations

The US new economic policy and the Smithsonian Agreement

Just a few years after it achieved full operation in 1958 the Bretton Woods system started to show strains. With the decline of sterling the system had become a gold dollar standard whereby the United States pegged the price of gold and the rest of the world pegged their currencies to the dollar, whose value in gold, fixed at $35 per ounce, had been kept unchanged since 1944. From the 1950s onwards the balance of payments of the United States was in the red. If the US balance of payments deficit was a means of providing liquidity to the international system, its persistence and expansion could engender fears in the convertibility of the US currency and, although no IMF article prevented the United States from devaluing the dollar, the US monetary authorities were loath to resort to devaluation for fear of undermining confidence in the system.[11] To keep the balance of payments deficit under control would imply stricter fiscal and monetary policies that the US authorities were not willing to adopt as they might reverse the sustained growth achieved since the beginning of the 1960s. On the other hand, the overvaluation of the dollar had its advantages as it allowed US nationals to buy foreign goods and assets cheaply, as the MNC expansion bears out. In the absence of a corrective mechanism a series of international ad hoc arrangements soon became necessary.[12] In 1961 the London Gold Pool was created to lessen the risk of a sharp drop in gold stocks. The following year a swap network between the Federal Reserve and the central banks of many industrialized countries was put in place. To this was added the issue of US Treasury special certificates and bonds, known as Roosa Bonds, denominated in the currencies of the European central banks and treasuries to provide the foreign countries concerned with an investment medium for past or present balance of payments surpluses. Finally, when in March 1968 a larger than expected balance of payments deficit prompted a rush to sell dollars, the Gold Pool was disbanded to be replaced by a two-tier arrangement whereby the central banks of the industrial countries agreed not to carry out market transactions in gold, using the metal only for official transactions among themselves. These measures, on the one hand, buoyed the dollar value up in spite of the growing US balance of payments deficit; on the other hand, they signified the unofficial inconvertibility of the American currency. The international arrangements were accompanied by domestic measures in the US aimed at preventing capital outflows.[13] The Interest Equalization Tax, enacted in 1964, was imposed on purchases by Americans from foreigners of new or outstanding securities issued on behalf of a borrower resident in any industrial nation so as to increase the cost to foreigners of long-term financing in the US. Since 1965, the US monetary authorities had issued guidelines to the commercial banks to limit the increase of their foreign claims and guidelines envisaging a similar ceiling were issued for non-bank financial institutions. A set of voluntary controls on direct investments abroad was imposed in 1965 and was converted into mandatory restrictions in January 1968.

The balance of payments problem prevalently originated in the outflow of long-term capitals and in military expenses, which were partly offset by a positive current account balance. After being positive for a short spell at the end of the 1960s, in 1970 the balance of payments sharply worsened and a large outflow of short-term capitals was recorded, while at the same time the economy fell into its second recession since 1958 (Table 1). In the following year the economy recovered but the balance of payments deficit grew by over 200 per cent and for the first time the merchandise trade balance went into the red, along with the current account balance (Table 2). The room for manoeuvre left to the government was not large as severe monetary discipline to reverse the growing outflow of capital could jeopardize recovery in the months immediately preceding the presidential election year. The secretary of the Treasury, John Connally, made it clear that the United States was no longer prepared to bear disproportionate economic costs and that the other members of the Western block had to share the burden by more effectively opening their markets to US products.[14]

The benign neglect policy followed by the Nixon administration made the expectation of a future realignment of the dollar a self-fulfilling prophecy for both the monetary authorities of the main trading partners of the US, which ended the defence of the American currency, and the traders in the foreign exchange market, who had been launching attacks against the greenback since the beginning of 1971.[15] The end of the Bretton Woods monetary system, established by international agreements in July 1944, was the result of a set of unilateral measures implemented by the US executive 17 years later. In his 'Address to the Nation outlining a new economic policy' on 15 August 1971, Nixon claimed that his success in creating what, in his opinion, was a more favourable environment for ending the hot war in Vietnam, offered the opportunity to give the American economy a new start, for which it was also necessary that the Western allies took their fair share of the burden in the management of international economy.[16] The measures announced by the president can be divided into two groups. On the domestic side, Nixon announced a series of initiatives to stimulate the economy, keeping employment at a high level and fighting inflation. Among the fiscal measures were a tax credit on new equipment to increase productivity and generate new jobs, the repeal of excise tax on automobiles and the acceleration of income tax exemptions whose pressure on the budget were to be offset by a $4.7 billion cut in government spending through a postponement of pay rises and a 6 per cent cut in government personnel. To balance the budget, but not without effects on the economy of many developing countries, the president also ordered a 10 per cent cut in foreign economic aid. The only measure directed at contrasting the creeping inflation – the implicit price deflator grew by 6.1 per cent in 1969, 5.4 per cent in 1970 and 5 per cent in 1971 – was a freeze on all prices and wages for a period of 90 days accompanied by a call for a voluntary freeze on all dividends payable by US corporations.

Although it was not among the measures announced by the president, the government soon forwarded to Congress a fiscal stimulus bill destined to stir up a hornet's nest in US relations with its trading partners. As noted in the preceding chapter, the weight of direct taxation in the US system was disadvantageous to US firms' exports compared to those from countries relying on different forms of taxation. The solution worked out by the US Treasury was to carve out a special tax regime in favour of those companies engaged in export activities. The January 1972 DISC Law allowed exporters to create domestic paper shell affiliates, known as 'Domestic International Sale Corporations' (DISCs*)*, to be used as a conduit for exporting goods actually sold by their parent companies. One half of the DISC's profits were deemed distributed back to the parent exporter, while the remainder would not be taxed until distribution to the parent. As intended by the US executive, very soon tax experts and accountants understood that the deferral could be indefinitely extended, thus actually coinciding with an exemption as no interest accrued on the deferred tax. In practice, the scheme allowed a deferral/exemption on 25 per cent of the exporter's total export profits, later reduced to 17–18 per cent.[17]

The second array of measures directly affected international trade and currency relations. Nixon announced a temporary suspension of convertibility of the dollar into gold and other assets in order to protect the reserves of the United States from further draining and to let all other countries take note of US desire to achieve significant improvements in its position and of the need for a reform of the international monetary system.[18] The temporary suspension was presented as the result of speculative attacks on the dollar. Indeed, net short-term capital movements had jumped to over $10 billion in 1971 and were the main negative item in the balance of payments. However, the president did not mention any specific monetary measure to attract foreign capitals or to curb the drain from the US. On the other hand, as noted above, disguised de facto inconvertibility of the dollar had marked the monetary history of the previous decade. Suspension of convertibility, which was in force for a temporary but indefinite period, was aimed at forcing the US's main partners in the international monetary system to give up the defence of their existing pegs, as the dollars they acquired were made inconvertible into gold and thus less desirable to hold. Concurrently, the US government imposed an additional tax of 10 per cent on goods imported into the United States to be in force, like the inconvertibility, for a temporary but indefinite period. The surtax covered about half of US imports, applying only to products on which duties had been reduced under reciprocal trade agreements with the exception of items subject to mandatory quota restrictions. The import surcharge was evidence of a link between monetary and trade problems as it was clearly directed at improving the trade balance by making foreign goods less competitive. In Nixon's words, it was 'an action to make certain that American products will not be at a disadvantage because of unfair exchange rates'. The president added that 'when the unfair treatment is ended, the import tax will end as well'.[19] The administration's objective was to achieve a $13 billion improvement in the basic balance (comprising current transactions and long-term capital movements) substantially through a surplus in the trade balance that could more than offset the negative tendency in capital movements.

The measure by itself was neither extraordinary nor unprecedented. For instance, a temporary surcharge on imports was introduced by the British Labour government when the pound came under pressure in late 1964. What was different was the weight of the two countries in the post World War Two international economy and the way the measure was justified. The UK government claimed that the surcharge had a defensive goal, aimed at avoiding devaluation. The US made it clear that the repeal of the surcharge was conditional on a parity realignment whose burden had to be borne prevalently by its trading partners.

The United States hoped that the realignment could be achieved through a revaluation of the US trading partners' currency. A devaluation of the US dollar could be carried out unilaterally but was difficult to justify politically. The West European countries indicated, however, that the United States should raise the price of gold as part of a prospective multilaterally agreed exchange rate adjustment and this approach was supported by the IMF.[20] Although it had no operational significance, as the dollar was no longer officially convertible into gold, the gold price rise allowed the European central banks to maintain the local currency value of their reserve assets, avoiding the legal and political difficulties of making book losses on their reserve holdings.

The standoff between the United States and its West European partners was ended by a meeting between Nixon and his French counterpart, Georges Pompidou, in the Azores. Pompidou rejected the idea of a floating system, an alternative already keenly considered by the US, but declared he was prepared to help establish new parities provided they reflected relative economic strength.[21] The French president also insisted that the new parities should be defended.[22] The meeting was followed by negotiations within the Group of Ten that led to the Smithsonian Agreement of 18 December 1971. In return for the repeal of the 10 per cent surcharge, revaluation of currencies ranging from 7.5 per cent to 17 per cent was agreed.[23] The US price of gold was raised from $35 to $38 per ounce, but the dollar remained inconvertible.

However, in the course of the talks on currency realignment, the American representatives, probably aware that the prospective currency arrangement was not enough to secure the hoped-for reversal of the current account deficit, made it clear that the resolution of the international monetary crisis had to be complemented by trade negotiations. During the Rome G–10 meeting on 30 November 1971, Connally pointed out that the areas for discussion had to be and were three: currency realignment, burden sharing (of defence expense) and trade, the latter topic to be addressed by negotiations between the United States and Canada, Japan and the EC.[24] The demands on the EC concerned in particular several aspects of the EC agricultural policy and the Community preferential arrangements with third countries. The Special Trade Representative, William Eberle, was sent to Brussels in December for preparatory talks. The Community accepted to start prompt negotiations on specific trade topics with its transatlantic partner, once the parity realignment had been put in place and the 10 per cent surcharge repealed and on the basis of reciprocity and mutual advantage, that is, concessions were not to be unilateral. On the other hand, the parties agreed that, in line with the issue of monetary realignment, where a multilateral approach had been preferred to bilateral deals, by 1973 a full-scale review of the entire trading system was to be set in motion.[25]

The advent of the floating exchange rate regime

The Smithsonian Agreement not only established a new set of parities but also widened the trading bands surrounding the new central rates from 2.25 per cent to 4.5 per cent. This meant that a European country's currency could fluctuate from ceiling to floor by 4.5 per cent against the dollar, but that the currencies of two European countries would fluctuate by 9 per cent against each other if one rose from floor to ceiling while the other fell from ceiling to floor. [26] This ran counter to the scheme of the Werner Report of October 1970 according to which the EC central banks had to restrict the margin of fluctuation between Community currencies and subsequently from 1974 would progressively exclude autonomous parity changes. In April 1972 the EC members inaugurated a regime, known as the 'snake in the tunnel', by which their currencies would jointly fluctuate against the dollar by 4.5 per cent (the tunnel) while the fluctuation between member countries' currencies was to be kept within the narrower limit of 2.5 per cent (the snake). The three prospective members of the EC, Denmark, Ireland and the UK, joined the arrangement, along with Sweden and Norway, but the UK retired in June, followed by Ireland. Italy left the snake in February 1973.

In March 1972 the US Congress passed the law authorizing the Secretary of the Treasury to implement the dollar devaluation agreed at the Smithsonian meeting. However, soon after tensions on the greenback started again and on 29 July the Federal Reserve Bank of New York sold about $32 million in foreign currencies to support the Smithsonian rate and thus withstand a first assault on the dollar. As noted by Tew, the absence of a firm commitment to defend the Smithsonian Agreement and the knowledge that many in the US administration and banking were ready for a transition to floating, while others believed that larger currency changes were needed to restore equilibrium, led the market to expect another devaluation of the American currency.[27] Indeed, in 1972 an improvement in the balance of payments was registered but it was not brought about by a return of the trade balance to the red. On the contrary, in January 1973 the Department of Commerce announced that in the previous year the merchandise trade deficit had soared to $6.4 billion from $2.3 billion in 1971, that is, an increase of more than 175 per cent. The European Community could now boast a surplus of ECU 996 million in its trade with the United States. The worsening of the US merchandise trade in spite of the devaluation could at least be partially explained by the J curve effect which determined a soaring import bill in US dollars. This was because the US demand for foreign products did not adjust speedily enough to their new price, while US exports failed to rapidly attract foreign demand in spite of their lower price in terms of other currencies. The consequent lack of confidence in the permanence of the Smithsonian central values triggered a run on the dollar. In the first ten days of February 1973 the West German Bundesbank bought $6.1 billion and the Japanese central bank $1.2 billion. On 10 February the Japanese authorities closed the exchange market and suspended their support for the dollar. After a series of secret rounds of consultations of the under-secretary for monetary affairs of the US Treasury, Paul Volcker, in Bonn, London and Tokyo, the representatives of France, Italy, the UK, the US and West Germany met in Paris on 12 February to revise the Smithsonian pegs. The revision was carried out by changing the US dollar's par value from 38 dollars an ounce to 42.2 dollars an ounce, while leaving the gold value of other currencies unchanged. This meant a devaluation of ten per cent of the dollar relative to the currency of its main trading partners. Seven months later the US Congress ratified the rise of the official price of gold. Yet, in February and March 1973 a further run on the dollar occurred, which resulted in the abandonment, wrongly thought to be temporary, of pegging on the dollar. After two meetings in Paris, France, Germany, the Benelux countries and Denmark agreed to proceed with a joint float in which they were joined by their snake partners, Sweden and Norway, while the other EC members continued to float individually as did Canada, Japan and Switzerland. None of these currencies was pegged to the dollar.

The events from August 1971 to the middle of 1973 showed a clash of perspectives and approaches in which the US viewpoint prevailed de facto. For the United States the first cause of the US deficit lay in the desire for surpluses in the rest of the world rather than in the budget deficit and the relaxation of monetary policy in the early 1970s.[28] The United States, therefore, did not believe that severe domestic fiscal and monetary measures were urgently necessary to restore competitiveness to the American economy so as to rebalance its trade and financial relations with its main trading partners. Instead, the burden of readjustment had to be born by the surplus countries. For instance, at the 1972 annual meeting of the IMF the Secretary of the Treasury, George Shultz, proposed a reserve indicator system under which countries would be obliged to adjust when their reserves passed certain specified points. The alternative approach, regarded with growing sympathy in Washington, was to accept floating rates through which the value of a currency was to be dictated, at least partially, by the market. Both approaches were looking for an automatic mechanism which could remove the currency undervaluation that allowed some countries to constantly achieve a trade surplus which, in turn, entailed hoarding of international reserves.

The European countries, whether in surplus or deficit, resented the monetary dependence implied by the dollar standard, while viewing the growing volatility of the international monetary market as a threat to their integration goals. The 'snake in the tunnel' was a tentative response to that perceived threat. However, their position was far from monolithic. The main concern for Germany was to prevent the inflationary bias inherent in the current system. Thus the Federal Republic's main aim was to establish effective control over the volume of global liquidity, which, in turn, also meant the creation of a system of asset settlement that could neutralize the pressure generated by future US deficits. France was a strong advocate of fixed parity, which, however, did not necessarily coincide with a dollar-centric system. At the December 1971 Azores meeting Pompidou bargained the acceptance of new parities with the maintenance of a revised fixed parity system that had to reflect relative economic strengths and at the Paris meeting 14 months later Giscard d'Estaing defended the same pattern. It is likely that in France's eyes adherence to fixed exchange rates would compel the United States to share the burden of economic adjustment. Besides, the volatility of the main reserve currency was bound to affect the stability of the European currencies. On the other hand, it cannot be said that the French were unsympathetic to the aim of ensuring that surplus countries played a proper part in the adjustment process, as shown by the disputes on the adjustment process with West Germany and by the fact that the French tabled a proposal for a reserve ceiling beyond which reserves would have to be deposited in a special account with negative interest rate in the IMF.[29] Nor was French allegiance to the fixed exchange principle unconditional as borne out by the fact that the franc was allowed to float out of the snake when market pressure developed in January 1974. By June 1972 Britain was converted to the idea that floating was the best available option. Although the June 1972 float was described as temporary, the government showed no hurry to re-peg and declined to participate in the joint float against the dollar operated by other EC partners.[30] Initially the pound was allowed to find its own level but in May 1973 the Bank of England started to intervene in the market, at first to moderate upward pressure on the British currency and later to support it. Analogous interventions were carried out by other central banks and by the end of the year a managed floating regime was the rule, one way or another, in the industrialized countries.

National product, trade growth and inflation build-up

Despite the currency turmoil, both 1972 and 1973 were marked by a very strong GDP growth rate in the OECD countries and by a sustained increase in world trade, accompanied, however, by accelerating inflation. After the slump of 1970, the US economy started its recovery in the second half of 1971 and strengthened in the following two years, reaching its peak in the first half of 1973. While in France 1973 marked the fifth year of increase in general demand, in West Germany, Japan and the UK the acceleration in growth rate started only in the second half of 1972. In the United States and in France investments in plant and equipment represented the main driving force in the expansionary phase, while the growth of the West German economy was provided by the external component. The continuous increase in West German exports, despite the appreciation of the Deutschmark, could be explained by the fact that relative price rises in the period were far smaller than the cumulative revaluation of the DM and by the characteristics of German exports heavily weighted in favour of machinery often sold in fairly monopolistic markets.[31] In the other OECD countries demand was mostly boosted by domestic consumption.

The recovery coincided with and contributed to an upsurge in international trade that grew approximately by 17 per cent in 1972 and 36 per cent in the following year, compared with a 9.3 per cent average in the 1960s. This growth can be attributed to a large increase both of trade volume and of international prices, estimated at around 14 per cent and 20 per cent respectively in 1973. Various factors contributed to this expansion: the high rate of economic growth, coupled with the coincidence of the boom phase of the cycle in most industrial countries, at least since the second half of 1972; the distribution of income in favour of a number of developing countries; and greater participation of socialist countries in world trade. The price rise was preceded and accompanied by monetary expansion, as the combined growth of the nominal money supply (M1) in eleven major industrial countries almost doubled between 1970 and 1972. On the other hand, the acceleration of inflation increased the demand for international liquidity, while the US decision to sever the link between gold and the dollar eliminated the principle factor limiting the supply of liquidity.

The parity changes that had taken place since December 1971 fully manifested their influence on the pattern of world trade in 1973. The growth rate of United States exports was roughly three times as large as in 1972, while the volume of imports rose at half the rate of the previous year. With the exception of Germany, the trade balance with the EC member states and the whole of

Europe, which was negative in 1972, showed a substantial credit for the US. A particularly dynamic sector was agriculture.

The early 1970s also witnessed a shift in the terms of trade between the industrialized countries and developing countries that exported raw materials. The international prices of raw materials started to rise in 1968 but they gathered considerable speed in the second half of 1972. The hike was due not only to the faster growth of economic activity in the main industrialized countries, but also to structural factors such as the increasingly oligopolistic nature of the primary products market occasioned both by the growing number of multinational corporations and by agreements among producer countries. However, the attempt of the countries exporting raw materials was also a defensive move, as is borne out by the price acceleration in 1972. Primary products, including oil, were generally priced in US dollars, a currency whose value was falling. The developing countries' reserves were in US dollars or British pounds. Their imports were affected by an accelerating inflationary process and were quite often from countries whose currencies were appreciating against the greenback. The hike in one essential import, food, was particularly strong as the United States had difficulties in coping with soaring demands for its farm products.

The year 1973 was the annus mirabilis of American agriculture, ushering in nine years of farm products export boom. In 1972 exports had already grown by over 20 per cent rising to \$9.4 billion and the Secretary of Agriculture, Earl L. Butz, confidently predicted that they would reach \$11 billion by 1973.[32] His forecast was dwarfed by the accounts: in 1973 exports grew by 88 per cent, reaching \$17.7 billion (Figure 4). About 60 per cent of the increase was caused by increased volume, the remainder coming from higher prices. The \$9.26 billion positive farm trade balance showed an improvement of over 215 per cent. In the following years it remained the strong point of the US trade balance, while the fortunes of manufactured goods declined. Net farm income, already on the rise in 1972, jumped by 78 per cent in current dollars and by 68 per cent in real terms to \$33.3 billion and \$25.1 billion respectively (Figure 4). However, this success was short-lived as growing production expenses started to erode the earnings from the following year onwards.

With the exception of World War Two, US agriculture had been marked by excess capacity even before the slump of the 1930s, to deal with which government restrictions on farm outputs were adopted. By 1973, however, the higher level of exports had eliminated almost all excess capacity and the government accelerated the implementation of policies encouraging all-out production. The reasons for this change were several. Backstage there was a slight gap, which had however a cumulative effect, between production and consumption that was traced back to the 1950s. World food production outside the US grew by 2.95 per cent per annum between 1950 and 1972, whereas in the same period consumption grew by 3 per cent per annum.[33] The gap was particularly wide in certain key food products like wheat and coarse grains where the US was the dominant producer. According to the International Wheat Council, in the market year 1972–3 wheat production fell to 337 million tons, contracting by over 7 million tons relative to the previous year. [34]

In the early 1970s demand for food produce in the international market also increased in response to contingent factors like shortages in the Central Plan economies, in particular the Union of Soviet Socialist Republics (USSR) and China which were affected by bad weather. In the summer of 1972, following a poor harvest, the Soviet Union entered the American market and purchased some $750 million worth of wheat and feed grains over a three-year period. The July 1972 deal bolstered the policy of détente which the two blocks were pursuing at that time. In the years preceding the Afghan crisis, exports to Eastern Europe and the USSR increased by 41.9 per cent annually.[35] The new trade bonds with the USSR and its satellite countries did not bring about a significant improvement in the US balance of payments. The Soviet Union sold some gold, exerting modest downward pressure on world gold prices and thereby supporting the dollar-gold parity, but its interest as a major gold producing nation was not to stem the rise in world gold prices. It preferred to borrow Eurodollars in the West European market and in February 1973 it was able to obtain substantial loans at a modest 6 per cent interest rate.[36]

Also contributing to the pressure on the market was the growing need for food products in some fast growing economies in East and South-East Asia and the hike in world population which grew by 75 million in 1972 alone. The depreciation of the dollar, whose multilateral trade-weighted value fell by 21 per cent between 1970 and March 1973, also contributed to encourage demand for American produce, first preceding and then partially offsetting the price hike.

In this favourable context the administration pursued a policy aimed at making US agriculture more respondent to market signals.[37] The Agriculture and Consumer Protection Act of 1973 allowed farmers to plant any crop they chose on the acres outside the portion of the base acreage they had to keep fallow if they agreed to participate in farm support programmes. Loan rates for non-recourse loans administered by the Commodity Credit Corporation (CCC) were fixed well below the foreseeable market price, having, therefore, only a safety net function. This made 1974 the first year in which a farmer was not assured of direct payment regardless of the market price level. On the other hand, the 1973 Act added an income support regime to the price support mechanism for crops and cotton, based on target prices related to changes in production costs adjusted for yields. According to the new regime, a deficiency payment would be made if the average market price during the first five months of the marketing year were below the target price. The new regime was not as market-neutral and budget cost-effective as one might have expected. Indeed, it was bound to increase budget costs, at least in times of low average market prices, since, in contrast to a pure loan rate regime, the burden on the taxpayer was not shared by domestic consumers forced to buy agricultural produce at higher prices. Besides, it did not reduce incentive to overproduce, as target prices could result in total returns for farmers above those provided by the equilibrium market price and, because of the expansion of local production, would interfere with international trade.[38] As noted by the Deputy Director of the Cost Stabilization Program, deficiency payments applied to portions of the crop required for domestic and export use would result in a more direct subsidy to exports. It was, therefore, to be expected that: 'Such a program would invite criticism from those countries whose producers would be affected by this competition. This could seriously impair our posture in upcoming GATT negotiations'.[39]

On the other hand, the export expansion and the consequent disappearance of excess capacity in agriculture brought about strains for the domestic food market. In 1973 the food component of the consumer price index rose by over 19 per cent accordingly reducing the purchasing power of American consumers. The large exports of feed grains and oilseeds raised the cost of livestock production. Beef producers, whose profits were squeezed first by the ceiling price on red meat and then by the general freeze on food prices, were no longer able to pay world prices for the available supplies of soybean products and started to slaughter breeding animals.[40] On 27 June the government imposed export embargos on soybeans, cottonseed and their derivatives. A month later the embargos were replaced by export licences, which, however, were also applied to other farm commodities, livestock feed, edible oils, peanuts and animal fats. By October the restrictions were lifted but the incident provided ammunition to the advocates of a special treatment for agricultural trade, particularly numerous in the EC and Japan. Indeed, the embargos were evidence of the danger of unconditionally relying on free imports from countries allegedly endowed with a comparative advantage and of the wisdom of actively pursuing a policy of self-sufficiency.[41]

The road towards a new round of multilateral trade negotiations in the GATT

After the shock announcement of a new policy for the United States and, therefore, for all the industrialized nations in August 1971, faced with the prospect of a 10 per cent surtax on about 87 per cent of EC exports to its main trading partner, the European Commission argued that the measure would threaten a stable upwards trend in trade between the two areas, whose balance had increasingly been in favour of the United States. It also contended that the surcharge, which threatened to wipe out most of the concessions negotiated in the Dillon and Kennedy Rounds, was not in conformity with GATT rules and that it was inappropriate, given the nature of the United States' balance of payments problems and the undue burden of adjustment placed on the import account with serious effect on the trade of other GATT parties.[42] A GATT working party was set up, of which both the United States and the EC member states were parties along with other countries. The working party, obviously with the contrary view of the United States, urged the US to repeal the 10 per cent surcharge as soon as possible. However, the IMF representative testified that, although a corrective adjustment in the pattern of exchange rates would be preferable, given the low level of US international assets and the high level of its reserve liabilities, in the absence of other appropriate actions the import surcharge could be regarded as being within the bounds of what was necessary to prevent a serious deterioration in the United States balance of payments position. Moreover, the US did not fail to point out that, given the findings of the IMF, it was 'entitled under GATT Article XII to apply quantitative restrictions to safeguard its external financial position but had chosen instead to apply import surcharges, which were less damaging to world trade.' [43]

The 10 per cent surcharge was repealed on 20 December soon after the Smithsonian Agreement and at the same time the European Commission and the United States started bilateral commercial negotiations. The talks ended on 11 February 1972 with limited concessions by the EC, mostly addressing American grievances on transatlantic farm trade.[44] No engagement was made with regard to the thorny reciprocity issue in the preferential agreements with the Mediterranean and ex-colonial countries. They marked, however, the assent of the EC to the US executive's opinion, in line with the recommendations of the Williams Commission, that a multilateral revision of the international trade regime was needed. The really noteworthy result of the talks was a joint declaration by which the United States and the Community recognized the need for a comprehensive review of international economic relations with a view to negotiating improvements in the light of the structural changes which had recently occurred. These covered 'inter alia' all elements of trade, including measures which impeded or distorted agricultural, raw material and industrial trade.[45] The multilateral negotiations which, within the GATT framework, were to begin in 1973 – subject to the required internal authorizations – had to aim at the expansion and ever greater liberalization of world trade and improvement in the standard of living of the people of the world, paying special attention to the needs of the developing countries, goals that could 'be achieved "inter alia" through the progressive dismantling of obstacles to trade and improvement to the international framework for the conduct of world trade'.[46]

Thus the transatlantic trading partners acknowledged that their conflicts could be properly and lastingly solved only within the context of multilateral negotiations aimed at curbing obstacles to trade and improving the rules of the world trade game. It seems, however, that the parties to the declaration, and in particular the EC, saw these two objectives as part of a greater puzzle in which variables other than trade liberalization were to be taken into account. This wider context – with reference to which the term 'inter alia' could be explained – was also likely to include the reshaping of the world monetary system on more stable bases.

The 'declaration' along with a Japan – US statement [47] having a similar content was hailed by the GATT Council at its 7 March meeting.[48] However, the EC–US Joint Declaration had a jarring note. On agriculture the Community stated that 'in appropriate cases' the conclusion of international commodity agreements was also one of the means to achieve expansion of world trade and improvement in standards of living. The United States dryly answered that 'such agreements do not offer a useful approach to the achievement of these aims'. In other words, the viewpoints of the United States and the Community on how to achieve a better environment for farm trade seemed to be irreconcilable and, therefore, on one key point of the talks the two parties had to agree to disagree.

The United States' stance

The US protectionist lobbies did not give up. In 1971, Senator Hartke's and Representative Burke's Fair Trade and Investment bill called for quotas on all imports based on the 1965–9 average and for a set of measures, including the withdrawal of tax benefits to discourage American investments abroad, especially by MNCs. The stated rationale for the bill was the constant gap between US imports and exports. Even though the bill failed to make significant progress and was fiercely opposed by the administration, its rationale was shared by many in Congress and to a certain extent by the executive. Although they were more and more focused on Japan, US grievances were also directed to the EC. In the first place, the US assumed that the disappearance of its trade surplus was the upshot of currency undervaluation and unfair practices from both Japan and the EC. Secondly, the Common Agricultural Policy was accused of fostering expensive overproduction in the Community, while preventing American farm products from acquiring a share of the EC market commensurate to the US comparative advantage. Thirdly, alleged EC restrictions diverted Japanese exports towards the US market. Finally, the network of agreements signed by the Community, in particular with the Mediterranean countries and the former colonies, which provided for reciprocal preference, allowed tariff-free entry of EC industrial products in the markets of these countries, displacing, in the US view, competing American products. This would be inconsistent with GATT Article I on MFN (Most Favoured Nation) treatment despite the inexistence of a customs union or a free-trade area given the non-fulfilment of the requirements of Article XXIV of the General Agreement for their actual establishment. This was because the developing countries which were parties to the agreements would never be able to dismantle all their restrictions on EC goods.

His standing and room for manoeuvre boosted by a sweeping endorsement by the electorate in the 1972 presidential election, on 10 April 1973, Nixon proposed a Trade Reform Act to Congress and asked for wide negotiating authority in view of the approaching GATT round.[49] The details of the government bill will be analyzed in great detail in the following chapter, as it was only in December 1974, four months after Nixon's resignation, that at the end of a long and uneven journey the US Congress approved the bill, though without substantial amendments to the original proposal. The bill, which partly resubmitted the proposals put forward four years earlier, had the following goals: negotiating for a more open and equitable world trading system; strengthening the US ability to deal with unfair competitive practices and rapid increases in imports which threatened the disruption of the US market; managing more efficiently the US trade policy and using it effectively to fight inflation and improve the balance of payments; and enhancing the contribution of trade to the development of poorer countries.

With particular regard to the issue of negotiating authority, in contrast with the previous requests, the bill did not set a limit in the percentage change of the tariffs subject to negotiation, thus maintaining full freedom to raise a duty to any level the president wished or eliminate it altogether. As regards non-tariff barriers, Nixon found it impossible to come up with a common standard that would lend itself to a new delegation of authority. The main problem lay in the fact that the elimination of such barriers quite often required changes in domestic laws, whose uncertain implementation would make foreign governments reluctant to accept concessions subject to congressional delay and opposition. The administration suggested a new optional arrangement under which the president would give advance notice to the Congress of his intention to negotiate an agreement so as to allow the lawmakers to make their views known. After the negotiation the agreement would be submitted to Congress along with the implementing legislation. If not rejected by a majority vote, it would then enter into effect within 90 days. Advance authority was asked only to deal with some specific customs matters primarily involving customs valuation and the marking of goods by country of origin. The authority would be granted for five years on both tariff and non-tariff barriers. On agriculture, Nixon stressed that the executive expected the round to achieve the expansion of agricultural trade, arguing that the concerns of all nations for farmers and consumers could be best met by greater reliance on free market forces. He also made it clear that he did not believe that agriculture should have a separate place in the negotiations as barriers to agricultural trade were either tariff or non-tariff in nature and could therefore be dealt with under a general framework which would encompass other primary products as well as manufactured goods. Finally, Nixon called for presidential authority to extend Most-Favoured Nation (MFN) treatment to any country when he deemed it in the national interest. MFN status was a condition for the implementation of the US–Soviet trade agreement of October 1972. The agreement was the cornerstone of the détente policy with the Soviet Union which was not a party to the GATT. Moreover, if the agreement did not enter into force the USSR would not have to repay its World War Two lend and lease debt of $722 billion.

However, the request for negotiating authority was made at a moment in which Nixon's personal authority was shaken as his administration was embittered over the so-called Watergate scandal. On 11 December the House passed the government bill with amendments.[50] It rejected the president's request for unlimited authority to raise or lower tariffs, setting limits to his power according to the tariff rate to be reduced. It adopted the procedure for prompt consideration of non-tariff barrier agreements briefly outlined above, but rejected Nixon's request for advance authority on matters concerning customs valuation practices and rules of origin. However, a main reservation, the so-called Vanik Amendment, was made with regard to the authority to give MFN trade status to the Soviet Union. Although the president was given authority to grant MFN status to countries that were not GATT parties, particularly Communist countries, for the Soviet Union the status was made conditional on the relaxation of its policies discouraging Soviet Jews from emigrating to Israel, actually preventing the coming into force of the US–Soviet trade agreement. In turn, the Senate postponed any decision on the governmental bill until 1974. Thus, because of an issue unrelated to the GATT negotiations, the American executive could not enter the round it had helped to launch with the full authority it had requested and with definite terms of reference.

The EC's stance

In October 1972 the European Summit requested the Commission to work out an overall approach of the Community to the coming trade round in the GATT, establishing 1 July 1973 as the deadline for its submission to the European Council.

A first Memorandum was sent by the Commission on 4 April .[51] In keeping with a Council Resolution of 13 December 1971 and with the Summit communiqué, the Commission expressed the view that the imminent negotiating round had to have two general goals. The first was the pursuit of trade liberalization on the basis of reciprocity and mutual advantage for all parties. The second was greater participation of the developing countries in international trade and the achievement of better economic equilibrium with the industrialized world. The Commission, however, was careful to stress that the participation of the Community to the negotiations would not jeopardize the advantages already enjoyed by those countries with which the EC had special relations. In other terms, their margin of advantage in trading with EC member states relative to the generality of developing countries was to be preserved.

As regards the main aspects of the negotiation, the Commission did not consider the complete elimination of all customs duties as a realistic approach. There were two main obstacles: the role of customs duties in protecting sectors that in quite a few countries were experiencing difficulties in withstanding foreign competition; and the lack of harmonization of national policies concerning taxation, social security and measures to stimulate economic development. On the other hand, every tariff reduction method had to take into account the considerable differences between average customs duty levels in the developed countries as well as their different structure, since some countries applied tariffs of a roughly homogeneous level to all products while others applied very high tariffs to some products and much lower ones to others. What was to be worked out, therefore, was a mechanism that could at the same time reduce the overall level and level off the differences. However, the general scheme should not prevent the parties from seeking, on a reciprocal basis, greater concessions on individual items, which could even imply the abolition of customs duties.

The Commission's approach to non-tariff barrier negotiations was less specific, since negotiators would be confronted by a set of problems wider than those concerning tariff barriers. First, the existence of a great variety of different kinds of barriers, classified by a GATT committee under nearly 30 chapter headings, rendered a solution for all the listed measures problematic and made it preferable to select a restricted number of non-tariff barriers on which the negotiations should be focused. Secondly, reciprocity was harder to assess and this made it necessary to come up with a wide range of solutions to make up a well balanced package of concessions, while there was the possibility that not all the negotiating parties would be willing or could take part in the agreement. In this context, before entering negotiations the Community and its member states had to fulfil two tasks. The first was to select those non-tariff barriers whose suppression or regulation was in the Community's best interest. On the other hand, as such measures were in most cases imposed and administered by the member states rather than by the Community itself, it was necessary that the former agreed as soon as possible on a sufficient number of negotiable measures so as to offer adequate reciprocity in return for concessions by the trading partners. Finally, in order to secure the greatest possible participation of the GATT parties to such agreements and to prevent the worsening of the existing imbalance it was to be made clear that the advantages derived from solutions comprising obligations going beyond the existing GATT rules would be reserved to those countries which in practice abided by those solutions. In short, the Commission was suggesting, as was the case for the US Congress, the conditional application of the MFN clause.

On agriculture the Memorandum reiterated the Community's stance that, although the objectives of the negotiations were to be in keeping with the general approach of the round, that is, trade expansion and barrier reduction, they also had to take into account the sector's specific characteristics: the universal existence of support policies and the instability of world markets. In the Commission's view, the condition for expanding trade was stability of world markets and the best way to achieve this objective was a code of good conduct on export practices, aimed at introducing market discipline. Within the domestic sphere governments should intensify structural reforms so that marketing policies and price policies were based to a greater extent on economic considerations. On the other hand, for products such as cereals, dairy products and sugar the Commission suggested the negotiation of international arrangements, which should provide a price mechanism and adjustment of supply including measures of storage. The Community was to pledge to apply the instruments of its CAP in a way consistent with its multilateral commitments. However, taking into account the criticism of the Economic and Social Committee and some member states, the Commission amended its draft, stressing that 'the principles of the CAP should not be called into question'. Thus, on agriculture the memorandum seemed to meet French farm market philosophy and policies. France, which in the 1960s had carried out structural reforms aimed at transforming peasant farming into modern agriculture, in the 1970s was eager to secure its present and prospective share in the world market, while guaranteeing its role as main supplier in the EC market. These objectives made it favour forms of multinational cooperation and orderly trade conduct rather than the elimination of trade barriers and the retreat of government from the domestic market.

Like the United States, the Community was concerned with the upsurge of imports that could cause market injury to the domestic industries of its member states. The Commission suggested that the provisions of GATT Article XIX should be kept in force, but, given the difficulty of their effective implementation, that they be accompanied by a complementary mechanism, which should especially allow selective application of safeguard measures and suspension of the affected trading partners' compensatory rights.

Specific advantages had to be provided to the developing countries through improvements to the Generalized System of Preference, with the inclusion of a greater number of processed agricultural products and the widening of duty-free quotas, and through a more flexible application of the rules to be established on non-tariff barriers.

The Commission was careful to stress that its memorandum was based on the assumption that parallel machinery would be developed in the monetary sector to guarantee its long-term balance and stability, the absence of which would jeopardize the effectiveness of any wide-ranging agreement in the field of trade.

Similarities and differences of the preparatory stage to the new GATT round in the two areas

What were the similarities and differences between the preparatory stages to the new GATT round in the United States and in the EC, and why was the US executive able to take part in the opening phase of the negotiations without receiving negotiating authority from Congress? As regards similarities, the answer is simple and to a certain extent tautological. The stated aim of both parties was a more open and equitable world trading environment resulting in the general improvement of the world economy and in which the needs and expectations of the developing countries should be particularly taken into account. That was, after all, the core of the 11 February 1972 EC–US Declaration that paved the way to the launching of the round. The basic difference between the Commission's Memorandum and the US president's request for trade negotiating authority in the Trade Reform Act lay in their function and in their context. The negotiating authority requested by Nixon was directed at providing the executive with room for manoeuvre with regard to two sets of subjects on which authority was conferred on Congress by the US Constitution or by statutes. In the case of tariffs, Article 1, section 8, clause 3 of the Constitution empowered Congress to regulate commerce. However, since the Reciprocal Tariff Act of 1934, the US Congress had granted the executive the power to reduce customs duties up to a certain rate. It was, therefore, an a priori authorization. Once the authorization was granted the executive was free to choose the terms in which the prospective reductions could be applied: it could be an item by item reduction, an across the board cut, and so on. In the case of non-tariff barriers, since these obstacles resulted from the existing provisions of law, as every international agreement to be implemented implied the modification of a statute, the negotiating authority was directed to find a system by which the implementing legislation could be passed without bringing up for further discussion what had already been agreed by the executive in the negotiations. Otherwise, the other parties could never be sure whether the concessions they had made were grounded on reciprocal advantages. In this case, however, there was to be an agreement between the executive and Congress on the topics to which the new simplified legislation could apply. Thus, in both cases the US negotiators were able to play a primary role in the opening phase of the Tokyo Round not only because they were one of the main trading partners and the new round originated from a US proposal, but also because the initial stage only set the framework of the negotiations. Indeed, the actual start of the talks was postponed for over one year awaiting negotiating authority to be granted by US Congress and it was only when the House and the Senate conferred the authority that the attitude of the lawmakers and also of the executive towards the various items already debated in Geneva took complete, though not definite, shape.

The context in which the Memorandum from the Commission was worked out and approved was different. Article 113 of the Rome Treaty entrusted the Commission with the task of conducting negotiations on trade matters. However, the power of the EC executive was not open-ended. Article 113 of the Treaty of Rome provided that when agreements with third countries were to be negotiated in order to implement the Community Common Commercial Policy, the Commission should make recommendations to the Council, which should authorize it to open the necessary negotiations. The article also stated that the Commission should conduct the negotiations in consultation with a special committee appointed by the Council to assist it in the negotiating task within the framework of directives issued by the Council, the so-called Article 113 Committee, which was composed of senior civil servants (or their assistants) from the interested ministries of the member states. Thus, although formally an advisory body, the Article 113 Committee, whose members were national representatives, acted as a link between the Commission and the Council and, as its recommendations were often regarded as a preview of Council position, the Commission complied with them.

When in October 1972 the Paris European Summit entrusted the Commission with the task of defining a global approach to the GATT negotiations, it also stated that the strategy worked out by the Commission had to be submitted to the Council for approval by July 1973. Actually, as noted above, the Commission modified its Memorandum before submitting it to the Council for its final approval, which is indicative of a complex process of redaction that had to balance the not always reconcilable directives of the member states. Therefore, the Memorandum outlined the negotiating objectives of the Community, without, however, entering into the details. By approving the document the Council simply countenanced the line of action submitted by the Commission. On the other hand, as noted by the Commission itself, the 'overall approach to trade' was not a mandate to negotiate, nor did it provide specific negotiating directives on the various items of the forthcoming talks.[52] Besides, while the 'overall approach' was quite specific on items such as tariff reduction and harmonization, the safeguard clause and, in particular, agriculture, it postponed the outline of the EC negotiating stance on non-tariff barriers to a subsequent stage.

The launch of a new trade round

In the absence of negotiating authority to the president which would have helped define the United States' scope and approach to the GATT talks on tariff and non-tariff barriers and in the absence of any directive to the Commission on what the non-tariff barriers negotiations should be concerned with, in the run-up to the opening of the Tokyo Round there were only two areas of open disagreement between the US and the EC: trade in agriculture and the link between the prospective multilateral talks and the ongoing upheavals and negotiations in the monetary sector. A third potential area of disagreement concerned the manner and extent of tariff cuts, but it was to be expected that differences on this topic would be left to a later stage of the negotiations.

During the July meeting of the Preparatory Committee, the EC delegation circulated a 'Statement by the European Economic Community on the General approach adopted by the Council of Ministers on the forthcoming multilateral trade negotiations', which addressed, among other things, the question of the relation between trade negotiations and developments within the monetary system.[53] The text of the Statement on this point had previously been debated in the European Council where the Commission had suggested a reference to the need for parallel efforts to set up a monetary system shielding the world economy from the shocks and imbalances which had recently occurred and to the necessity that progress in the monetary field should be borne in mind by the Parties to the General Agreement, both at the beginning and during the course of the negotiations. France proposed a harder and more pressing statement which labelled the actual start of trade negotiations as unrealistic until the necessary steps had been taken to allow the exchange market to reflect the parity grid agreed in Paris in March 1973. A compromise was finally reached adding a paragraph stating that there were prospects for the establishment of a fair and durable monetary system based on fixed but adjustable parities, the general convertibility of currencies, effective international regulation of the world supply of liquidities and a reduction in the role of national currencies as reserve instruments.[54] The United States replied that an efficient monetary system was conditional on the adoption of trade measures which would facilitate the adjustment process as well as upon concurrent efforts to provide for trade liberalization and an improved framework for trade relations.[55]

In spite of the various differences in attitude there was no clash between the transatlantic parties. On the contrary, one senior member of the Commission delegation in Geneva related that in the last phase of the preparatory talks to the September ministerial meeting in Tokyo, the American delegation showed a strong desire to smooth over the points of dispute with the Community, avoiding any criticism of EC trade policy, and the CAP in particular, as it had done in the previous stages.[56] Thus, with regard to the agricultural trade and monetary system issues the Declaration approved by the Ministers at Tokyo on 14 September 1973 was a compromise in which the Community did not have to make any significant concessions.[57] Regarding agriculture, the Declaration called for an approach to negotiations which 'while in line with the general objectives of the negotiations, should take account of the special characteristics and problems in this sector'. As regards the link with international monetary arrangements, the Ministers recognized that the policy of liberalizing world trade could not be carried out successfully without parallel efforts to set up a monetary system shielding the world economy from the shocks and imbalances which had previously occurred, but also acknowledged that the new phase in the liberalization of trade, which it was their intention to undertake, would facilitate the orderly functioning of the monetary system. No reference was made to any agreed parity grid.

The Tokyo Declaration did not make any reference to the elimination of tariff barriers suggested by Japan and the Scandinavian countries, but in line with the Community's perspective simply referred to negotiations on tariffs based on appropriate formulae of as wide application as possible. On non-tariff barriers the Declaration pledged to reduce or eliminate non-tariff measures or, when this was not possible, their trade-distorting effects. However, the measures in question were not listed. The Ministers also agreed that the negotiations could concern the coordinated reduction or elimination of all barriers to trade in selected sectors. As requested by the EC, the adequacy of the multilateral safeguard system under GATT Article XIX was to be examined.

A Trade Negotiations Committee (TNC) was established with the task of elaborating detailed plans for the negotiations, working out appropriate procedures and supervising the progress of the negotiations. The Committee whose membership was open to all governments taking part in the talks and to the EC had to begin work by 1 November 1973. The deadline for the negotiations was set in 1975, a date that turned out to be overly optimistic, also because negotiating authority was still to be granted to the US executive. To avoid delays the parties agreed to concentrate their work in this first phase on the analytical and statistical aspects of the negotiations. The Commission decided not to table for the moment any substantive proposal not to allow the American negotiators to change their position on the pretext of new conditions attached to their mandate by the US Congress. On the other hand, the Commission suggested that the EC negotiators should be given specific directives which had to take into account the discussions on the trade bill in the US Congress, nevertheless avoiding the risk that they be left behind by the Americans in establishing their negotiating stance.[58]

Thus the spirit of the Tokyo Conference reflected the favourable but increasingly overheated climate of the world economy in which income and trade were strongly growing and there was a close correlation between the two. This meant that the voices of those calling for fewer barriers to trade were not drowned out by the complaints of import competing industries. Moreover, import liberalization began to be seen as an antidote against inflation by increasing the availability of goods at better prices and by generating major pressure for production efficiency. The performance of American farm trade made the United States consider the idea that the dismantling of CAP was still a priority but a less immediate one. On the other hand, the hostility of many European countries against the floating rate regime was waning as the West European countries, including the hardliners in the EC were, willingly or unwillingly, accepting a floating system as the normal course of currency management. The attitude changed when only a month later the so-called oil crisis ushered in a period in which inflation was no longer the unwelcome companion to growth but went hand in hand with recession.

3

Crisis and Unstable Recovery (October 1973–December 1976)

The economic conjuncture and its impact on domestic and international policies in the United States and in the European Community

The years 1974 and 1975 witnessed an unprecedented slump on both sides of the Atlantic which had its impact on trade relations between the United States and the EC member countries, as well as between the two areas and the Rest of the World. Contrary to previous slumps in the nineteenth and twentieth centuries, the reversal of the upwards phase that had marked most of the 1950s and 1960s was accompanied by an inflation upsurge that hit the EC member states and the US, although with different strength and duration. Indeed the years following 1973 are remembered as the years of stagflation. They are viewed as the outcome of changes in the economic trend that characterized the 'golden age' of the two previous decades in terms of productivity, trade expansion and management of fiscal and monetary policy. However, as already noted, this term can be apposite to the performance of the European economy, with the remarkable exception of Great Britain, but not to the performance of the US economy which, by the close of the 1960s, saw its predominance over the Japanese and Western European partners shrink, not only because Japan and Western Europe were fast closing the productivity gap, but also because overall productivity in US industry was decelerating. Secondly, in Western Europe too by the end of the 1960s, the golden age had lost much of its lustre. On both sides of the Atlantic the beginning of the 1970s saw a robust upsurge in the economic cycle, along with, it is true, a price hike which, however, was far below the inflation rate in the years following the start of the oil crisis (Tables 1, 10 and 22). It must also be noted that after the 1974–5 decline, the recovery that marked the following three years in the US was characterized, in contrast to most EC member states, by a growth rate comparable to the recovery of the early 1970s and to the years of highest growth in the previous decade.

The onset of the oil crisis and the disparate responses of the industrial countries

As often in the declining phase of a cycle, the 1974–5 slump was triggered by an exogenous factor. The exogenous factor was the so-called oil crisis set off by events that took place in the last quarter of 1973. The oil crisis took partially different features in the US and the EC member states, although its impact on the economies of both sides of the Atlantic was broadly similar. Thus, it caused different responses in political and economic terms, as context and constraints were not the same in the United States and in the Western European countries.

The EC member states were traditionally heavily dependent on foreign oil supply. Only the UK, Germany and Belgium had a sufficient alternative source of energy in coal, whose exploitation, however, was becoming increasingly expensive relative to oil imports, while the Netherlands had good gas reserves. Although the United Kingdom had the medium-term prospect of becoming an important oil producer itself, at the time of the crisis it was no exception, its problems being exacerbated by a lengthy dispute between the Heath government and the National Union of Miners which had curtailed its supply of alternative energy source, coal. The United States, the main oil producer, but at the same time the dominant oil consumer, after 1970 had passed rapidly from a position of relative oil supply independence to a position of relative oil supply dependence. In spite of new discoveries on the North Slope of Alaska and on the Outer Continental Shelf, oil production slowed down in the 1960s and early 1970s, also hampered by a variety of environmental restrictions and governmental controls, while no significant progress took place in the development of alternative sources of supply. In contrast demand for fuel kept growing, stimulated by oil and gas prices which remained below the market clearing price.[1] In April 1973, the system of import quotas adopted in 1959 to limit dependence upon foreign sources supply was definitively abandoned in favour of a flexible import fee. Imports of crude oil and refined products in the US rose from 22 per cent of domestic consumption in 1969 to 36 per cent in 1973.[2]

At the same time the oil producing countries had been constantly strengthening their sway over the market. The Organization of Petroleum Exporting

Countries (OPEC) was established at the Baghdad Conference in September 1960 with the objective of resisting pressure by the oil companies, the so-called 'Seven Sisters' in particular, to reduce oil prices and payments to the exporting states. It had an original membership of seven countries, but by 1973 the organization had acquired a membership of 13 states. Most of these countries had been able to replace the royalty system with a majority share in the oil companies, which entailed a direct control on quantities produced, while Algeria, Libya and Iraq proceeded directly to nationalization of the more important companies operating on their soils. The foregoing, coupled with growing demand for oil, offered a good chance to impose higher prices. The Tehran and Tripoli agreements of January and February 1971, of the OPEC members to impose a substantial price increase, soon turned out to be exceedingly moderate. In fact the increase was more than offset by the depreciation of the dollar, the currency in which oil prices were fixed, and by growing inflationary pressures characterizing the world economy since 1972, which increased the price of imports for the oil producing countries including food and materials essential to their development programmes. The break-out of the Yom Kippur War in October 1973 allowed the OPEC members to raise the posted price of oil by 70 per cent to US$5.11 per barrel while implementing measures to increasingly cut supply.

The OPEC decision overlapped with the embargo imposed by the Organization of Arab Petroleum Exporting Countries (OAPEC) to put pressure on those Western countries that appeared to support Israel in the conflict. In the Kuwait meeting on 24 and 25 December, the OAPEC cut oil exports by a minimum of 5 per cent and subdivided the importing countries into four categories: a) countries that had severed diplomatic relations with Israel, including the United Kingdom, France and Spain, which were to be preferentially supplied according to their need even if that exceeded the 1973 level of oil exports; b) friendly countries, such as Japan, Belgium and West Germany, that had adjusted their policies so as to favour the Arab position to which supplies would be secured at the September 1973 level; c) unfriendly countries like the United States, the Netherlands, Portugal and South Africa, to be placed under total embargo; d) neutral remaining countries not belonging to the previous groups which were to receive a prorated share of the remaining Arabian oil supply and were subject to the general cutback.[3] On 17 March, 1974 the OAPEC members, with the exception of Libya, lifted the embargo, but by then oil prices had quadrupled to nearly US$12 per barrel. Thus, as Venn points out, a clear distinction must be drawn between the 5 month embargo, which only affected a few countries, only one of which was a EEC member state, and the oil price crisis which was brought about by the policy that OPEC as a whole was able to establish also thanks to the embargo itself.[4] That policy also presupposed agreed control of oil supply, but agreements of this kind were rarely implemented effectively.

The November 1973 call from Secretary of State Henry Kissinger for a united front of oil importing countries under the leadership of the United States met with a lukewarm response from the EC countries. The Community member countries, as well as Japan, which was even more dependent on supply from the Middle East, tried to establish bilateral agreements with the oil producing countries of North Africa and the Middle East to secure oil imports at good terms in exchange for high technology exports.[5] France in particular, unwilling to sacrifice its long-lasting political and economic links with the Arab countries, tried to scupper the US project for a coalition of oil consumers under its leadership.[6] The February 1974 Washington Energy Conference, summoned by the United States to establish consumer cooperation in place of bilateral deals, was attended by all main oil importing countries, including France, but failed to achieve a unified consuming nations policy towards OPEC and OAPEC. Yet, the participants agreed on a number of principles, such as the need for conservation, emergency sharing and development of new energy sources, and on the establishment of an Energy Coordination Group. These principles were rendered more operative when in November 1974 the OECD members, with the exclusion of France, agreed to implement a joint programme under the aegis of a newly established International Energy Agency (IEA), which provided for an emergency petroleum allocation scheme, including oil sharing, demand restraint obligations, an extensive information system on the oil market and long-term cooperation on energy research to develop hydrocarbon and alternative energy sources. However, the launch of the new programme, prevalently aimed at dealing with emergency situations and the IEA establishment, did not result in a qualitative leap in the coordination among consumers. Bilateral agreements with several oil producing countries remained the dominant approach of the EC member states, and the United States, having set aside the goal of a unified consumer coalition under its leadership, soon started to develop a network of bilateral relations with the so-called 'moderate oil producers' in the Middle East, at the centre of which was Saudi Arabia.

The common pledge to curtail consumption and develop alternative sources of energy production did not result in a unified policy and each IEA member implemented its own measures and achieved different results. The outcome was markedly different on the two sides of the Atlantic.

In November 1973 Nixon declared that by the end of 1975 oil imports would be reduced by one million barrels per day through energy conservation and enhanced domestic energy supply. Things turned out differently. With the aim of preventing windfall gains for domestic oil producers and curbing the inflationary impact of the increased cost of energy, the oil policy measures that were actually adopted ended up by implicitly taxing domestic producers and subsidizing consumers and importers. The result was lower levels of production, more consumption and higher imports, thus increasing the bill paid to the OPEC countries.[7] Before the occurrence of the oil crisis, the Cost of Living Council had established a distinction between 'old oil' and 'new oil', whereby a ceiling price was set for oil in stock, while new and imported oil was allowed to seek a market-clearing level. After the end of the oil embargo, the Entitlements Program, implemented in November 1974, provided that refiners who purchased price-controlled oil had to make an income transfer to refiners who purchased uncontrolled or imported oil. Finally, the Energy Policy and Conservation Act brought more domestic crude oil under control and fixed a \$7.66/bbl price ceiling from February 1976 which could rise ten per cent a year. Domestic consumers paid a composite price based on a weighted average of low-priced domestic and high-priced imported oil. As a result, in spite of a slight decline in 1974 and 1975 on account of the oil embargo and what could be more properly called 'slumpflation', US oil consumption between 1973 and 1978 grew from 17,308 thousands of barrels per day to 18,847 thousands of barrels per day and total imports grew from 6,256 thousands of barrels per day to 8,363 thousands of barrels per day.[8] Imports as percentage of demand grew from 36.1 per cent to 44.4 per cent, whereas in 1970 they had accounted for only 23.3 per cent.

The performance of the EC was more cautious. After the 1974 shock which witnessed a 146 per cent growth rate under the pressure of the quadrupling of the oil price, the fuel bill grew by only 18 per cent by 1978 (Table 18). In quantitative terms the contraction was remarkable, although it was helped by the slump and the slackening of the economy after the 1976 recovery. Petroleum consumption in West Germany, France and the UK declined respectively by 3.6 per cent, 6.4 per cent and 14.7 per cent, while imports fell by 6.5 per cent and 13.2 per cent in West Germany and France, plummeting by over 41 per cent in Britain.[9] However, the success achieved by the EC member states was not the result of a unified policy entrusted to a supranational entity. Although the Commission reviewed the overall energy position in the Community, the individual members maintained full control of their domestic and foreign policy in pursuit of their national energy interests, nor was there any pooling of energy sources.[10] In particular, the United Kingdom made it quite soon clear that it was not willing to surrender control over North Sea oil. France used state-owned or controlled companies to exploit foreign oil resources and developed a domestic nuclear energy programme. Italy did not depart from its policy of friendly relations with the oil producers maintained through the state-owned ENI, which in the two previous decades had often been at odds with the main oil companies.

Economic recession and recovery

The undeniable fact that the sudden hike in the oil price ushered in a prolonged slump along with an upsurge in inflation proves that the upheaval in the oil market had a role in the economic crisis characterizing 1974 and 1975. However, this does not shed much light on the importance of the oil factor in the recession plus inflation process as other elements of greater weight might have been at play.

A Marxist commentator claims that 'the 1974–5 recession was a classical overproduction crisis and the outcome of a typical phase of decline of the rate of profit', which pre-dated the leap in oil prices following the Kippur War.[11] Certainly, the movements around the trend had become more pronounced and more frequent since the late 1960s and the overheating of the economy in 1972–3, following the decline of 1970, made it possible to foresee a marked slowdown in the following years. And there is no doubt that the 1974–5 recession ushered in a lowering of the general trend. With reference to inflationary pressures, Aldcroft argues that the leap in oil prices cannot be regarded as the initial cause of acceleration of inflation or as the main contributor to its perpetuation in the 1970s, and that instead 'a secular upward trend in inflation from the mid-1960s had superimposed on it a cyclically or partly cyclically generated price boom in the early 1970s'.[12] Yet, there is no denying that the oil crisis in its various aspects and stages deeply affected the main features of the stagflation and its severity. For instance, in the United States a soft landing of the economy could have occurred under different circumstances. In fact, the Economic Report of the President for the year 1973 relates that as early as the second and third quarters of the year there were signs of deceleration in the growth of output and demand.[13]

Rostow points out that overall the OECD countries suffered total output declines in 1974 and 1975 twice the level that could be directly attributed to the rise in the oil price, while the inflation rate after 1972 was greater than what could be directly attributed to the rise in food and energy prices. However, the scholar adds that the effect on GDP of the rise in the oil bill was compounded by policies of fiscal and monetary restraint, while the inflation leap caused by the hike in basic commodities was also the outcome of the attempt of the labour unions to protect the real wage of workers from the explosive increase in the price of basic commodities.[14] All this suggests that if the oil price rise and the other threats of the oil crisis to the economies of the OECD countries are viewed as an independent variable affecting income and inflation along with several other independent variables – including fiscal and monetary policies as well as firms' and trade unions' decisions on investments and wage and price rises – in assessing the weight of the former in the causal process, one must also consider their influence on concurrent causes. Put more simply, it is arguable that the oil crisis had a direct impact on the industrialized countries' economy, but above all contributed to the economic environment that, in turn, induced the monetary and fiscal authorities on both sides of the Atlantic to take the measures that triggered the slump or made it worse.

The quadrupling of oil price affected the OECD members' economy in a plurality of ways, although their impact was not uniform. In the first place, the quadrupling of the oil price caused a diversion of expenditures in the oil-importing countries from domestically produced goods to imported petroleum products, whose immediate result, in the absence of an equivalent decline in the price of other consumer goods, was a reduction in the available income. A French economic historian put the transfer of wealth to the oil-exporting countries between 2 and 3 per cent of the Federal Republic of Germany's GDP, that is, a burden of the same order as the Dawes Plan war reparations.[15] The worsening of the terms of trade compelled oil consumers – manufacturing industries in particular – to pay higher prices for equal or even declining quantities, and in order to foot the bill the industrial countries had to withdraw resources from the domestic economy. This, combined with a lack of compensating increases in productivity and real wage resistance, resulted in lower profits and hence fewer investments, which, in turn, led to a fall in output and productivity growth.[16] As the oil-exporting nations did not increase their imports correspondingly, aggregate demand was bound to decline in the oil-importing countries unless the reduction was offset by domestic policy action. But the room for manoeuvre left to their governments was quite limited as they operated in an already inflationary environment and any income support measure might have resulted in the acceleration of inflation.

Secondly, increased oil prices had an impact on the general price level through various channels. There was a direct impact arising from the higher prices that consumers had to pay for petroleum products, such as gasoline and heating oil, and there was an indirect impact through the price increase for other goods of which oil was an input. Finally, the higher price for oil heightened the demand for substitute sources of energy driving up their prices. According to the 1974 Economic Report of the President, 'the increase of the price of gasoline from October 1973 to August 1974 added between 1 and 2 percentage points to the rise of the consumer price index in Great Britain, Italy and the United States'.

Thirdly, the increase in the price of oil led to a deficit in the current account of the oil-importing countries and a matching surplus in the current account of the oil-exporting countries. The latter, however, in the short-run were precluded from significantly increasing their demand for imported products by the confinement of income gains to narrow segments of their population, or by the long lead time in developing major projects needing imports from industrialized countries. The OPEC countries' trade balance surplus amounted to 102 billion dollars in 1974, compared with 22 billion the previous year, while the industrial countries' deficit more than tripled.

The amount of the current account deficit and its impact on the economy was not the same among the OECD members. As noted by Thirlwall, if a country gets into balance of payments difficulties before reaching its short-term capacity growth, then demand must be curtailed, thus discouraging investment and slowing down technological progress.[17] However, the constraint is not immediately felt, or is felt to a lesser degree, by those countries whose currencies are considered reserve currencies. Indeed, the United States benefited from short-term capital inflows as the oil-exporting countries invested part of their financial surpluses in its capital market. For most other countries the best way to ease the constraint imposed on the growth level by the balance of payments was to increase their exports, with the caveat, however, that the same rate of export growth in different countries could not necessarily permit the same rate of growth of output, because the import requirements associated with growth differed from country to country.[18]

There was, thus, the temptation for many countries affected by the oil crisis to resort to export incentives and import restrictions to prevent deterioration in their trade and current account balances. To prevent an escalation of trade-distorting actions the OECD members at their annual Ministerial Meeting in May 1974 agreed on a declaration setting forth their intention to avoid new import restrictions, artificial export stimulations and export restrictions for a period of one year. The declaration, known as the 'trade pledge' was renewed at the Ministerial Meeting of 1975 and at subsequent OECD meetings. However, there is no certainty as to whether the members of the Paris Organization stood by their commitment.

In the United States, the country in which stagflation was first experienced, the crisis was not brought about by current account constraints. After the recovery of 1973, the US merchandise trade balance went back into the red in 1974, but the losses caused by soaring oil import expenditures were partially offset by fast growing exports to Western Europe boosted by the dollar devaluation. In 1975, the current account balance reached a surplus unprecedented in monetary terms and the trade balance became positive again despite the impact of the oil bill thanks to sustained exports but above all to a contraction of imports brought about by the slump. The US slump was caused by its inability to fight inflation without compromising growth and employment. As noted by Alex McLeod, the simultaneous achievement of multiple policy goals by demand management requires as many effective and non-redundant policy instruments as policy objectives and the attainment of each objective must be influenced by at least one instrument. Besides, each instrument must also be capable of differentially affecting progress towards separate objectives.[19] The problem with the use of fiscal and monetary policy to simultaneously curb inflation and increase national product and consequently employment is that, although the time and the impact of their effects may differ, they proceed in the same direction resulting either in an expansion or in a contraction of real as well as nominal income. As the United States had to rely on the usual instruments of 'total' demand management, while the causes of its troubles were several, it was not able to achieve a satisfactory balance between price stability and growth and unemployment reduction.

At the beginning of the recession inflation was perceived as the most acute problem. The US consumer price annual growth rate had already increased from 3.5 to 5.4 per cent between 1972 and 1973 but it ballooned to double figures the following year (Table 22). The wholesale price for manufactured goods hit 19 per cent (Table 23). In addition to disruption of economic activity, the energy crisis erased all hopes of controlling inflation through wage and price control programmes. In turn, inflation curtailed real purchasing power as real wages fell by 5 per cent during the year. Presenting his programme to check inflation and encourage growth, President Ford exhorted the nation to 'whip inflation now (WIN)' as a scourge threatening to destroy the American way of life[20]. The overall contractionary fiscal policy was accompanied by a monetary policy that continued the move toward restraint begun in 1973. The rate of growth of money sharply declined in the second half of 1974 and the M1 growth rate became actually negative in the first quarter of 1975, just when the US economy was reaching the trough of the cycle. The slump first hit housing and then spread to other sectors, prominent among which were automobiles and clothing. In 1974 GNP declined by 0.6 per cent and GDP by 0.8 per cent (Table 1). Industrial production fell by over 12 per cent in the last quarter of the year and, even worse from a human and political perspective, unemployment rose to 7.2 per cent in December reaching 8.5 per cent by March 1975. In 1975 GDP and GNP declined respectively by 0.9 per cent and 1.2 per cent. During the months of the recession the capacity-utilization rate dropped to 68 per cent from 83 per cent at the beginning of the period. Nominal unit labour costs added to inflationary pressures as the growth of compensation per hour markedly exceeded the growth of output in the two recession years (Table 8).

In January 1975 President Ford called for tax reductions to fight the recession and Congress backed him. In December 1975 the tax cuts were renewed. As government expenditures also increased, the Federal budget deficit jumped from $11.5 billion to $69.3 billion, thus rising from a modest 0.8 per cent of the GDP to a non-negligible 4.5 per cent (Table 9). In 1976 a robust recovery (5.5%) seemed to be firmly established and consumer prices abated to 1973 levels under the effect of the recession, the monetary squeeze and the end of the oil hike. Yet, inflation was still high and the unemployment rate stood at a high 7.8 per cent, not far from the trough rate of the previous year. Meanwhile the merchandise trade balance had markedly returned to the red under the impact of growing imports, oil in particular, even though the current account balance was still positive (Table 2). The onset, duration and severity of the slump were not uniform among the EC member countries, which makes us think that the causes of the recession were not identical.

West Germany managed to escape the balance of payments constraint that affected most other EC member countries. Its trade balance remained healthy in spite of an export decline in 1975 (Tables 11 and 12). The slowdown in 1974 can be primarily attributed to the restrictive monetary policy adopted by the Bundesbank till the end of 1973 in the wake of the breakdown of the Bretton Woods system to combat inflation which in that year had already hit 6.9 per cent.[21] The restrictive policy sustained the appreciation of the Deutschmark vis-à-vis the US dollar, thus curbing the oil bill and with it inflation. However, investment contracted by almost 10 per cent in 1974 ushering in a slowdown which turned into recession in 1975 when the spreading slump caused exports, the engine of German economic strength, to decline for the first time in over 20 years. Thus, it was not the constraint imposed by the surge of import value in the balance of payment but the decline of main components of demand, nominally investments and exports, that brought about the slump. In 1975 the German monetary authority adopted a cautiously expansionary stance, while the fiscal authority continued the countercyclical course already adopted in 1974 and the fiscal deficit reached an unprecedented high of 5.8 per cent of GDP (Table 19). In 1976 the economy fully recovered with a 5.1 growth rate not lower than the 1960 average (Table 10), fuelled by the resurgence of exports and the recovery of investments. However, the expansionary momentum slowed down quite soon.

There was greater volatility in the course of events in Italy, the UK and France which, in turn, showed many similarities. In particular, the Italian economy, in spite of the oil crisis, went on growing in 1974, although at a rate lower than the previous year: 4.1 per cent and 7 per cent respectively (Table 10). Industrial production also continued to grow (Table 20). Inflation, however, jumped to over 19 per cent and the trade gap widened at an unprecedented rate (Tables 11, 12 and 22). Thus, in line with the model developed by Thirlwall, the gaping current account deficit, which in 1974 exceeded US$8 billion, forced the Italian central bank to tighten credit conditions to reduce private demand.[22] The credit squeeze helped reduce the trade deficit and abate inflation, though not significantly nor durably (Tables 22 and 23). At the same time the Italian GDP plunged by a stunning minus 3.6 per cent (Table 10) while the fiscal deficit soared to over 13 per cent of GDP under the combined pressure of lower revenues and higher expenditure to subsidize declining industries and contain unemployment (Table 19). To redress the current account balance without penalizing growth, the Italian authorities tried to boost exports by resorting to devaluation. At the beginning of 1976, after a 40 day suspension of the foreign exchange market, the lira depreciated by about 30 per cent on average. The manoeuvre raised the competitiveness of the Italian products despite the continued rise of the cost of labour (Figure 3) and in the short-run the Italian GDP recovered by a robust 5.9 per cent, while the import bill and inflation remained high.

The recession started earlier in the UK than in Italy but was less severe, while the 1976 recovery was less pronounced (Table 10). Inflation, whose average was 5.1 per cent in the 1961–73 years, ballooned to 16 per cent in 1974 and hit 24 per cent in 1975 and did not fall below 16 per cent the following year, thus remaining well above the EC average along with Italy (Table 22). The initial impact of the oil crisis on the trade balance was even more severe than in Italy, but in 1975 the import bill went down, partly because of the prolonged slump and because North Sea oil began to flow (Table 12).

The first impact of the oil shock on France was to accelerate the overheating of the economy, stimulating in the first semester of 1974 both the demand for consumer goods and investments; but the monetary and fiscal squeeze carried out in June 1974 drastically altered the economic environment hitting both above-mentioned components.[23] On a yearly basis, GDP grew by 3.2 per cent, while inflation jumped to 13.7 per cent (Tables 10 and 22). Exports grew by a robust 33 per cent but imports soared by 47 per cent (Tables 11 and 12). In 1975 the GDP growth rate was almost nil and import value slightly declined but inflation remained above 10 per cent. In September 1975 a plan was adopted to boost the demand by public investments, by the reduction of fiscal pressure and interest rates to stimulate private investments and by social aids. The outcome was not convincing as there was a strong recovery, but at the price of a rate of inflation higher than the EC average, and the worsening of the trade balance, which forced the French government to abandon once again the European Snake.[24] In September 1976 the new French government introduced a plan, known as Barre Plan, primarily directed at stabilizing the economy and curbing inflation. The set of measures helped to improve the trade and current account balances but the GDP growth slackened, the rate of investment decreased and unemployment remained high relative to the years prior to the oil crisis, while inflation did not significantly abate.

Considering all the EC member states, the oil crisis swelled their trade deficit: the gap between imports and exports grew by over 280 per cent between 1973 and 1974 and quadrupled two years later (Tables 11 and 12). The main cause was obviously the impact of the energy bill, as the share of fuel products rose from 11.7 per cent of the whole of commodity imports in 1973 to 20.5 per cent in 1974, declining only slightly in the following two years (Table 18). Obviously the picture was not uniform. The Federal Republic of Germany, although its exports contracted in 1975, was always able to keep a positive trade balance and the Netherlands improved it thanks to its energy exports, while the other EC countries saw their trade gap worsen in spite of the growth of their exports. Countries with sources of oil and gas like the UK and the Netherlands suffered much less than the other Community members from the burden of the energy bill or even benefited from its rise.

After the 1973 peak the following three years witnessed a decline in intra-EC trade (Table 16). This can be explained by the ballooning of the oil imports from the OPEC countries, to which corresponded the need to reorient EC exports of equipment and consumer products toward those countries. The Community trade gap with the United States almost quintupled between 1973 and 1976

(Tables 13 and 14). The share of exports from the EC member countries to the United States over their total exports declined from 7.5 per cent in 1973 to 5.5 per cent in 1976 while the share of imports remained constant at just over 8 per cent. Conversely, the share of US imports from the EC declined from 23.3 per cent in 1973 to 14.7 per cent three years later, and the share of exports to the Community decreased from 24 per cent to 21 per cent.[25]

The initial phase of the multilateral trade negotiations

The change in the economic environment was to have a delaying impact on trade negotiations as the negotiators were faced with economic decline, rising unemployment and, for the first time in 1975, with a 5 per cent contraction in world trade volume, which had almost tripled in the preceding 14 years, all but quadrupling in manufacture exports. While in 1973 the predominant economic problem for the OECD countries was inflation and, therefore, cutting trade barriers was seen as an opportunity to counter it, in the following years the industrial countries plunged into the worst recession after World War Two and 'the old pressure to limit imports and thus export unemployment returned'[26]. Other factors, which were linked to domestic developments in the US, hindered progress. In the first place, the US executive received trade authority more than a year after the official opening of the negotiations. Secondly, the attention to the GATT negotiations of the new president, whose accession to the presidency was due to his predecessor's misfortunes, was distracted by the forthcoming 1976 elections which was also a factor that made too clear a stance on several issues in the multilateral trade talks a dangerous course.

The Trade Act of 1974 and the granting of negotiating authority to the US President

As noted above, the multilateral talks launched by the September 1973 Ministerial Conference in Tokyo were kept in a preparatory stage awaiting Congress's grant of negotiating authority to the US executive. The negotiating mandate was expected to provide a clear signal of the American stance in the negotiations as well as of the room for manoeuvre allowed to the executive. Congress cleared the bill on 19 December 1974, just before the end of the second session of the 93rd Congress and the bill was signed into law by Gerald

Ford on 3 January 1975. The delay was formally caused by a peripheral controversy over restriction on Jewish emigration by the Soviet Union to which the administration wanted to grant MFN status, but actually it was the result of the declining authority of a presidency crippled by impeachment. It also concealed substantive issues of trade authority allocation on which the Senate's attitude was less compromising than the House's. The Jewish emigration obstacle was overcome by a compromise authorizing the president to waive the bill's ban on trade concessions to Communist countries that restricted emigration if he received assurances that practices were implemented to allow freedom to expatriate.

The legislation, entitled the 'Trade Act of 1974', has been labelled as 'essentially liberal'.[27] This judgement can be accepted only with some caveats. The Act is divided into six Titles of which only the first, dealing with negotiating authority, can be labelled as 'essentially liberal', although its provisions were far from being unconditionally free-trade oriented and many of the administration's preferences to secure room for manoeuvre in the multilateral negotiations did not meet with unconditional Congressional acceptance. Many other Titles contained provisions aiming at unilaterally opposing alleged unfair trade practices by foreign competitors or directed to providing more protection to those sectors of the economy allegedly hit by foreign competition or to make quasi-judicial remedies already in force, like antidumping and countervailing measures, stricter, more effective and more easily accessible.[28] Indeed, although openly protectionist proposals, such as the Hartke and Burke bill, were rejected, the legislation was adopted in a moment in which the economy was hit by the second recession in just four years and unemployment was increasing. The Senate Report pointed out that during the 1960s and early 1970s US pre-eminence in the world economy had declined as compared with Western Europe and Japan. It was then arguable that much of world economic history in the years following the Trade Expansion Act of 1962, considered the climax of the US drive to secure a freer and fairer world trade, 'has been unfavourable to this country, largely because of the antiquated rules of the international trade and monetary systems and the related lack of genuine cooperation and reciprocity in international economic relations'.[29]

Negotiating authority to the president was granted for tariff cuts, following the long-established rule of allowing the executive to negotiate cuts and implement them by self-executing presidential order. The Trade Act authorized the president to eliminate tariffs on goods carrying duties of 5 per cent or less and to reduce higher tariffs by as much as 60 per cent, subject to commensurate actions by other countries. The provision widened the administration's room for manoeuvre at the multilateral talks by negotiating tariff cuts modulated according to their level at the opening of the negotiations. Indeed, while the United States and the EC had comparable average duties of 6 per cent to 7 per cent, 12 per cent of US tariffs had a rate not lower than 20 per cent. On the other hand, the Act authorized the president to increase tariffs by 20 per cent of the 1973 rates or 150 per cent of the 1934 rates, whichever was the higher.

Things were much less simple with regard to non-tariff barriers (NTBs), as in this area future international deals would overlap with often quite complex domestic rules, which, in most cases, till that moment had not been affected by international commitments, whereas domestic interest groups had swayed their draft.

The administration had proposed an arrangement, accepted by the House of Representatives, under which the president would give notice in advance to Congress of his intention to negotiate an agreement so as to allow lawmakers to express their views. After the negotiation the agreement would be submitted to Congress along with the implementing legislation, entering into effect if not rejected by a majority vote within 90 days. In short, Congress would have been given an advisory function plus a power of veto to be exercised in a short span, but no positive approval of the agreements was envisaged. This approach would have satisfied the other parties to the negotiations, afraid that the NTB agreements could be blocked or deprived of content by the US Congress in the ratification stage. The lot of the limited number of non-tariff issues dealt with in the Kennedy Round, the American Sale Price system in particular, did not bode well. Formally Congress maintained veto power, but this would have cast on it full and, even worse, open responsibility for scuttling a deal laboriously worked out by the United States and its trading partners.

The Senate was not satisfied with the arrangement as the quasi-automatic implementations of multilateral trade agreements would impinge on its power to regulate, and to regulate in detail, matters that had often quite a weight on the domestic economy. The implementation of a tariff barrier agreement would simply require the lowering of a duty. The implementation of an NTB agreement would often entail a complex grafting on the legislation already in place. On the other hand, it was clear that Congress could not have an autonomous role in negotiating with foreign countries. The compromise worked out envisaged a greater voice for Congress in shaping an international agreement that could satisfactorily be implemented in the domestic legislation, but no power of amendment or deferral. The Trade Act of 1974 thus required the president to notify Congress at least 90 days in advance before entering into an NTB agreement and, following such an agreement, to transmit a copy of it along with the draft of the implementing bill and a statement of the reasons as to how the agreement served the interests of the United States. Congress had 90 days (60 for non-revenue bills) to decide on the legislation, but could not introduce amendments. This in practice meant that the Special Trade Representative had to work closely with the House Ways and Means Committee and the Senate Finance Committee during the transmittal phase. To this end delegates of both the House and Senate were accredited to the US delegation to the trade negotiations and the chairmen of the Ways and Means and Finance Committees were authorized to designate members to be official advisers of the delegation in Geneva.

The Trade Act also gave a direct role to interest groups in the NTB negotiations by creating a system of private sector committees to supply advice and information for US negotiators. The Act provided for the creation of an Advisory Committee for Trade Negotiations (ACTN) composed of 45 members appointed by the president, representing labour, industry, agriculture, small business, consumer interests and the general public. The ACTN, presided over by the US Special Trade Representative, would convene in Washington and in Geneva as well. At a level below the ACTN the legislation called for the creation of general policy advisory committees for industry, labour and agriculture and for a series of advisory committees to be established at a sectoral level. Thus, the reform relieved Congress of the pressure of interest groups and arguably diminished the lawmakers' power as mediators of such interests in drawing up statutes. Conversely, the interest groups were now able to make their voice heard directly, becoming a major interlocutor of the executive, and of the Special Trade Representative in particular, in the course of the multilateral negotiations.

The stated overall objective of the trade negotiations was to obtain more open and equitable market access and the harmonization, reduction, or elimination of devices that distort trade in every area. The Senate Report stressed that, as far as was feasibly possible, the process of harmonization, reduction or elimination of agricultural trade barriers should be undertaken in conjunction with industrial trade liberalization.[30] This meant that, in contrast with the EC perspective, although certain particular features of the farm sector could be recognized, this should not entail separate negotiations for agricultural trade. On the other hand, for some industrial sectors, such as steel, aluminium, electronics, chemicals and electrical machinery, sectoral negotiations could be carried out which should result in equivalent competitive opportunities for the developed countries within each sector. The Senate also made it clear that benefits and obligations of non-tariff barrier agreements should be limited to the parties of such agreements in order to encourage all trading nations to commit themselves and to avoid free-lancing in the hope of obtaining benefits without reciprocal engagements.[31] Finally, the Trade Act directed the president to seek reform of the GATT to promote the development of an open, non-discriminatory and fair world economic system. Among these principles particular attention was given to the revision of the decision-making procedures of the GATT, the establishment of international procedures for consultation among countries on trade issues and for the resolution of commercial disputes, the reform of GATT Article XIX on safeguard measures with the view to making it more flexible. In response to the particular difficulties of the economic situation in 1974, Congress also called for strengthening of the rules directed to assure access to supplies including procedures governing imposition of export controls and sanctions on those countries that denied fair and equitable access to supply sources. However, the Trade Act of 1974 and the reports of the Ways and Means Committee and of the Finance Committee were silent on issues such as customs valuation, public procurement, import restrictions and technical barriers to trade, which would figure prominently in the negotiations in Geneva.

Along with the draft of the US goals and strategies in the multilateral negotiations, the Trade Act set a series of domestic measures nominally directed at strengthening the protection of the US economy and of its industries against the pressure exerted by the international economic environment, whether its causes were labelled as unfair or otherwise.

As requested by the executive, the legislation relaxed the criteria for industries to be allowed relief from import competition, providing for an affirmative determination wherein the International Trade Commission (ITC) found that increased imports were a substantial cause of injury rather than a major cause as in previous laws.[32] At the same time the administration's room for manoeuvre was curtailed as the president could waive such relief if he found that it was not in the national interest but, if he did so or provided ways of relief other than those recommended by the Commission, he had to report his reasons to Congress which could override his decision by a concurrent resolution. Also the criteria for adjustment assistance to industries, firms and workers affected by foreign competition were made more elastic by the requirement that imports 'contribute importantly' to their difficulties. The Act, under Section 122, also required the president in case of large balance of payments deficit to proclaim for up to 150 days corrective action, including import surcharges of up to 15 per cent and temporary quotas, unless he determined that such measures were contrary to the national interest.

Under Section 301 of the Act the president was given authority to retaliate against 'unjustifiable or unreasonable' restrictions imposed by foreign countries that burden or restrict US commerce, both in goods and services, or access to supplies, whether through high tariffs or non-tariff barriers, including subsidies and import and export quotas. The term 'unjustifiable' referred to restrictions which were illegal under international law or inconsistent with international obligations. The term 'unreasonable', however, referred to restrictions which were not necessarily illegal but which nullified or impaired benefits accruing to the United States under trade agreements or which otherwise discriminated or burdened US commerce, opening the door for affirmative findings even if no treaty or international law provisions were violated. The section allowed the president to suspend trade concessions, impose new higher tariff rates on a selective basis, or take other retaliatory actions, including the imposition of antidumping duties or countervailing measures or even exclusion orders which barred a product from being imported into the United States. Although any decision on unjustifiable or unreasonable restrictions was the executive's responsibility, the procedure of ascertainment could be initiated by the petition of individual parties seeking recourse against foreign actions adversely affecting their interests.

The Trade Act introduced a host of amendments to the 1921 Antidumping Act directed to make the remedy more effective.[33] A deadline of six months, or nine months in most complicated cases, was applied to antidumping investigation and the right to judicial review of negative findings on dumping was given to United States industries petitioning against allegedly unfair imports, whereas previously the right to appeal positive decisions was only conceded to importers and foreign producers. Secondly, the Act tightened the net to catch allegedly unfair foreign competitors. Under GATT Article VI and subsection 205 of the 1921 Act, dumping was defined as selling goods in foreign markets at prices below those charged at home, and only in the absence of such domestic prices could the comparison refer to 'the cost of production of the product in the country of origin plus a reasonable addition for selling cost and profit'. The new statute, however, went a step further, providing that the Treasury Department conducting a dumping investigation should disregard home market sales at below the full cost of producing the article, relying instead on the constructed value (i.e. the estimated cost of production and marketing, plus a profit margin) whenever such home sales were made in substantial quantities over an extended period of time and did not allow recovery of all costs in a reasonable time. This new procedure allowed proof of dumping even though home market prices in the country of origin were not above export prices. If the non-defined 'reasonable time' was interpreted as also including cost recovery in the short-term, the new regime could result in an unbearable burden on foreign exporters during a period of widespread and prolonged recession, since in a recession average costs rise because fixed costs must be distributed over a smaller volume of sales. In order to pass the test foreign producers unable to recover costs at home had to sell at rather higher prices in foreign markets, which in practice meant that their products were destined to be outcompeted by US goods.[34]

Time limits were also established for countervailing duty proceedings, thus preventing the Treasury Department, considered by the lawmakers as too soft in opposing foreign subsidization, from stretching out or shelving countervailing duty investigations.[35] On the other hand, the Trade Act of 1974 introduced a temporary provision that allowed the Treasury Department to waive countervailing duties during the trade negotiations. However, the House bill was amended by the Senate making the Secretary of the Treasury's discretionary authority conditional on three requirements aimed at acting as stick and carrot for other participants to the multilateral negotiations on subsidies: the foreign government had taken steps to reduce substantially or eliminate the adverse effect of the bounty or grant; there was a reasonable prospect that an NTB agreement would be negotiated; and the imposition of duties would be likely to jeopardize the satisfactory completion of the negotiations.

The Trade Act was also an occasion to tighten the rein in applying the Generalised System of Preferences in favour of developing countries. In 1971 GATT members, agreeing on a request from United Nations Conference on Trade and Development (UNCTAD), enacted a waiver to the MFN which permitted tariff preferences to be granted for ten years to developing country exports, without reciprocity and without extending the concession to other developed countries. The new statute contained several exclusions some of which were opposed by the administration. The exclusion from receiving generalized preferences concerned Communist countries as well as any country which entered into a cartel to withhold supplies of vital materials or to charge monopolistic prices, including first and foremost the OPEC members. The exclusion also applied to those countries that expropriated the property of US nationals and to those that applied reverse preferences to imports from other developed countries, that is the developing countries that had entered into a preferential agreement with the EC.

The EC Council's directives for the GATT negotiations

The directives issued by the EC Council for the GATT multilateral negotiations in April 1975 were much less far-reaching as they merely elaborated, with no relevant amendments, the main points of the 'Overall Approach' already approved by the Council two years earlier.[36] Besides, as admitted in the document introduction, although the directives were viewed as sufficiently specific to allow the Community to embark on the negotiations with a clear idea of its objectives, they did not aim at predefining a line of action on the detailed aspects of the negotiations, as such a move would have been inadvisable at a stage in which the general context of the multilateral talks was not yet clear. However, the directives stressed the Community's stance on a series of negotiating issues. In particular, for industrial customs tariffs the Council's objective was a significant lowering of duties which, however, was to lead to their harmonization, that is, resulting in the levelling of the differences between the maximum and the minimum rates in the various tariffs. As regards non-tariff barriers the directives stressed the need for a case-by-case approach concentrating on the measures likely to create the greatest obstacles to international trade. The directives also made clear that, at least in some cases, the MFN principle should be made conditional on the participation to the agreements.

With specific reference to countervailing measures, the EC Council stressed that such measures should be applied by all GATT parties, including the United States, only when they were fully justified in terms of already existent GATT rules and consistent with the injury criterion established by GATT Article VI. In exchange of a satisfactory agreement on countervailing duties the Community was willing to negotiate rules on direct export subsidies for industrial products other than basic materials. Reading between the lines it meant that the Community was not disposed to a deal on agricultural subsidies or on domestic subsidies even if applied to manufactured products. On agriculture the directives emphasized that the tensions of the previous two years had turned a period of surplus characterized by increasing competition among exporters into a period of scarcity marked by concern over security of supply, which showed the need for an expansion of trade based on stable world markets. This goal was to be achieved through a set of multilateral agreements covering the main commodities, i.e. wheat, maize, sorghum, barley, rice, sugar and dairy products, and involving the major producing and consuming countries. For dairy products the agreements had to be based on the establishment of minimum and maximum safeguard prices and on preferential purchase and sale obligations, while for the other products, price arrangements were to be accompanied by coordinated national stockpiling policies. For products other than those subject to international agreements, the expansion of trade had to result from coordinated actions from importers and exporters directed at securing the orderly functioning of the market.

Subjects of discussion in the early stages of the Tokyo Round

The bestowal of negotiating authority on the US president signalled the effective start of the discussions but was far from entailing a breakthrough. On the other hand, as noted by Winham, despite the lack of overall progress, the early period of the Tokyo Round opened up a large range of areas for formal negotiations, as some of these areas had already been the subject of talks in the GATT even before the launch of the Tokyo Round.[37]

In February 1975 the Trade Negotiation Committee (TNC) created six specialized subcommittees which conformed to the negotiating areas outlined in the Tokyo Declaration:

group on tariff negotiations
group on reduction or elimination of non-tariff measures and their trade-distorting effects
group for the examination of the sector approach as a complementary negotiation technique
group for the examination of the multilateral safeguard system
group on agriculture negotiations
group on tropical products negotiations.

Later in the year the non-tariff measures group was subcategorized into five subgroups: quantitative restrictions; technical barriers to trade; customs matters; subsidies and countervailing duties; government procurement. The agriculture group was subdivided into three subgroups: grains; meat; and dairy products.

No progress was made on tariffs as the members of the group, rather than engaging in negotiations of substance, remained stalled in theoretical discussions about the approach to tariff cuts, with the EC and other Western European countries arguing that duty reductions should go hand-in-hand with tariff harmonization, whereas the United States seemed to favour linear reductions. On non-tariff barriers the interest groups, both in the EC and in the United States, started lobbying the EC and US executives even before the outset of the negotiations. Many EC industries complained that a host of non-tariff measures on government procurements, quantitative restrictions, antidumping and countervailing proceedings as well as on product standards and customs assessment, had been lowering their foreign market share. The main target was the United States whose domestic legislation was accused of imposing undue burdens on foreign exporters.

On subsidies the European Commission suggested that a list of always prohibited export support measures should be drawn up, while a second, non-exhaustive, list should enumerate subsidies prohibited only if they resulted in export prices lower than domestic market prices. Export credit and export insurance should not be prohibited but could be subject to a good conduct agreement. Domestic subsidies should under no circumstances be prohibited, being only subject to an improved notification and consultation procedure to deal with cases that could affect trading partners' interests. The EC complained that the US countervailing measures did not conform yet to GATT Article VI because of the Grand Father clause as they were applied irrespective of proof of damage to domestic industry.[38] The EC also argued that the implementation of the Kennedy Round Antidumping code by the United States was not fully consistent with the provisions of the code and with GATT Article VI because the US authorities applied too wide criteria in ascertaining when dumping occurred and when the domestic industry was hit. The United States rejoined that the real problem was dumping and subsidization and that, therefore, alleged inconsistencies of its regime with GATT rules would become irrelevant once a satisfactory solution to the mentioned trade-distorting practices had been found. In contrast to the EC, the US negotiators called for stricter regulation not only of export subsidies but also of domestic support measures, even prohibiting those able to significantly distort trade.

As regards quantitative import restrictions, while the United States favoured their gradual phasing-out, the attitude of the EC Commission was more prudent. In the first place, the regulation of these restrictions remained mostly under the jurisdiction of each member state until a uniform regime was adopted across the Community, although the Commission was confident that this regime could soon be implemented. On the other hand, the EC executive argued that concessions on quantitative restrictions had to be contingent on the adoption of more elastic criteria on the application of the Safeguard Clause under Article XIX of the GATT and on the satisfactory result of its bilateral negotiations with Japan and with the East European countries.

The subgroup on customs matters dealt prevalently with the methods to be used for determining the value of imported goods for the purpose of imposing duties. GATT ArticleVII required customs valuation to be based on the 'actual value of imported goods', i.e. the actual price at which the product is offered for sale in the ordinary course of trade under fully competitive conditions, but it did not shed light on the methodology to be followed for the assessment. The EC member states followed the Brussels Convention on valuation of goods and, along with most participants in the Tokyo Round, assessed imports according to the Brussels Definition of Value (BVD). Under this method, the value for customs purposes should be the normal market price, defined as the price that goods would fetch on sale in the open market between a buyer and a seller independent of each other. Other countries, among which the United States, followed different systems. The United States accused the BVD of being based on a notional approach, focusing on what the value would or should be rather than on what it was.[39] However, the US regime was not an example of administrative simplicity as it allowed for a multitude of assessment criteria according to needs and products, which could be basically grouped in five methods of valuation: export value (actual export price of freely offered goods); foreign value (price in the exporting country's market); United States value (price of comparable imported products in the US); cost of production (estimated cost of production plus profit); and American sale price (price of comparable goods produced in the United States). It was the latter method that, although applied to a limited set of imported products, was seen as the main irritant by the EC exporters as the ASP did not reflect prices charged by them but by the US industry, quite often resulting in an unfair evaluation of the imported goods. As previously noted, the US executive had on many occasions called for the repeal of such a method, but Congress had denied its assent. However, by 1975 the main beneficiary of the method, the chemical industry, had signaled its willingness to accept the repeal of the ASP in exchange for higher duties and the US customs authority was arguing that life would be easier if a simplification of the existing methods were carried out. Also the EC Commission had started to view a multilaterally agreed customs valuation reform as an opportunity for strengthening its grip on the functioning of the customs administration in the Community. Indeed, although a common tariff regime had been introduced in 1968, its administration continued to be carried out by the customs services of the member states and the Brussels Definition of Value appeared to give them discretion in following their traditional paths on evaluation.

Both the United States and the EC, as major exporters of finished and semi-finished products, had an interest in an agreement that could secure outlets in a new main section of the developed countries' economies: public procurement.

Negotiations on public procurements were already carried on in the OECD and many member states believed that they could be continued in the OECD in parallel with the GATT talks. The prospective agreement would then be included in the Tokyo Round final package and would be opened for accession by the GATT parties that were not members of the Paris Organization. The major aim of the EC in the negotiations had been, long before the start of the Tokyo Round, the abolition of the 1933 Buy American Act which provided that goods purchased with federal funds for government use or for construction of public works must be of domestic origin as long as the American firms' bid did not exceed their competitors' offered prices by a given percentage (originally 25 per cent and later 6 per cent, except for Department of Defense procurements). The European Commission and the EC member states also feared that the United States would try to limit its commitments appealing to national security reasons, or arguing that many groups of potential buyers were not under Federal jurisdiction or belonged to the private sector even though they exercised public functions, while many American firms could bid for public procurements within the EC through their subsidiaries in the EC member states. On the other hand, the Community was handicapped in its negotiating position by the lack of a general discipline on public procurement bids among its member states. It was only in December 1976 that a draft Directive submitted by the Commission was finally approved by the EC Council, with an effective date in 1978.

Greater progress was made on so-called technical barriers to trade, that is, on product standards inhibiting the free flow of goods, whether intentionally or unintentionally, where negotiators took advantage of the existence of a draft code prepared before the start of the Tokyo Round, which was used as a starting point for discussions. Negotiations covered such topics as testing and certification by governmental bodies and included the areas of packaging, labeling and marking of origin.

As was to be expected, most of the skirmishes concerned agriculture. Here, the EC contended that agriculture had a unique position in the world market and that multilateral negotiations should focus on the stabilization of the market for the main farm products. Conversely, the United States, though recognizing that the sector had its peculiarities and trade stabilization was important, argued that in the long-run market equilibrium would be brought about by liberalization of world trade and, therefore, by the elimination of protective barriers and distorting subsidies.[40] The creation in February 1975 of an 'agriculture' group within the TNC was a favourable starting point for the Community. There was, however, the problem of the relationship of this group with the other groups in the TNC and in particular with the group on non-tariff measures, whose jurisdiction would also cover import restrictions and subsidies. Before the formal establishment of the 'agriculture' group, France, the main producer and exporter in the Community, had requested that the EC negotiators should make a declaration on the role of the prospective group, stating that it should have 'responsabilité globale et exclusive' (global and exclusive responsibility) on farm issues. However, a softer statement proposed by the Commission, to be circulated by 'note verbale', was finally agreed by the EC member states which assigned to the group 'responsabilité globale et principale' (global and main responsibility).[41] The position of the United States was that negotiations on agriculture should take place primarily in the groups on tariff and non-tariff measures and other functional groups, on the assumption that the objective of the negotiations in agriculture and industry alike was liberalization of trade restraints and that this task could best be accomplished through an across-the-board approach to these issues. In May 1976 a compromise seemed to have been reached according to which the agriculture group would treat tariff and non-tariff measures relating to agriculture in conjunction with the work in the groups on tariff and non-tariff measures.[42] The United States interpreted the compromise as allowing any participant to the round to raise a matter relating to agriculture in other groups, thus ruling out exclusive jurisdiction for the 'agriculture' group. As expected, the EC rejected such an interpretation. A new compromise proposal put forward by the United States in September 1976 was also rejected by the EC. This proposal suggested that consultations on agricultural restrictions could be held under the auspices of the 'agriculture' group so long as the results of the consultations were reported simultaneously to the subgroup on quantitative restrictions and any other relevant group or subgroup.

The same kind of problem about objectives and relations with other negotiating instances emerged in each of the three subgroups on grains, meat and dairy products. The disagreement was particularly manifest in the grains subgroup where the Community proposed the negotiation of a comprehensive international grains agreement that would stabilize prices within a wide band by means of stocks operated by the participating countries, whereas the US along with the other main producers saw trade expansion and liberalization as the major goal.

Bilateral agreements and disputes in the framework of GATT

The issue of tariff compensation following the enlargement of the European Community

Efforts to avoid confrontation and postpone the unsettled differences without papering them over marked the negotiations on compensatory tariff reductions required of the EC under GATT Article XXIV: 6 as a result of its enlargement to nine members which were conducted in the GATT framework but were substantially bilateral. The mentioned article required customs unions, such as the EEC, to negotiate tariff compensation when the expansion of a common external tariff resulted in the increase in national rates of duties previously applied by the acceding countries. As noted in Chapter I, the accession of the United Kingdom, Denmark and Ireland, generally entailed lower tariffs in manufacture imports and higher barriers on farm imports.[43]

In the negotiations, which formally opened in January 1973, the EC initially argued that the tariff reductions implemented by the three acceding countries outweighed the tariff increases and, therefore, little or no compensation was due. The United States, along with other exporters, maintained that since it had bargained and paid for the lower tariff rates previously applied by Denmark, Ireland and the UK, it was entitled to receive compensation through EC tariff reductions on items of interest to its exporters.

In December 1973 the Community made a global offer of tariff reductions on items of interest to many countries, which, however, was found to be insufficient. The April 1974 decision of the EC Council of Ministers to be open to further settlement efforts resulted in an intensification of the dialogue between the Community and the United States which led the following May to a bilateral settlement. The US obtained concessions not only on some industrial products, but also on a number of agricultural products like tobacco, oranges and grapefruits. No concessions, however, were obtained on the item of main interest for US farmers, cereals, and the two parties agreed to continue discussions with a view to seeking agreed solutions to the problems of international trade in grains through international negotiations. Other countries like Canada, prevalently farm exporters, were not able to reach an agreed settlement on their demand for compensatory tariff adjustment and finally lodged a complaint in the GATT for violation of Article XXIV.

The use of the GATT to attack trade policies on the other side of the Atlantic

On the other hand, the launch of a new multilateral round in the GATT, the bite of the recession and the call for more decisive and prompter response to allegedly unfair practices by foreign competitors in the Trade Act of 1974 meant that the GATT increasingly became the arena for legal confrontation between the United States and the EC and, to a lesser extent, Japan. Until 1972 the legal disputes between the transatlantic partners did not result in a demand for formal legal rulings with the establishment of a panel or the complaint was dropped before the panel gave its rulings. However, in 1973 the EC lodged a formal complaint in the GATT against the Domestic International Sales Corporations (DISC) legislation, which, as noted in the previous chapter, provided fiscal incentives to US exporting companies.[44] The EC argued that the DISC provisions violated Article XVI: 4 of the General Agreement as the regime conferred an export subsidy on US producers by allowing a continuous deferral of their foreign sale income tax liability or, in any case, by the exemption of the compound interest rate on the deferred tax.[45] The United States countered that the territoriality principle, adopted by certain EC member states, led to equivalent economic distortions as it allowed European producers to reduce their overall tax liability by organizing foreign branches or subsidiaries in low-tax countries and using transfer price.[46] The US accepted the creation of the panel, but on condition that a single panel should entertain the European complaints together with the American ones. It was a clever tactic which worked in the short-run. Three years later, in a highly politicized report, the panel, in a Salomonian way, held that neither the DISC regime nor the territoriality principle was fully consistent with GATT Article XVI. This gave the US substantial diplomatic leeway, as the repeal of the recently adopted DISC provisions was conditional on the surrender of the long-standing territoriality approach by its EC counterparts. However, the US legal position was strongly criticized by the majority of the other GATT members as the DISC regime was a blatant subsidy, whereas the territorial system of income taxation had been an integral part of many developed countries' fiscal regime long before the existence of the GATT.[47] This simple truth was finally recognized by the Parties to the General Agreement. After a five year stalemate, in December 1981 the Council adopted the four reports but with the understanding that 'with respect to these cases, and in general, economic processes (including transactions involving export goods) located outside the territorial limits of the exporting country need not be subject to taxation by the exporting country and should not be regarded as export activities in terms of Article XVI: 4 of the General Agreement'. This implicitly acquitted the European countries' regime based on the territoriality principle.[48]

In the United States the new section 301 of the Trade Act allowed several industries to put pressure on the executive to defend their rights against 'unjustifiable or unreasonable restrictions imposed by foreign countries' and in 1976 the Ford administration filed two complaints in the GATT against the EC involving short-term trade measures in the agricultural sector to alleviate surplus situations in sectors benefiting from CAP support.

Thus, the dispute settling apparatus of the GATT became the arena in which the United States turned the spotlight on the inconsistency of the CAP with already established GATT rules, while the EC and its member states tried to show that the United States, though a self-proclaimed opponent of government intrusion in the economy, in particular through subsidizing measures, was itself a subsidizer, being only able to conceal its policies in a more sophisticated way than its trading partners.

4

The Slackening Of Growth in the EC Countries and the Strengthening of Protectionism on Both Sides of the Atlantic

Differences and similarities in the economic trend of the transatlantic economic areas and their impact on the EC and US economic policies

The economy that in 1976 was fast recovering in all OECD countries from 1977 was characterized by a divergent tendency in the industrialized countries as, while the United States continued to grow in the two following years approximately at the same rate as in 1976 (Table 1), the growth rate in the EC member states markedly slowed down, with the exception of Ireland and Luxembourg (Table 10). Also, Japan experienced a deceleration of its rate of growth.

When the new president, Jimmy Carter, took office in January 1977 the rate of unemployment was 7.4 per cent, a level of joblessness that the Democratic executive could not but consider unacceptable, being only one point below the 1975 peak. The Tax Reduction and Simplification Act passed in May 1977 increased the personal standard deduction and provided additional funds to states and localities. Later the administration increased spending on public works and on public service employment. The fiscal deficit of the two previous years was not curtailed (Table 9) but the economy kept growing and by 1978 the rate of unemployment was reduced to a still high but more acceptable 6.1 per cent. From 1977 onwards, the favourable picture was marred by the worsening of the balance of payments. The merchandise trade deficit soared by 228 per cent relative to the deficit of the previous year, which, in turn, was much higher than in 1972, that is, the year in which the effects of the dollar devaluation had not yet been felt, while the current account balance, positive for the last four years, turned into a deficit of $14.5 billion in 1977 and $15.4 billion the following year (Table 2). As shown by Table 3, only a part of the trade deficit can be attributed to constant US thirst for imported oil, although only between 1976–7 crude petroleum imports grew by one-quarter. The deficit for the whole of the industrial supplies and materials group doubled in the same period; the deficit for non-food consumer goods except automotives doubled between 1975 and 1977 and trebled a year later. The same trend characterized the automotive sector. The deficit with Germany, which had been cancelled in the previous year, reappeared in 1977 and further grew in 1978, but overall the negative balance with the Federal Republic remained a modest portion of the US trade deficit. The deficit with Japan more than doubled between 1976–8, accounting for over a third of the US merchandise trade deficit (Table 4). A cursory analysis of the causes of the deficit, that is, without considering its various components, does not point to the non-competitiveness of American products in terms of costs. On the contrary, it appears that the competitive edge provided by the 1971–3 devaluation of the greenback had not been eroded. For instance, the unit labour cost in manufacturing of the main US trading partners, estimated on a dollar basis, rose much more quickly than in the United States (Figure 3). It is, therefore, arguable that at least part of the deficit was the result of the discrepancy between the speed and extent of the recovery in the USA and in the other OECD countries. The path to a sustained, non-inflationary growth in all industrialized countries, also capable of avoiding dangerous gaps among their balance of payments, was seen in the coordination of their policies, in particular those of the United States, Japan and West Germany. The 'Locomotive' approach, which was the official Group of 7 (G7) philosophy, was that a satisfactory pace of global recovery could be achieved only if the major industrialized countries, that is, initially Germany, Japan and the United States adopted a stimulative stance in their domestic stabilization policy. In turn, such a policy would not only bring about export-led expansion in the weaker countries but would also loosen domestic policy constraints linked to balance of payments deterioration risks. The apparently rational picture was spoiled by the fact that the three engines forming the locomotive had different levels of inflation and above all of unemployment, which was higher in the United States than in the other two countries, and their priorities in fighting the two ills were different. Both Germany and Japan were wary of relying on domestic stimuli to the economic recovery, also because, as in the past, their recovery, modest though it was, was export-led. The German monetary authorities, in particular, were worried about measures that could rekindle Germany's traditional bogyman: inflation. The May 1977 Downing Street Summit committed the G7 governments 'to targets for growth and stabilization which vary from country to country but which, taken as a whole, should provide a basis for non-inflationary growth worldwide'. The Summit declaration also stated that the governments of countries pursuing stabilization policies, designed to provide growth without inflation, would continue to pursue those goals, whereas countries that had adopted reasonably expansionist growth targets would keep their policies under review and, if needed, adopt further measures to contribute to the adjustment of payments imbalances. It seems, therefore, that Japan's and West Germany's policies received full endorsement while the United States was required to implement adjustments in case of worsening of its balance of payments.

Attitudes substantially changed at the time of the Bonn Summit in August 1978 as the pace of recovery had not shown any significant improvement in most EC member countries where the unemployment rate was approaching that of the United States, which in turn was declining. The Bonn declaration pointed at unemployment as the main evil, to combat which the G7 governments would build on the progress already made in curbing inflation, pursuing, however, higher economic growth. In this context West Germany's Chancellor, Helmut Schmidt announced that his government would propose to the German parliament additional fiscal measures of up to 1 per cent of Gross National Product. According to a political scientist, by so doing under the cloak of an international commitment Schmidt, backed by the Social Democratic Party, also in view of the approaching 1980 election, wanted to overcome the resistance of the junior partner in the government, the Free Democratic Party, represented by the Finance Minister, as well as of the business and banking communities.[1] Actually, the German government's fiscal stimulus had already secured the bolstering of a Community commitment as the EC Summit held in April at Copenhagen had called for a growth rate of 4.5 per cent throughout the EC by 1979, while the GDP growth of Germany, by definition the Western Europe Locomotive, in 1978 was not expected to exceed 3 per cent.[2] The Japanese Prime Minister Takeo Fukuda stressed his governments' efforts to increase by 1.5 percentage points the growth rate of the previous year, mainly through the expansion of domestic demand, and pledged to increase imports through the same channel. The US president announced that his government had already taken measures to prevent its fiscal stimulus from reigniting inflation by reducing expenditure projection for 1978 and 1979, while a very tight budget was prepared for 1980. Carter also committed the US executive to introduce measures directed to curb the US dependence on imported oil by the end of the year. Actually, the programme, whose cornerstone was the decontrol of oil prices, had been hailed at the Downing Street

Summit, but was soon bogged down on account of opposition in Congress and in the administration as well, as some of Carter's political and economic advisers deemed that such a measure could rekindle an inflation that had abated but did not give any sign of disappearing. In any case, price deregulation was bound to stir up resentment from the average American who had long taken cheap consumption of oil for granted. The renewed pledge in Bonn offered Carter the international backing that enabled him to push through the reform, also assisted by the announcement that the EC member states had agreed during the European Council held in Bremen the previous week to reduce the Community's dependence on imported energy to 50 per cent by 1985. Although with a delay of five months from the deadline indicated at the G7 Summit, price decontrol in the US began on 1 June 1979, with all controls to end by October 1981. It must be noted that the administration was careful enough to schedule the final stage of the alignment to world prices well after the November 1980 presidential election.

Growth and recession in main US and EC industries and measures adopted to support them

The recovery, whose strength was different in the United States and in Western Europe, concealed areas of decline and expansion bound to have an impact on their economic policies and on the multilateral negotiations.

The sectors experiencing grave difficulties were shipbuilding, in particular in the EC, textiles and steel, while agriculture and aircraft industry acquired growing importance in the expansion of US and EC trade. In line with the teaching of international political economy, the crisis that affected the first three sectors fostered protectionist tendencies on both sides of the Atlantic. Yet, the sheer fact that the success of the latter two sectors was inextricably linked to public support both in the US and in the EC, although with different levels and different kinds of intervention, hampered trade liberalizing agreements and only postponed the confrontation between the two areas, for agriculture until the early 1980s and for aircraft until the twenty-first century.

Shipbuilding

As noted by Lindert, the United States shipbuilding industry was never able to effectively compete with the United Kingdom shipbuilding industry and the chance to gain ground on the British was seized by other European nations and later by Japan. The United States, therefore, satisfied itself with isolating a non-competitive industry from foreign onslaughts.[3] Thus, there was no question of any new difficulties for the American industry in the 1970s. A serious decline was, instead, experienced by the EC industry, unable to withstand competition, not only from Japan but also from some newly industrialized countries in a global environment dominated by overcapacity. Order books in the international market swelled unprecedentedly between 1970–73 as a result of optimistic forecasts of the world economy and of speculative demand. To meet orders received in 1972–3, annual world production in the period 1974–6 grew to approximately 20 million cgrt (compensated gross registered ton).[4] Production in the EC countries had not kept pace with the buoyant world market, as its share had steadily declined from 70 per cent in 1955 to 23.3 per cent 20 years later, while that of Japan had jumped from 12 per cent to 50.6 per cent.[5] The 1974–5 slump, although not the only cause of the decline, put an abrupt end to the rosy expectations. By 1977 new orders had fallen to 14 million cgrt and had started to cause overcapacity problems even to Japan. A year later they plummeted to just 10.8 million cgrt (–23 % relative to 1977 and –32% relative to 1976). Production fell from 22.1 million cgrt in 1976 to 16.5 million cgrt in 1978 (–25%).[6] The recession was forecast to extend well into the following decade. The EC shipyards were hit more than their competitors as their share of world newbuilding completions declined to 21 per cent by 1978. Already in 1975 the decline was affecting 8.3 per cent of the workforce in the shipyards of the EC member countries. In 1978 employment in new shipbuilding fell to 155,840 units, with a 25 per cent decline relative to 1975 and a similar trend characterized all other sectors of shipyards.[7] The member states at national levels reacted by supporting their shipyards, i.e. placing orders for naval vessels and, above all, through financial intervention aimed at overcoming the price advantage of Japan and of the Newly Industrialized Countries (NICs). These efforts, however, ended up by keeping afloat an industry affected by overcapacity but without effectively tackling this problem.

The EC intervened by issuing directives aimed at harmonizing state intervention in the sector and reducing the level of aids which were damaging intra-Community competition. The stated aim of the Community was to make the EC shipyards more competitive in the world market, thus providing a more significant proportion of the member countries' fleets. Since demand for shipping was declining, because of the continuous impact of the oil crisis, the European Commission suggested that financial measures should be taken to stimulate demand and to orientate it towards local production. Nevertheless, restructuring and curtailment of production potential had to be accepted. The European Regional Development Fund provided financial support to the regions, prevalently located in France, Germany, Italy and the UK, where there was a high concentration of shipbuilding to create or preserve jobs and to assist the execution of industrial infrastructure projects. Obviously, the Community's efforts to buoy up, restructure and render its shipbuilding industries more competitive was open to the accusation that reorganization of the shipyard industry would interfere with the market, distorting competition with other producers. Under the auspices of the OECD 'general guidelines for government policies in the shipbuilding industry' were agreed by the EC member states together with the other members of the Association of West European Shipbuilders (AWES) and by Japan with the stated aim of pursuing the reduction of production capacity so as to restore in the medium-term the balance between supply and demand, while maintaining fair competition. The OECD agreement was made more effective by pressure on Japan to bear a satisfactory share of the consequences of the crisis under threat of unilateral protective measures. Japan agreed to raise its export prices by 5 per cent and introduce a series of measures of voluntary restraint vis-à-vis some EC member states, which, however, was far from bringing balance back in the market.

Steel industry

Similar problems were experienced by the US and EC steel industries in the period ushered in by the oil crisis. The years 1973–4 witnessed a strong expansion in steel demand which entailed major expansion projects as producers were forecasting an upwards trend for the following decade. After a decline in 1975, world consumption slowly recovered in the second half of the 1970s until it exceeded its 1973 level by a meagre 3.7 per cent in 1980. However, the overall trend masked more ominous developments for the industrialized countries where consumption annually declined by 2.4 per cent.[8] As a result the steel industry on both sides of the Atlantic experienced significant losses and overcapacity. The American and Western European problems were rendered more acute by the fierce competition of Japan and some NICs. The United States, which accounted for over 48 per cent of world production in 1950, accounted for 21.6 per cent 20 years later and for just 14.1 per cent in 1980.[9] By 1960 the US had become a net importer and by 1980 its net imports amounted to 12.4 million tons of steel products. Japan, which accounted for only 2.6 per cent of world output in 1950, accounted for 16.1 per cent in 1970 and 15.5 per cent ten years later, and its net exports soared from 0.4 million tons in 1950 to 22.3 million tons in 1970 and almost 35 million in 1980. The EC remained a net exporter but its share of the world product, after climbing to over 29 per cent in 1960, declined to less than 18 per cent 20 years later.

The changing production pattern of steel trade flows is primarily explained by changes in relative costs in favour of Japan and the NICs vis-à-vis their competitors in the United States and Europe. US costs relative to Japan went from being slightly lower in the mid-1950s to over $100 per ton higher in the mid-1970s and by 1976 the Japanese industry was 13–7 per cent more productive than its American competitor in converting inputs into steel.[10] In spite of the recovery of the economy, the steel industry experienced low capacity utilization, significant job losses and declining profits. The industry's difficulties were exacerbated by imports which, during 1977, rose 35 per cent by volume and covered 17 per cent of domestic consumption. It was, therefore, natural to claim that in a sluggish world market, foreign competition was taking the form of major price reduction which was quite often bound to result in sales below production costs.[11] In September 1977, an interagency task force, headed by Treasury undersecretary Anthony Solomon, was established to examine the steel industry's problems. The task force recommended measures to encourage modernization of steel making facilities; assistance to firms and workers in adjusting to import competition; review of the environmental regulations applying to the steel industry; and above all the establishment of a trigger price mechanism for monitoring imports into the US and initiating expedited antidumping investigations. The trigger price mechanism (TPM) was approved by Carter at the end of 1977 and was formally initiated the following February in the investigations on the 32 categories of steel products marketed in the US. It was based on the full cost of production by the most efficient foreign steel producer, Japan, plus the cost of bringing the imported products into the United States. The TPM was not considered a minimum price system as the importers were free to sell steel in the United States below the trigger price as long as they were selling above 'fair value' as defined by the Antidumping Act. It indicated, however, when an imported product was likely to be sold at less than fair market value, thus automatically opening an investigation unless the exporter had received a pre-clearance. In other words, importers of foreign steel at better prices than increasingly costly US products were warned that they were embarking on a dicey adventure. It was, therefore, much more consistent with prudence to buy American products.

Things went comparatively worse for the EC member states as the downturn did not mean the worsening of a long downwards trend but the inversion of a phase of expansion culminated in 1974. In 1977 the Community's production of crude steel amounted to just over 126 million tons, compared with 134 million in 1976 (–6%) and 155.6 million in 1974 (–19%). The rate of utilization of production capacity was approximately 60 per cent and the rate was even lower in Germany, Belgium, Denmark, Luxembourg and Ireland. Steel imports increased by 67 per cent compared with 1974 and the proportion of consumption covered by imports jumped from 5.8 per cent to 10.4 per cent.[12]

The EC steel industry had set up a cartel, which fixed minimum prices and quotas of production and exports within the Community. Derogating the General EC rules on competition, the steel cartel was allowed under the 1951 ECSC Treaty. The effectiveness of a cartel depends on two factors: its comprehensiveness and unity; its ability to prevent the entry of foreign competitors into its market. Within the EC the effectiveness of the cartel was put into question by competition from the so-called Bresciani firms (from the name of a town from the industrial North of Italy). These small and efficient firms were able to produce at much lower costs than big German and particularly French steelmakers and, therefore, were threatening their markets. The growing inflow of steel products from a wide range of countries was even more dangerous.

As was predictable, since the crisis was more unexpected and was deeply felt in all the Community member countries, the measures adopted were even less consistent with the principles of free trade and free market which, after all, was the philosophy to which both sides of the Atlantic claimed to adhere. As the system by which steel producers could voluntarily undertake to limit supplies of certain products did not prevent the deterioration of the market, in May 1977 the Commission, endorsed by the European Council, adopted a package of measures which were further expanded in December, to reorient and reshape the steel industry and to protect it from foreign competition. These measures, known as the 'Davignon Plan', after the commissioner for Industrial Affairs, provided for mandatory minimum prices for products under stiff competition like concrete reinforcing bars and hot-rolled wide strips and called for guidance price for other products, combined with voluntary production quotas. Concurrently an import control programme was initiated. Like the TPM in the United States, the programme employed a system of basic prices reflecting the lowest production costs in the exporting country in which normal conditions of competition prevailed, but went further than the American regime, as it provided for the levy of provisional duties on imports below basic price without need for prior enquiry.[13] Steel exporting countries were, however, exempt from the basic import price system if they negotiated voluntary export restraint agreements. Fifteen countries providing about 75 per cent of EC imports, including EFTA members and Japan, agreed to a VER as of 1 January 1978.

On the other hand, one of the declared objectives of the plan put forward by the Commission – whose policy, unlike the United States', along with protectionism, was also characterized by a high degree of dirigisme – was to bolster the profitability of the EC steel industry by a severe curtailment of its capacity in order to achieve balance between offer and prospective demand.[14] According to the Commission's estimates, the latter could regain its 1974 level, that is the highest level ever met by member states' supply, only in 1989. Thus the 1979 capacity was forecast to exceed foreseen production needs for 1983 by 13 per cent for crude steel and 15 per cent for laminated products, which, taking into account the cuts already carried out by the firms concerned, made a further reduction of about 20 million tonnes necessary. The foregoing would have required a restructuring policy involving the reconversion of industrial plants and workers to other sectors to be financed by the Community budget and stricter rules on subsidies provided by member states as they would distort competition and hinder the capacity cut process.

If the measures adopted by the Community were definitely inconsistent with the GATT provisions, they did fit with the understanding worked out in the OECD where, at the initiative of the United States, an Ad Hoc Group on Steel was formed to identify structural problems of the sector on a worldwide basis and to provide a forum for discussion. The Group, which in late 1978 was replaced by a standing Steel Committee, focused on three main areas: steel trade, steel prices and longer-term structural changes in the industry. At a meeting in November 1977 the Group agreed on a number of principles to guide governments in dealing with the steel sector's problems: worldwide rationalization of the sector was needed and the burden of adjustment was not to be shifted from one producing nation to another either in the short or the long-term; immediate measures to keep domestic firms afloat had to be consistent with the longer-term need to rationalize the industry while maintaining free and fair flow of trade and, therefore, 'unilateral' quantitative restrictions were to be avoided; in spite of slack demand, the parties to the understanding were to refrain from cut price competition that could affect the industry of the other parties, which was a warning not to exploit cost advantages under threat of countervailing measures.[15] To render the commitment more effective and to prevent freelancing, a monitoring mechanism was established which aimed at identifying incipient problems and facilitating 'rational investment decisions through increased transparency'.

The dealings in the OECD were obviously influenced by trilateral talks held by the US with its EC and Japanese counterparts. This may explain why the United States, while pressing foreign exporters with quasi-judicial antidumping proceedings, refrained from large-scale actions involving presidential decisions. For instance, President Carter decided in January 1978 to discontinue review of a complaint filed by the American Iron and Steel Institute under section 301 of the 1974 Trade Act alleging substantial diversion of Japanese steel to the US market as a result of a voluntary restriction agreed with the EC. The president noted that there was no sufficient evidence of significant diversion of Japanese steel towards the US and that, at any rate, adequate relief could be obtained through the antidumping complaints filed by the steel industry.[16] However, there is no evidence that the activities in the OECD and the tripartite talks resulted in or aimed at the establishment of an international steel cartel. The Americans, for instance, were not prepared to impose a curtailment of capacity on their industry. No deal on market shares is traceable. The EC steel producers looked favourably to the re-birth of the voluntary restraint arrangement expired in 1974, which would have provided a limited but not threatened share of the US market, but this policy was not followed by the Commission. On the other hand, the absence of a stable outlet in foreign markets, and the United States was a main importer of EC steel products, meant that the forecast of excess capacity made by the Commission could prove optimistic and that, therefore, more severe rationalization measures were needed.

Textile and clothing industries; synthetic fibres industry

The aftermath of the first oil crisis also witnessed a surge in import restricting policies within the textile and clothing industries. The new trend was the outcome of the worsening condition in Western European countries, although the US was not coy to exploit the advantages offered by the EC call for greater control over developing country exports. While the United States had actively pursued bilateral agreements during the first period of the Multifibre Arrangement, the EC had not implemented a consistent textile trade policy and was paying the price.[17] In 1977, the United States had agreements with 18 countries, covering approximately 77 per cent of its imports of cotton, wool and man-made fibre textiles and apparel and was actively negotiating new bilateral agreements. The EC had been slow in exploiting the room for manoeuvre offered by the MFA, as most of the voluntary restraint agreements signed with developing countries did not come into force until 1976, that is, two years after the MFA took effect. Moreover, the quantities stipulated in many bilateral agreements were relatively large and numerous concessions had to be given to those countries with which the EC had signed preferential agreements. The EC trade surplus for manufactured textiles and clothing of over $900 million in 1971 turned into an $846 million deficit in 1975, and in terms of tonnage this deficit rose from 163,000 tons in 1974 to 383,000 tons in 1975 and 600,000 tons in 1976.[18] Between 1971 and 1977 530,000 workers left the textile and clothing industries, while over 700,000 workers were either unemployed or working short-time. [19]

The negotiations for the extension of the MFA offered the industrial countries an opportunity to curb textile and apparel inflows. The 1973 MFAs, though imposing import limits on all kinds of textile products, provided for a 6 per cent annual rate of growth for individual countries that was in line with the normal increase of their exports. When the Arrangement was renewed in 1977 with reference to the 1978–82 period, although it still envisaged the above-mentioned growth rate, it did allow the importing countries to set lower limits through bilateral negotiations. The EC, at the behest of France and the United Kingdom in particular, required that the exporters of the largest developing countries reduce their 1978 exports of textiles and clothing to the Common Market below the 1976 level. Likewise, the United States reached agreements with Hong Kong, Korea and Taiwan to freeze their 1978 exports of textiles and clothing at the 1977 level and then to increase the exports of a number of sensitive items at a rate substantially less than 6 per cent.

The difficulties of the textile industry contributed to worsen the prospect in the EC member states of the synthetic fibres industry which was affected by the economic decline triggered by the first oil crisis and by the consequent explosion of overcapacity, estimated at around 30 per cent in 1977. The EC Commission urged the member countries not to provide aid which would create new production capacity. In turn, the main producers in the Community resorted to the establishment of a semi-official cartel similar to the regime in place in the steel industry. This informal understanding, which was based on a concerted reduction of production capacity and production quota allocations, was tolerated by the Commission in spite of its dubious conformity with EC rules on competition.

Civil transport aircrafts

The US predominance in the civil aircraft market continued throughout the 1970s, but the EC industry gradually increased its presence in the market. The orders and deliveries of American jet aircrafts up to December 1974 outshone their European competitors by a ratio of 5.3 to 1.[20] However, between 1970 and 1975 the American market shrank from 64 per cent of the world market to about 46 per cent, while the EC market rose from 14.7 per cent to 17.6 per cent and that of the other Western European countries from 6.3 per cent to 8 per cent. On the other hand, the share of European products on the various markets fell substantially: from 33 per cent in 1970 to 22 per cent five years later and from 2 per cent to just 0.3 per cent of the US market.[21]

Nonetheless, prospects for the EC industry started to become brighter in the second half of the decade without direct involvement of the EC, but thanks to cooperation among the industries and governments of some member states. The first main example was Concorde, which entered service in 1976. This new aircraft was the product of an Anglo–French government treaty, combining the manufacturing efforts of Aérospatiale and the British Aircraft Corporation. The main enterprise was, however, the Airbus. Airbus Industrie was formally established as a Groupement d'Interêt Économique (Economic Interest Group) in December 1970 as a result of government initiative between France, Germany and the UK that dated back to 1967. The members of the Group were Aérospatiale, Deutsche Airbus, Hawker Siddeley and Fokker-VFW, and they were joined in October 1971 by the Spanish company CASA. In January 1979 British Aerospace, which had absorbed Hawker Siddeley, acquired a 20 per cent share of Airbus Industrie. The first production model, the A300B2 entered service in 1974. Initially the success of the consortium was poor, but orders for the aircraft picked up as Airbus succeeded in targeting airlines in America and Asia. By 1979 the consortium had 256 orders for A300, while a more advanced aircraft, the A310, had been launched the previous year. By the early 1980s the European Industry led by Airbus had become a main competitor of the American giants, Boeing, McDonnell Douglas and Lockheed.

Both the United States and the European states involved in the Concorde and Airbus projects were lavish in providing financial aid, but the means of support were different. In the United States the federal government intervened primarily by means of military purchases and military research and development contracts which provided a basis for many large-scale civil engineering projects. In the Community, government support was given through purchases and Research & Development (R&D) contracts, later followed by reimbursable launch investments. In case of a legal conflict involving governments on both sides of the Atlantic, it would have been easier for the US to deny that it was financially supporting its civil aeronautical industry as the aid it received was just a by-product of military contracts. The European member states could reply that their support was only the result of ordinary purchases and that, at any rate, subsidies bestowed on their national industries were domestic subsidies that were not aimed at distorting competition in world trade.

Agriculture

The aftermath of the 1974–5 depression saw the continuation of the farm products export boom in the US, although at a growth rate lower than in the years between 1971 and 1974 (Figure 4). The growth was due to an increase in export volume rather than to an increase in prices. which were often marked by a declining trend. Exports, which as expected, showed a very strong correlation (0.99) with gross farm income, in 1978 accounted for over one-fourth of a fast growing gross income while, on average, they had made up just one-eighth of it in the 1960–70 years. The scenario was less bright for the net farm income in constant dollars. Indeed, after reaching a $25.9 billion peak in 1973, with an over 100 per cent increase relative to 1971, the net income of the whole sector constantly fell and in 1977 was much lower than in 1965, totalling less than $11 billion, though recovering the following year. The decline was the upshot of the faster growth of the non-farm components of the gross product such as wages paid to farm workers, rent on land owned by non-farm operators and inputs provided by other sectors. On the other hand, the net farm operator income per farm significantly improved compared with the previous decade, due to the continuing decline in the number of farms, from almost 4 million in 1960 to about 2.7 million in 1977.[22] However, in 1977 also the net farm income per farm was somewhat lower than four years earlier as the 1973 bonanza slowed down the exodus from agriculture and the prices paid to non-farm sectors were biting. In other words, the export boom was not enough to prevent the malaise of farm operators, or at least a number of them, as borne out by the numerous demonstrations of protest, which manifested striking similarities with those organized on the other side of the Atlantic.

It is in this context, less positive than the one in which the 1973 farm law was drafted but much more favourable than the one which characterized the US farm industry during the Reagan years, that the Food and Agriculture Act of 1977 was approved. The 1977 Act envisaged six main policy instruments for the crops that constituted the bulk of American exports, wheat, feed grains and cotton: loan rates; target prices and deficiency payments; land set-aside and diversions; crop acreage reductions; land diversion payments; and an extended farmer-held grain reserve programme. In particular, as for the 1973 statute, the loan rates, that is, the support prices provided by the Commodity Credit Corporation, were kept below market prices and, therefore, were not destined to impinge on the export propensity of US farmers. Judgment is much less clear-cut with regard to target prices. The latter, introduced in the 1973 legislation, were used to determine deficiency payments per unit of eligible production which were the new main instrument of income support for American farmers. The deficiency payment was the difference between the target price and the market price or the loan rate, whichever the higher. The target prices fixed by the 1977 Food and Agricultural Act, as amended by the Emergency Agricultural Act of 1978, were higher than market prices and loan rates, in particular for wheat, thus entitling farmers to an integration of their income. As the Food and Agricultural Act stipulated that deficiency payments be proportional to production rather than tied to allotments fixed on an historical base, they were likely to increase supply on a greater scale than set-asides and acreage diversions designed to reduce production. Therefore, the income support programme left the United States open to the charge of dumping, thus weakening its call for reform of the EC's CAP that it was accusing of trade distortion through subsidization. Besides, as it was a form of direct income support, it increased the pressure on the budget when the prevailing policy called for the curtailment of fiscal deficit.

Yet, there is no denying that the CAP was bound to raise the worries of the United States as, assisted by scientific progress enhancing productivity, the Community was fast reaching self-sufficiency in main farm products sectors and by 1979 sugar and butter exceeded self-sufficiency by 20 per cent (Figure 5). Surpluses entailed the need for storage and disposal in markets outside the EC. The CAP mechanism started, therefore, to cause costs that were no longer exclusively borne by consumers but by the tax payers, straining the limited budgetary resources bestowed on the EC by its member states. But progress towards self-sufficiency was not uniform in all member states, some of which reached and exceeded self-sufficiency in most products covered by the CAP long before others which remained net importers. France, in particular, by far exceeded self-sufficiency in all kinds of grains, especially wheat, along with sugar, cheese and butter by the early 1970s. The aim of achieving balance in farm trade, underlying the 'Loi d'Orientation Agricole' (Law of Agricultural Orientation) of 1960, by the mid–1970s was replaced by the goal of becoming a net exporter.[23] This objective was made possible by membership of the EC within which France had a positive farm trade balance while it was still a net importer vis-à-vis the countries outside the Community which, however, also provided many products that France was unable to grow. Therefore, for France it was not just a question of successfully competing in the world market but of safeguarding the non-tariff barriers that prevented third country competitors from displacing it in its preserve, the European Common Market. France was not the only great farm product exporter in the Community. In 1972 the Netherlands exceeded self-sufficiency in butter by over 200 per cent, in cheese by over 100 per cent and in veal by a modest 1,700 per cent. Germany in 1978 exceeded self-sufficiency only in rye (6%), sugar (29%) and butter (35%). As West Germany was the main exporter of industrial products in the EC it would have been foreseeable that the Federal Republic might be inclined to sacrifice the preservation of the CAP to favourable deals in other areas of the multilateral negotiations that could enhance its predominance in manufacturing exports. Yet, the German farmers had a staunch ally in the Minister for Agriculture, the liberal democrat Josef Ertl and were among the main beneficiaries of the European Agricultural Guidance and Guarantee Fund (EAGGF). Besides, if it is true that manufactured exports dwarfed the agricultural exports of the Federal Republic, to deduce that the latter were irrelevant would be misleading. If intra-EC exports are included, West Germany numbered among the main farm product exporters of the 1970s and by 1977 it had outstripped traditionally big exporters like Australia and Canada.

As was to be expected, the United States attacked various EC programmes adopted under the Common Agricultural Policy. The principal examples of this policy can be found in the NFDM and MIP disputes. In 1976 the National Soybean Processors Association filed a section 301 petition against an EC scheme requiring the mixing of non-fat dry milk (NFDM), a product increasingly in surplus in the Community, into livestock feed, allegedly displacing a substantial amount of vegetable proteins mainly imported from the US. The United States requested the submission of the issue to a GATT panel which in 1978 declared the EC measure inconsistent with its obligations under the General Agreement. The opinion of the panel was solicited by the United States, albeit the NFDM compulsory requirement had already been repealed after the European Court of Justice found it illegal under the Treaty of Rome. On the other hand, since not all of the surplus non-fat dry milk had been disposed of, the Community replaced it with a domestic subsidy system. Following another 301 petition, the US lodged a complaint in the GATT against an EC programme which had established minimum import prices (MIP) for tomato concentrates and imposed a system of licencing and surety deposits on some processed fruits and vegetables of interest for American exporters. However, the opinion of the panel was only partially favourable to the United States as it found that the MIP was inconsistent with the Community's obligation but that the import licencing surety bond system was not.

First attempts by the EC and the US to manage bilateral trade with Japan on a comprehensive scale

The measures described above were confined to single industries. However, from the middle of the decade the problem started to be perceived no longer as concerning one or more domestic industries, but the entire economy and the cause was no longer attributed to a plurality of separate foreign industries but to a single economic entity: Japan. The total US merchandise trade deficit with its Asian partner soared from a manageable $1.4 billion in 1973 to $8 billion four years later and $11.6 billion in 1978 (respectively 26 per cent and 34 per cent of the total US deficit).

Actually, it was difficult to point the finger at particular failings in Japanese trade policy as a whole, that is, its lack of consistency with fair play rules in international trade. During the 1950s Japan adopted a strategy of export promotion and import control, but this policy was gradually abandoned in the 1960s when a growing number of non-traditional sectors of the economy achieved competitive advantage in the absence of governmental assistance, and the demand for import restrictions in the United States and Europe became stronger and stronger. In 1968 the Japanese government announced a programme of liberalization on 60 items and partial liberalization on 12 by the end of 1971. At the end of 1972, when pressure on the yen mounted despite realignment, the government cut tariffs by 20 per cent and even adopted measures to control the rise in the export of certain products to particular countries.[24] By the mid–1970s tariff rates in Japan, averaged over dutiable imports and over all imports, were lower than in the US.[25] Thus it was reasonably arguable that the loss of share by the United States in nearly all categories of trade in modern manufacturing was due to the lack of competitiveness of US companies relative to the Japanese industrial juggernaut rather than to deliberate policies of the Japanese government.[26] The same could be said of the growing trade gap between the EC and its Far East trading partner.

This is not to say that all barriers to imports from the United States and elsewhere had fallen. The Japanese approval procedures for product marketing hindered imports more than the explicit and independent procedures across the Pacific and public policy companies, including the Telephone and Telegraph Public Corporation or the National Railways, went on using product specification that hampered bids from outsiders, thus favouring Japanese firms and in turn making them more competitive in the international market.[27] It is arguable that the removal or the ease of these restrictions should have formed the subject of concessions in the ongoing multilateral negotiations. A possible compensation might have been the repeal of the Buy American Laws. On the other hand, the gaping deficit was perceived in Washington as a bilateral and urgent issue and the outcome of the Tokyo Round negotiations was still an uncertain prospect.

The US executive effectively exploited the bugbear of protectionist feelings in Congress which were bolstered by the remedies introduced by the Trade Act of 1974 which required the president to adopt temporary corrective actions, including import surcharges and quotas, in case of large balance of payments deficit and, under section 301, gave him authority to retaliate against 'unjustifiable or unreasonable' restrictions by foreign countries that hampered US trade. The United States started to complain that economic relations with Japan were threatened by the stress placed on the world monetary system by Japan's persistent and large current account surplus and by the widespread feeling that it was not giving US exporters equitable access. To make amends for its alleged trade sins, in a meeting on 13 January 1978 between the new US Special Trade Representative, Robert Strauss, and the Japanese minister for External Economic Affairs, Nobuhiko Ushiba, Japan pledged to adopt measures for the stimulation of the economy, aiming at a target of 7 per cent growth rate in the fiscal year 1978 so as to increase imports and to implement specific measures to improve market access.[28] The measures adopted by Japan to increase imports ranged from tariff reduction on $2 billion of imports to the removal of quotas on 12 products and to quota increases for a series of products of particular interest to American farm exporters. As was to be expected, a joint Trade Facilitation Committee was set up with the task of solving problems of market access on a case by case basis and of sponsoring a variety of trade development activities. Government and industry buying missions to promote exports to Japan were organized. But the Japanese authorities went further. Realizing, perhaps with the help of hints from their American counterparts, that the root of US malaise was not so much lack of equitable access to the Japanese market but the swell of Japanese exports to the American one, at the Bonn Summit Japanese prime minister, Takeo Fukuda stated that, to cope with the unusual trade surplus with the United States, his government was taking 'the temporary and extraordinary step' of calling for moderation in exports so as to keep their total volume in the 1978 fiscal year at or below the 1977 level. The outcome of the foregoing was modest. Despite the directives given to the Japanese industrial establishment and the measures envisaged in the joint declaration, the trade gap continued to grow in 1978 (+45%) and, although it declined the following year, it was still greater than in 1977.

Also, the EC tried to reach an agreement with Japan to reduce the rocketing deficit with its Asian trading partner. Indeed, the EC member states' negative balance increased seventeen-fold overall between 1970 and 1977, while that of the United States increased less than six-fold. Yet, the quantitative difference, which made the blow suffered by the EC heavier than the one borne by its transatlantic partner, was more than offset by a qualitative difference in favour of the United States. The EC lacked, among other things, the economic policy weaponry that had made the US request for a Japanese effort to close the trade gap credible and compelling. There was no section 301 and since balance of payments deficit was a matter for each member state, there was no provision authorizing the Community executive to impose surcharges and quantitative restrictions on Japanese exports. Thus, when in March the two parties met in Tokyo, the vice-president of the Commission, Wilhelm Haferkamp, could not draw any substantial commitment out of Nobuhiko Ushiba. The joint statement provided only vague generalities on the improvement of the international trade context and the assurance that the EC would doubtless benefit from the implementations of the pledges made by Japan on previous occasions and from the measures it was autonomously undertaking.[29]

A comprehensive assessment: To what extent was protectionism on the rise in the years following the first oil crisis and which forms did it take?

The foregoing sectorial analyses lead to the conclusion that the so-called stagflation years witnessed a rise in protectionist tendencies in the industrialized world, notably for the two transatlantic partners. Yet, this statement, which to a certain extent is borne out by the facts, could be misleading; it could hinder a clear understanding of the stance of the two parties in the concurrent multilateral negotiations in the GATT. Hegel, criticizing the 'absolute' theory in Frederic Schelling's objective idealism, said that it was like the night in which all cows are black. The same could be said of the above statement. Moreover, it could be suggested that it would lead to mixing allegedly inoffensive sheep with aggressive bulls. On the other hand, the sheep, inoffensive though they seem, could cause negative environmental effects and the apparently aggressive bulls could claim they were only reacting to a threat to their herd. In other words, was the weaponry used by the main trade competitors directed at favouring domestic producers over their foreign competitors or was it aimed at offsetting distortions often caused by trade disruptive practices adopted by the competitors themselves? In the first case, was there a substantial increase in such practices during the years following the oil crisis?

What has been said in the previous sections and chapters shows that the measures in question could be divided into two strands: those aimed at hindering the inflow of foreign products and those aimed at boosting domestic production, which in so doing could prevent imports of foreign like products or could outcompete them in foreign markets, including the market of importing countries. The first class, in turn, could be divided into tariff barriers which had been on the decline due to the various rounds of GATT negotiations, and non-tariff barriers.

The years under review witnessed a further decline in the implementation of safeguard measures in the US. Both GATT Article XIX and US legislation gave relevance to safeguard measures (also known as escape clause). This form of temporary protection was originally designed only to protect against import surges causing economic dislocation in excess of what had been anticipated by trade negotiators in offering concessions. Subsequently, however, these measures were increasingly used to protect domestic industries against increased import competition regardless of previous tariff concessions.[30] In particular, in US legislation, the link with serious injury or threat of serious injury had become increasingly weak: the 1951 trade law provided that imports had to cause or threaten serious injury; the 1962 Trade Expansion Act provided that imports had to be the major factor in causing or threatening to cause serious injury; the Trade Act of 1974 only required that the increased import be a substantial cause of serious injury. Yet, no relevant increase in the use of such measures can be detected in the years following 1974. Not only had serious injury to be proved but the remedy had to be applied in line with the MFN principle, i.e. it had to be applied to all exporting countries rather than the main exporter, and in the absence of compensation, retaliatory measures would be applied. Above all, the final decision on adopting the remedy was for the president who had to balance the interest of the industries affected by foreign competition with those of other industries interested in expanding their trade or acquiring cheaper inputs and with the need not to cause undue strains in relations with US trading partners. At the close of 1977 the US had in effect escape clause relief on just five products and three other safeguard measures were authorized the following year.[31] The trend was different in the EC where the number of safeguard actions soared from 2 in 1974 to 36 three years later, declining to 23 and 19 in the following years.[32]

Conversely, quota restrictions were rapidly increasing following the oil crisis. As is well-known, quotas, which were the trademark of Orderly Market Agreements (OMAs) and VERs, were prohibited by GATT Article XI, with the exception of clearly circumscribed cases in agriculture, and were only allowed by GATT Article XII to safeguard the balance of payments, a provision that was never invoked by the United States nor, after the 1950s, by the EC member states. Yet, quota restrictions became current currency in the 1970s under the cloak of a deal between importer and exporter, thus falling, with the exception of the textile arrangements, into a grey area outside the GATT purview. As related in Chapter I, import quotas were doubtless already applied in the 1960s, but after a pause in the first half of the 1970s they soared in number and value during the stagflation years. The rise does not seem to be directly linked to the general state of the economy, but to the declining health of some particular sectors, encompassing not only textiles and clothing or iron and steel products, but also chemicals, machinery and transport equipment as well as footwear and domestic appliances like TV receivers.

At EC level so-called bilateral trade agreements jumped from 3 in 1973 to 14 in 1975, 11 in 1976, 19 in 1977, 11 in 1978 and 15 in 1979.[33] However, in measuring the impact of such measures it should also be remembered that analogous restrictive measures could be taken by each member state. Italy, for instance, introduced 14 autonomous import quotas in 1977. Also, there was a surge in the imposition of quotas on the other side of the Atlantic. Apart from the quotas established within the framework of the MFA, an orderly marketing agreement was negotiated with Japan on specialty steel in 1976. Orderly marketing agreements were signed in 1977 with Japan on colour TV receivers, a sector in which the US had been the world leader until recently, and with South Korea and Taiwan on footwear. In the first instance, imports were limited to 60 per cent of the 1976 level until 1980. Regarding South Korea and Taiwan, quotas would apply until 1981, curtailing imports to a level below the 1976 value despite annual increases. In 1978, when imports of colour TV receivers from Japan were replaced by an inflow from Taiwan and Korea, voluntary restraint agreements were promptly negotiated with both countries.

Trends and features are even more clearly detectable in the upsurge of antidumping and countervailing measures. Antidumping measures are duties imposed on products exported at less than their normal value in the exporting countries. There was and still is controversy among economists on whether this practice should be condemned. After all, price discrimination, i.e. the ability to identify separate markets for a product and to charge a higher price in the market attaching greater utility to the product, is usually tolerated by competition law when the markets in question are located within national borders. Dumped products sold in a foreign market can benefit domestic consumers except in limited cases, such as predatory dumping, e.g. when differential prices are charged with the aim of driving domestic producers out of the market in order to ultimately raise them to monopolistic levels. On the other hand, dumping damages domestic producers of like products and it was the interest of the latter that was upheld by Article VI of GATT in 1947. The article provided that products are exported at less than their normal value if their export price is less than the comparable price in the ordinary course of trade (a concept that the article failed to define) when destined for consumption in the exporting country or, in the absence of such domestic price, is less than the cost of production plus a reasonable addition for selling costs and profit.

The US antidumping statute provided that antidumping duties could be applied if imports occurred at less than fair value. The concept of fair value substantially coincided with the concept of normal value as outlined in the GATT. Although the US statute only provided for injury caused by dumping, whereas GATT Article VI required material injury, affirmative decision in antidumping cases could not be taken for granted and resort to antidumping procedures was limited to individual cases of allegedly unfair competition from foreign firms. In other terms, it was not the main defence to protect declining domestic industries against foreign competition. Things, however, started to change in December 1974 when, in the middle of an unprecedented recession, the president was granted trade authority no longer limited to tariffs but incorporating the unexplored areas of non-tariff barriers. As noted in the previous chapter, a trade-off was expected between the granting of authority and the strengthening of the defence for domestic industries that had to compete with inflows of foreign products or could not find outlets abroad. One trade-off was the introduction of antidumping rules which were stricter and more favourable to domestic firms, including a shorter deadline for determinations in antidumping proceedings, the right of judicial review of negative findings and, in ascertaining 'fair value', the possibility to disregard persistent sales of the investigated merchandise in the home market at prices below cost of production.[34] Tightening the net allowed the US to accuse of unfair trade those foreign industries whose main fault was that they were able to successfully compete with US firms and to impose extra duties onto their exports. Thus, although the legal objective of antidumping and countervailing measures differed from that of safeguards, the former being directed against unfair trade, their economic objective tended to coincide, boiling down to protection from foreign competition through import restriction. However, antidumping did not have the limits of an escape clause: safeguards could only be implemented for limited periods, whereas antidumping had indefinite length once there was a positive finding. And whereas safeguards were subject to the executive's discretion, the quasi-judicial character of antidumping proceedings – in which the petitioner was a domestic entity and the defendants were foreign firms – ensured a binding result in case of positive findings.[35]

Apart from more favourable rules, a factor that increased the use of antidumping petitions was the depreciation of the dollar vis-à-vis other currencies and in particular the yen, which accelerated between 1976–8 (Figure 1). In spite of the yen appreciation, which entailed a rise of the Japanese unit labour cost on a dollar basis (Figure 3), the merchandise trade gap with Japan soared between 1975–8 (Table 4). Ito provides a convincing explanation pointing out that the yen appreciation was partially offset by the lower cost of imported components and, in particular, of raw materials most of which were priced in dollars, as well as by the adoption of partial pass-through practice in determining the price charged on export products. In order to keep the retail price constant in foreign markets so as not to lose market share, many Japanese firms lowered their profit margin for exports while maintaining or even increasing their profit margin on domestic sales.[36] The pricing to market system, which resulted in different prices in the domestic market and in the export market, unfortunately fell under the purview of the antidumping law whenever it injured domestic industries, which was not difficult to claim in a moment in which Japanese competition was becoming particularly effective not only in steel and motor vehicles but also in industrial plants and electronics. Thus, the rise in antidumping proceedings in the US was at the same time a byproduct of the dollar devaluation and its complement, which made life harder to those foreign exporters who were disposed to pricing to market whenever their products effectively competed with domestic industries.

In 1976 nine antidumping investigations were initiated on automobile imports from Canada, France, West Germany, Italy, the UK, Belgium, Sweden and Japan, involving over $7 billion of imports. However, the investigations were discontinued after receipt of satisfactory price assurances from foreign manufacturers. Twenty-nine investigations were in progress at the end of 1977 involving trade for over $1,960 million. Almost two-thirds of them, involving $1.7 billion, concerned steel products, 70 per cent of which were from Japan.

In the EC antidumping rules were first introduced by Council Regulation n. 458/68 of 5 April 1968, amended in 1973 and 1977. Some 60 antidumping proceedings were initiated under the mentioned Regulation, of which only five resulted in the imposition of antidumping duties as in most cases exporters subject to investigation signed price revision undertakings, that is, increased their export prices. In 1977 the Commission adopted antidumping rules specifically directed to products covered by the Treaty establishing the ECSC by introducing its Recommendation 77/320/ECSC, later modified in December to allow the imposition of provisional duties on steel imports not falling within a basic price system. Recommendation 77/320 and its amendment brought about a spate of self-limitation agreements with iron and steel producing countries. The foregoing seems, therefore, to indicate that also in the EC antidumping measures were nothing but a disguised tariff or a threat of one successfully transforming protection from unfair competition into a protectionist instrument.[37]

The idea, floated by the French government, of a multinational management of international trade, at least with regard to those industrial sectors most threatened by recession, did not receive any effective following. Yet, both the United States and the EC showed great sympathy for a managed trade with Japan directed at better balancing imports and exports, although the attempt was made under the cloak of presumed protectionist attitudes of the Japanese government and the insulation of the Japanese market from foreign imports.

Up to this point the United States and the EC seemed to be treading similar paths with regard both to the kinds of measures adopted and the objectives pursued. They parted company, however, as regards countervailing measures and subsidies. Along with antidumping investigations, the number of countervailing duty proceedings in the US increased in the stagflation years during which on the other side of the Atlantic the number and value of subsidization measures stepped up. In 1974, in the US, four countervailing duty orders and a negative determination were issued. Five countervailing investigations were launched. In 1977 12 petitions were filed and 14 final determinations were made, eight affirmative and six negative,while 11 other investigations were in progress covering trade for $57.2 million. In 1978 18 final determinations were issued, 11 positive and seven negative, while 20 investigations were pending. However, a relevant percentage of countervailing duties was temporarily waived in the course of multilateral trade negotiations until January 1979 under section 331 (a) of the Trade Act of 1974.

The increase in the number of investigations and affirmative decisions does not necessarily mean that countervailing measures had turned into a protectionist tool. It could be argued, as the Americans did, that countervailing measures were a necessary means to prevent unfair pressure on US industries as a result of more and more frequent trade-distorting practices adopted by other countries. On the other hand, American industries confronted by foreign competition, with the aid of the US trade courts, were able to expose to the countervailing authorities certain practices not condemned at the time by GATT rules. This was in particular the case of domestic subsidies. The first general US countervailing duty statute, the Tariff Act of 1897, only provided for the imposition of countervailing duties whenever a foreign government bestowed, directly or indirectly, any bounty or grant upon the exportation of any article or merchandise. The Tariff Act of 1922, however, widened the scope for countervailing measures covering any bounty or grant 'on manufacture or production as well as on exportation'. From 1922, therefore, subsidies that had no export-related performance requirements could also be considered countervailable. Until the 1960s the US administering authority had refrained from imposing duties to offset public support not related to exports. Things changed radically a few years later. In 1974 countervailing measures were imposed on rubber tires produced by a French company, Michelin S.A., in a factory located in Nova Scotia so as to benefit from a series of incentives offered by that Canadian provincial government. In this case, although most of the products would ultimately compete in the US market, the Canadian statutory provisions that allowed the countervailed subsidies in question provided no requirement of export capability for programme eligibility. Thus, the rationale for this kind of countervailing measure was that what is relevant is not the destination of the subsidy but the impact of subsidized export on the US market. And this test was made more severe for foreign exporters by the absence of a material injury requirement in the US statute.

Some import competing American industries tried to extend the boundaries of the US countervailing legislation without, however, receiving governmental endorsement. This was the case with consumer electronics, in particular colour television receivers, a sector targeted for export growth by the Japanese government in the 1960s, which made heavy inroads in the US market in the following decade. American firms petitioned for countervailing duty proceedings arguing that rebates of commodity tax on exports allowed by the Japanese authorities constituted subsidies. An analogous petition was made against EC rebates of the value added tax (VAT) for steel exports. The Treasury Department issued a negative determination in line with a long established practice in the US and in the GATT. However, US legislation was ambiguous on this issue and a leading American firm, the Zenith Radio Corporation, successfully appealed the negative determination in the Customs Court in 1976. In a rare instance, Japan and the EC joined forces claiming that classifying indirect tax rebates on exports as subsidies ran counter to GATT Article VI. The message did not go unheeded and in 1977 the Court of Customs and Patent Appeals reversed the Customs Court decision. That same year the Committee to Preserve the American Television Industry filed an Escape Clause petition arguing that Japanese exports caused injury to the American domestic industry. The president agreed with the claim of injury with regard to colour televisions but did not deem that 'safeguard' was the appropriate remedy, directing instead the Special Trade Representative to negotiate an orderly marketing agreement with Japan, which, as noted above, was duly signed.[38]

The EC had a system under Articles 92 and 93 of the Treaty of Rome to monitor and eventually prohibit subsidies bestowed by its member states, which at that time was applied quite leniently, but had no regime to countervail subsidized imports from third countries comparable to that in force on the other side of the Atlantic.

The United States, in its heavy use of countervailing proceedings, could claim, in contrast to most of its trading partners, that it was not a subsidizer. Subsidies amounted to only 0.5 per cent of US GDP in 1970 and declined to 0.3 per cent in 1975 and 0.4 per cent five years later, although it is extremely likely that the United States did not include its public support to industries like civil transport aircraft and did not take into account the numerous measures offered by state and local authorities to attract investments. [39] Conversely, the EC member states not only started from a much higher basis but showed a marked upwards trend in their degree of subsidization: the EC average, which was 2 per cent of GDP in 1970, jumped to 2.9 per cent in 1975 and 3.2 per cent in 1980; in France and Italy the rate grew respectively from 2 per cent and 1.5 per cent in 1970 to 2.5 per cent and 3 per cent in 1980; in the UK the rate soared from

1.7 per cent in 1970 to 3.5 per cent five years later, declining to 2.3 per cent in 1980.[40] The Federal Republic was on the lower echelon with a rate of 1.7 per cent of GDP in 1970 and 2 per cent in 1980. German scholars, however, contend that after the first oil crisis public subsidization took on a new qualitative dimension amounting to 4–5 per cent of German GNP.[41] Subsidization, which before had concentrated on sectors of the economy traditionally considered as needing assistance, like mining and agriculture, now extended to many other sectors including shipbuilding and to a lesser degree, steel. The same scenario characterized the other main Western European economies. In the UK the declining nationalized steel industry and the motor vehicle industry, where British Leyland was effectively state-owned though technically not nationalized, were heavily subsidized. In Italy, where the capital of most import competing industries such as those in the steel, chemical and shipbuilding sectors was directly or indirectly controlled by the state, government-controlled firms would receive financial support from the owner. It must also be noted that investments of Italian industries benefited from long-term subsidized credit supplied by special credit institutions. In France, automobile, data-processing, pulp and paper, steel and watch industries received various forms of government aid.

The amount of domestic subsidization was in inverse relation with the competitiveness of the firms receiving subsidies, with their numbers and with the level of EC tariff protection.[42] This does not imply that government support policies necessarily reduced non-tariff protection. On the contrary, most of the cases described above indicate that financial support to industries hit by foreign competition was part of a scheme in which import restraints played a large role, whether through quotas, antidumping proceedings or licences. In some cases the granting of subsidies was not linked to the displacement caused by competing foreign products, as the subsidies were granted to encourage investments in underdeveloped areas by offsetting the greater cost of the investment, or were granted to compensate for extra costs brought about by stricter requirements imposed on some industries. Likewise subsidies were bestowed to prevent firms from having to resort to laying-off their employees. All these kinds of measures could always be accused of artificially expanding production and by so doing impinging on the normal play of the market. The accusation, therefore, could be easily made that whatever their avowed purpose, most public aid 'would shore up, and hence protect, weak industries or weak firms that found it difficult to face foreign competition'.[43] The fact remains that, whatever their political persuasion, West European governments of the second half of the 1970s found it impractical to stop financial support to manufacturing industries and agriculture at a moment in which recovery could not steadily take off and unemployment was still high. When a few years later governments like those of Margaret Thatcher and Helmut Kohl came to power, though officially committed to freeing the economy from state interference or to balancing the budget, they found it difficult to reverse policy.

In short, though it may be precipitate to state that the increase in antidumping and countervailing proceedings on one side of the spectrum and in subsidies on the other was by itself clear evidence of rising protectionism, the foregoing demonstrates that there was an upwards trend in their use. The number of antidumping and countervailing proceedings increased and there's no denying that in many cases such proceedings were adopted to constrain imports regardless of their fair or unfair nature, stretching the boundaries established by GATT Article VI. In Western Europe, though it is doubtful that the trend was limited to the eastern side of the Atlantic, public authorities intervened more frequently and more generously to buoy up industries that in the aftermath of the oil crisis were experiencing financial strains and were losing ground to foreign competitors.

5

The Last Phase of the Uruguay Round

It now becomes apposite to precede the following sections with a methodological premise clarifying the questions to which this chapter purports to answer and, therefore, its way of proceeding. It goes without saying that this chapter does not aim at providing a detailed analysis of the results of the Tokyo Round from a legal perspective.[1] Rather it purports to answer two questions: did the long awaited conclusion of the round create a new setting for international trade, i.e. a legal environment enhancing free trade, or was this objective only partially achieved and if so to what extent? And second, did the results of the negotiations coincide with the perspective of the main actors, the US and the EC, and to what extent did they satisfy the interests of each of the two parties?

As expected, opinions on the results of the negotiations are not uniform, although each judgement has its caveat; in other words, the results were a failure, but not an extreme one; alternatively, the results could be classified as a success, but only under the specific circumstances.

Curzon Price argues that, 'although worse cases could be cited', the Tokyo Round was characterized by 'protracted negotiations which by any normal input/output measure have been extraordinarily unproductive and disappointing'.[2] This was because the negotiations were doomed by the steady advance of protectionism which was the natural result of a declining economic environment marked by a high rate of overcapacity which both the main parties were unable to redress. The European Commission stated that the conclusion of the Tokyo Round brought 'results which exceed appearances' not only with regard to tariff negotiations but above all to the non-tariff issues and that 'protectionism and world crisis were held in check', an outcome even more significant as it was 'achieved at a time of international economic recession'.[3] The Report of the President of the United States argued that 'in their entirety, the

Tokyo Round Agreements represent a new beginning to achieve and maintain an open and fair trading system'.[4]

A series of notations can be made on the above judgements. Certainly, as Curzon Price argues, the worsening of the economic environment imposed severe constraints on the drive to create a less protectionist environment for the world economy and trade management, but this does not imply that the deal could not encourage progress when the tide changed and prevent further deterioration of trade conditions when there was a downturn. On the other hand, the outcome of a negotiation must be measured not with reference to the moment in which the agreement is signed but to future circumstances which could significantly alter the economic environment in which the agreement must find its implementation. Actually, in contrast to what the EC maintained, the decisive moments of the GATT negotiations did not occur during a recession. Only some important sectors of the economy in the United States and Europe were in a declining trend and were thus in need of financial support or protection from foreign competition when the negotiations ended. The recession occurred when the agreements were to be implemented. It seems, therefore, that from the historical perspective the best way to answer the questions listed above is first to leave aside a general assessment of the round and to look at what was finally agreed as well as at what it was not possible to agree on, also examining, by focusing on the last phase of the round, the reasons for these outcomes and their possible impact on the management of world trade in future stages.

The re-launch of the multilateral negotiations under the Carter administration

The defusing of the agriculture controversy

The advent of the Carter administration and the nomination of a new Special Representative for Trade Negotiations, Robert Schwarz Strauss, an accomplished lawyer in fields not directly related to international trade, but also a cunning politician with long-standing good relations with Congress members, meant the relaunch of the multinational negotiations. It also meant an agreement with the EC that involved the US renouncing its efforts to significantly liberalize trade in agriculture by opening up the EC market and dismantling the CAP. Various factors can explain, also from a rational viewpoint, this turn in US strategy. First, if the United States wanted the commitment of its main trading partner to the 'locomotive' approach to sustain growth without trade disequilibrium and consequent currency instability, progress towards a mutually satisfactory deal on trade issues, based on perceived reciprocity, was a cornerstone in fostering wider cooperation. By the same token, prolonging the round stalemate on an issue to which the other main party in the negotiations appeared to give paramount importance, thus risking non-cooperation on other areas, was something to be avoided. Secondly, the need for improvement of the trade balance and for greater opportunities for those sectors with higher competitive capacity did not involve, or at least no longer involved, an enhanced contribution from agriculture. Certainly, as noted after the completion of the round by the Secretary for Agriculture, Bob Bergland, in contrast to the non-agricultural trade balance which had been in deficit for most of the decade, agricultural trade had posted a surplus for over 15 years and this surplus had been rocketing since 1973.[5] The share of US agricultural exports over world farm exports grew from 12 per cent in 1971 to over 16 per cent six years later.[6] But all this was due to the high productivity of American agriculture, assisted by a set of favourable circumstances, among which the devaluation of the dollar, and so the achievement did not appear to be conditional on a legal environment guaranteeing trade liberalization and the curbing of trading partners' protection and support policy. Besides this, room for further expansion was predictably not unlimited. From the 1950–4 base period to 1977 world production of all goods, agricultural and non-agricultural, had more than tripled in volume, while the volume of farm production had grown 75 to 80 per cent. During the same period world agricultural trade had nearly tripled in volume, but the volume of American farm exports had almost quadrupled.[7] No doubt, less than ten years later the scenario would have completely changed and with it the US attitude, but in 1977 the main problems concerned industrial trade and it was there that substantial gains had to be speedily sought.

In April 1977, during the talks that Strauss had in Brussels with Wilhelm Haferkamp and Finn Olav Guntelach, vice-presidents of the Commission respectively responsible for External Relations and Agriculture, agreement was reached on the need to conclude the GATT negotiations as soon as possible on the basis of an overall compromise embracing all the areas of the negotiations. A month later the Heads of State and Government participating in the Downing Street Summit stated that continuing economic difficulties made it essential to achieve the objectives of the Tokyo Round negotiations and 'to negotiate a comprehensive set of agreements to the maximum benefit of all'. As regards agriculture, the participants committed themselves to a mutually acceptable approach that would achieve increased expansion and stabilization of trade and greater assurance of world food supplies. The commitment made no further explicit reference to liberalization. In June and July the United States and the EC tabled convergent proposals.

The new terms of negotiations agreed upon by the two parties relied on an offer and request approach, covering both tariff and non-tariff barriers, with reference to single farm products. Lists of requests had to be submitted by 1 November 1977, but they could be modified and additional lists could be submitted as the negotiations proceeded. Offers had to be tabled by 15 January 1978.[8]

The formula simply meant that concessions, mostly in the form of tariff reductions and quota increases or repeals, should concern single products of interest for the parties involved in the negotiation. No agreement implying the general framework of agricultural trade was scheduled. Thus, no general reform of the various kinds of support, either in the United States or in the Community, was required. There was certainly the possibility that the negotiations on subsidies and countervailing measures could also address agriculture, but, given the rather vague GATT provisions concerning farm subsidization and the resistance of the Community negotiators to an agreement going beyond the border of trade in non-primary products, there was no likelihood that any significant provision on farm trade could be agreed.

The implication of the new terms of negotiations did not go unnoticed. A main exporter of farm products, Australia, remarked that because of an agreement between 'two of the major proponents of the negotiation .... what is now in prospect for agriculture is an item by item approach', destined to put countries overwhelmingly dependent on primary products exports, like Australia, at a disadvantage as 'we could not reconcile a multilateral and formula approach to reductions in barriers to trade in industrial products which form less than 6 per cent of our trade with developed countries, with a matched bilateral approach to trade in agriculture which forms 50 per cent of our total exports'.[9] However, Australia realistically declared that 'We are prepared to work with them towards a practical, realistic and balanced result on an item-by-item basis. To do otherwise would be merely obstructive'.[10]

On the other hand, discussions for a comprehensive arrangement of the market continued in the three product areas covered by the subgroups on grains, meat and dairy products, although relevant negotiations were conducted outside the Tokyo Round framework. In particular, negotiations for a new International Wheat Agreement (IWA) were conducted in the International Wheat Council

(IWC) under the auspices of the UNCTAD between late 1977 and the early weeks of 1979, during which period the GATT subgroup suspended discussions on this topic. As the Wheat Trade Convention negotiated during the Kennedy Round had soon collapsed when in 1968–9 contraction of demand, coupled by unexpected abundance of supply, resulted in a decline of price below the minimum level set by the arrangement, a new IWA was established in 1971, but with no pricing provisions.

The negotiations in the IWC under the aegis of the UNCTAD offered the advantage of more active participation of the developing countries than in the GATT and the presence of important members of the wheat market like Russia which were not GATT members. China, however, did not take part in the negotiations.

The Carter administration, which was more willing to explore an arrangement on wheat than its Republican predecessor, saw the IWC as an appropriate forum in which to negotiate an arrangement with stabilization, food security and burden sharing, leaving the issues of subsidization and access to the GATT negotiations.[11] In spite of these favourable premises, the IWA Conference, whose works officially started in February 1978, soon got bogged down in a multitude of issues on which the participants were not able to find practical trade-offs.[12] A consensus was quite soon reached that the operative mechanism for the new wheat convention should be a system of nationally held reserves whose accumulation and release should be triggered by the movement of price indicators specified in the convention. Accumulation of reserves would occur when the indicator fell to a pre-agreed low level and release would occur when the indicator rose to a high level. However, major exporters like the US, Canada and Australia favoured large reserves to moderate downward pressure on price when supply exceeded demand, while major commercial importers such as the EC and Japan demanded smaller reserves. The developing countries felt that large reserves could provide security against global food shortages. Likewise, the main exporters wanted a high minimum price to trigger the build-up of reserves, while the main commercial importers preferred a lower trigger price. The EC, which exported as well as imported, requested relatively higher prices than Japan and most developing countries. The developing countries also called for financial assistance to pay off the costs of acquiring reserves and improving storage facilities but the major trading countries, whether importers or exporters, were unwilling to satisfy such a request. Thus the IWA Conference concluded unsuccessfully in February 1979. For a moment the US and Canada together with Argentina considered an arrangement which would have excluded the importers but the Carter administration, hostile to an agreement that could be seen as a cartel by consumer nations, among which developing countries were the majority, abandoned the proposal.[13]

As regards dairy products, in late 1977 two proposals were put forward by the EC and New Zealand which led to a draft arrangement. The draft originally included such areas as maximum and minimum prices, but such provisions were dropped in 1978. On bovine meat the discussions were based on proposals put forward by Australia and the EC in late 1977. In particular, the EC proposal called for a multilateral framework arrangement which would provide for an information and surveillance system, multilateral consultations in crisis situations and consensus recommendations for joint action by all meat traders. The proposal also envisaged a framework of bilateral or plurilateral agreements between exporters and importers, including commitments on both export behaviour (i.e. voluntary restraints and export price agreements) and import behaviour (i.e. actions to improve conditions of import). The idea, however, was abandoned.

The removal of one of the main stumbling blocks in the negotiations paved the way to negotiating achievements in some other sectors of the Geneva talks, although in others progress was slower and more uncertain.

Industrial tariffs

Proposals for a general approach to tariff reductions had already been tabled in 1976. The United States, which had the highest and most frequent tariff peaks, had gradually accepted the idea of a formula aimed at duty reduction and harmonization but was recalcitrant to accept a significant curtailment of its highest tariffs. The tariff-cutting formula proposed by the United States envisaged that the percentage tariff reduction (Y) should be equal to one and one half times the initial tariff rate (X) plus 50, but with a ceiling of 60 per cent of the previous duty rate: $Y = 1.5\ X + 50;\ Y \leq 60\%\ X$.[14] It must be noted that the 60 per cent ceiling reflected the limit imposed by the Trade Act of 1974 which allowed the president to reduce duties over 5 per cent by a maximum of 60 per cent of the 1 January 1975 rate.

The US proposal was not welcomed by the other parties in the negotiation. The EC in particular noted that, although the formula suggested by the US delegation contained an element of harmonization, the 60 per cent ceiling considerably limited its effectiveness.[15] Indeed, if it was undisputed that the formula nominally cut the highest tariffs deeper, the gap with average or low rate duties remained. For instance, applying the 60 per cent maximum reduction rate, a 25 per cent duty would be reduced to a still high 10 per cent but a 6 per cent duty would be reduced to a modest 2.5 per cent – ineffective in discouraging imports. The Community, therefore, contended that the formula put forward by the United States, particularly with regard to industrial products, would impact prevalently where, as in the case of the EC, a high concentration of moderate tariffs could be found, that is, on those sectors that had already attained a non-negligible level of liberalization. It would be much less effective where, as in the case of the US, there was still a high proportion of protective duties and consequently international trade could not achieve its potential. What was needed in the EC view was a formula aimed at significant tariff reduction and harmonization but not fixed at a level where it would lose credibility being, consequently, eroded by a host of derogations and exceptions.[16]

For its part the Commission suggested a formula based on a reduction rate equal to the initial tariff ($Y = X$) repeated several times. However, by the beginning of 1977 most European countries, including the EC member states, were showing preference for the proposal put forward by the Swiss delegation which was based on the following formula: $Z = 14 \times X/(14 + X)$, where Z is the final duty and X is the initial duty.[17] The Swiss formula had a series of advantages. It was simple and direct as it determined the new tariff rate rather than the reduction rate and above all it was very effective in achieving harmonization since the reduction rate rose steadily as the initial duty increased. For instance, applied to an initial 5 per cent duty the formula gave a 3.68 per cent final duty, with a 26.32 per cent reduction rate, while applied to a 21 per cent duty it gave a final 8.4 per cent duty, with a 60 per cent reduction rate. On the other hand, the formula ensured that for very high initial duties, i.e. those above 100 per cent, final duty would not fall significantly below a 14 per cent ceiling.

During the talks with his counterparts in the EC Commission Strauss made a prudent but clear reference to the need for substantial tariff reduction with a sufficient degree of harmonization, thus making it implicitly clear that the US was willing to improve on its 1976 proposal. By 1978 only two main issues remained: which items were to be excluded from the application of the Swiss formula, and whether a parameter other than 14 – for instance, a parameter resulting in a lower level of approximation – should be adopted. But these issues turned out to be thorny.

Customs valuation

By the beginning of 1978 substantial progress had been achieved on the customs valuation issue. The EC had long defended the so-called 'notional' concept of valuation embedded in the Brussels Definition of Value according to which the price to be taken into account by the customs was the price at which the goods ought to be sold under a specified set of circumstances.[18] In particular the EC suggested that the customs value of goods should be the price on a sale for exports between unrelated parties. The approach presented some difficulties. Indeed, to establish the arm's length price for customs purposes was no easy undertaking and the assessment was bound to entail a certain degree of discretion, being consequently exploitable for protectionist objects. However, during 1976 and the first half of the following year, in the course of a series of visits from European Commission officials to Washington and debates within the Commission and among the member states, the EC gradually changed its stance in favour of the 'positive' concept, that is, the price at which imported goods are in fact sold under specified conditions, which was at the basis of the US customs system. The problem was that the 'positive' concept was at the basis of just one of the measurement criteria followed by the US customs statute which provided nine methods of valuation, some of which, the American Selling Price in particular, were notoriously used as a protectionist device. In November 1977 the EC submitted a draft customs valuation code which, as the EC negotiators did not fail to point out, was based on a 'positive' rather than a 'notional' approach.[19] The proposal put forward by the EC, which actually was a compromise between the two systems, adopted the price paid or payable for imported goods as the primary base for evaluation, even if the buyer and seller were related so long as such a relationship did not give rise to a non-allowed price reduction. If this method could not be applied, the proposal provided for a set of subsidiary criteria (price of identical goods; price of similar goods; price of the imported goods sold to an independent buyer less commissions and various costs) to be applied hierarchically. The draft also carefully listed the methods that should not be applied: the cost of production of the goods; the selling price in the country of importation of similar or comparable goods produced in that country; the price of identical, similar or comparable goods on the domestic market of the country of exportation; and the price of identical, similar or comparable goods sold to another country. It is to be noted that all the forbidden methods were part of the array of valuation criteria envisaged by the US legislation. The draft also stated that valuation procedures should not be used for antidumping purposes.

The EC proposal was overall favourably received and became the basis for the following negotiations.[20] However, sources of disagreement remained in areas like the need for separate rules for developing countries and methods for dispute settlement and a particularly thorny issue was found in the area of transactions between related parties.

Standards

The negotiations on technical barriers to trade went quite smoothly and the draft code tabled in May 1977 was similar in content to the text finally approved two years later also because the subject was rather technical and did not have a direct impact on sensitive issues. The negotiations, which covered such areas as testing and certification by governmental bodies, packaging, labelling and marking of origin, resulted in the basic agreement that signatories to the code would refrain from using standards as obstacles to trade.

Government procurement

The negotiators in the 'government procurement' subgroup were able to make substantial progress also because a lot of preparatory work had been done in the OECD where the negotiations involved the individual countries of Western Europe and America plus Japan. The United States supported the transfer of the negotiations to the Tokyo Round deeming that a larger forum would provide greater opportunities for tradeoffs and settlement, while some EC member states, in particular France, opposed the move.[21] The EC Commission supported the transfer, first because it was the Community negotiator in the GATT forum, whereas the OECD negotiations were conducted by the single EC member states, and secondly because its role in the GATT negotiations provided it with a better opportunity to push through a Directive for the coordination of public procurement procedures all over the Common Market.[22]

A first draft of the code was circulated in December 1977, followed by a second draft in July 1978. Progress was made on the issues of transparency, tender procedure and the value threshold for the application of the code, although some differences were not settled. During the negotiations efforts were made to establish a threshold low enough to accomplish the goal of opening-up the market but high enough not to cause difficulties to the authorities in the signatory countries. The United States favoured a low value threshold deeming that American companies could benefit from the fact that foreign procurement contracts tended to be much lower in value than those in the United States. Other industrialized nations, among which the EC, which had set a minimum threshold of approximately $250,000 in its good procurement Directive, favoured a higher value threshold.[23] Tender procedures remained a difficult issue till the end of the negotiations. The US proposal provided for two types of tender, 'public' (formal) bidding and 'informal' (negotiated or sole-sourced) bidding.[24] The EC along with Japan, in line with their domestic practice, favoured a tripartite system with 'open', 'selective' and 'single' tenders.[25] The open tender allowed all interested parties to bid, while in selective tenders only invited suppliers could do so. In single tendering procedures, permitted only in few cases, governmental bodies could deal with single suppliers. The disputes over transparency were resolved quite quickly. The United States pressed on this issue feeling that its procurement procedures were more open, and therefore fairer, than those of other industrialized countries, among which the EC member states and Japan. The thorniest issue remained the determination of the entities subject to the code. The EC was not disposed to make commitments on international tendering in areas such as energy, transportation and telecommunications. The United States, in turn, was not willing to extend the agreement to state and local government bodies many of which had enacted their own 'Buy American' laws. The July 1978 draft overcame the problem by adopting a system of offers and requests whereby each country would notify the others of those entities in its own country that would be subject to the code and those entities in other countries it would like to see covered.[26]

Subsidies, countervailing duties and antidumping measures

Progress in subsidies and countervailing measures was slow, but by the end of 1977 the United States and the EC were able to draw up a heavily bracketed 'outline of an approach' in which, although reiterating their viewpoints, some common ground was found.[27] The United States aimed at extending subsidy regulation to domestic support to non-primary products and at clarifying the rules on agricultural export subsidies in a way that could rein in their use. Although the US had already accepted the idea that causation of injury was necessarily to be part of an agreement on countervailing measures, it was not disposed to allow that subsidization should be the main, or even worse, the sole cause of injury and if the prospective code were not to reform the provision of GATT Article VI, according to which injury was to be 'material', this term should be interpreted restrictively. The EC was wary of commitments that could endanger its own and member states' policies to support industry in a presumptively limited period of difficulty, or in need of restructuring and policies to encourage business to locate to depressed regions. This had been even more necessary since 1975 because the recession had been followed by slow recovery and the unemployment rate remained high. After all, the adjustment assistance provided by the US government to industries and communities hit by foreign competition could be considered a form of subsidization and state authorities were not loath to offer incentives to attract business. On the other hand, the Community judged that, as material injury was already required by GATT Article VI for the imposition of antidumping and countervailing duties, there was no reason to view it as a bargaining chip in the negotiations, nor had it any sympathy for a watered-down interpretation of the requirement lest it allow leeway to the US authorities in their investigations against imported products accused of being dumped or subsidized.

The 'outline of an approach', jointly submitted by the US and EC delegations in Geneva, did not explicitly mention domestic subsidies, but confined itself to state that agreement should be sought not to use export subsidies on non-primary products and that an updated list of prohibited subsidies should be drawn up. The provisions on agricultural subsidies proposed by each delegation were bracketed by the other as the negotiators did no more than restate the traditional positions of the United States and the EC. As reported by two former high-ranking officers in the US delegation, the United States proposed a Supplementary Understanding on Internal Subsidies which stated that signatories would 'seek to avoid the use of subsidy practices in a manner that causes serious prejudice to the interests of other signatories' and provided an illustrative list of subsidies that could have an impact on the interests of other countries.[28] The proposal was not accepted by the other negotiators in the group. However, during the run-up to the Bonn Summit a new 'outline of an arrangement' was put forward by the US and EC delegations together with the delegations of Canada, Japan and the Nordic countries.[29] The new outline recognized that subsidies other than export subsidies were widely used as important instruments for the promotion of social and economic objectives of national policy and recognized the right of signatories to implement such subsidies, but contained in an Annex a list of internal subsidy practices which might have an adverse effect on the trade and production of other signatories. As was to be expected, the list was in brackets. On the other hand, as regards countervailing measures, requirements that subsidized products should be a principal cause or an important contributing factor of injury were also presented in brackets.

Safeguards

Safeguards remained one of the most controversial topics in the negotiations. The main stumbling block was selectivity. The EC backed by the 'Nordic Countries' group tried to push through a reform of GATT Article XIX which would allow selective actions against individual countries, subject to subsequent review by a GATT committee. The strongest opposition came from the developing countries which, having had to accept that they would not be entitled to any general exclusion from safeguard measures, argued that such measures should only be applied according to the MFN non-discrimination principle. The United States took a middle-ground stance, accepting the selectivity approach but only under exceptional circumstances to be ascertained by a GATT committee before the enforcement of any discriminatory measures. Another area of disagreement between the industrial and developing countries was the definition of 'injury' since, although the standard of serious injury provided by Article XIX was accepted, the parties disagreed as to the proper threshold for such a finding. Thus the draft text tabled in June 1978 was heavily bracketed and it contained a multitude of not easily reconcilable proposals on the issue of selective action.[30] In July both the American and the EC delegations held meetings with representatives of developing countries which, although stating that they were not opposed to all negotiations on selectivity, made it clear that they would not accept the EC version allowing unilateral action.

Aircraft

A late arrival in the negotiations was a proposal tabled by the United States for the elimination of tariffs and substantial reduction of non-tariff barriers on aircraft between the US and its main competitors on aircraft exports, i.e. the EC, Japan, Canada and Sweden. The United States was the leader in the sector accounting for 63 per cent of transport aircraft sales between 1973–7 and 28 per cent of general aviation sales in the same period. However, competition from the above-mentioned countries, quite often providing strong financial support to their national companies' production and export, was starting to make itself felt. The US was convinced that tariffs were not a serious obstacle to a continued high level of exports but non-tariff barriers could represent a threat. In return for the elimination of its 5 per cent duty on aircraft it called, therefore, for effective discipline on non-tariff measures going beyond the general agreements under negotiation in the round. The kind of measures the United States wished to subject to strict discipline included government-directed procurements, governmental subsidies, licence restrictions and mandatory subcontracts.

Naturally, the United States failed to notice that major manufacturers of aircraft like Boeing could receive a boost from their governments if their activities also embraced military equipment through sole-sourced bidding for high value contracts and Research and Development financing.

The final stages of the negotiations

On 13 July the delegations of the main trading nations issued what they called a 'framework of understanding on the major elements of a comprehensive package for the Tokyo Round', which was to be 'a reasonable basis for completing a mutual agreement in the weeks ahead'.[31] The document was endorsed three days later at the Bonn Summit by the heads of state and government who also set a deadline for the conclusion of the negotiations on 15 December 1978. The deadline, designed to add further impetus to the talks, proved too optimistic. The 'framework of understanding' took stock of the progress achieved but also of the work that was yet to be done. As noted above, the main differences concerned the prospective codes on subsidies and countervailing duties and on safeguards. Concerning industrial tariffs, though the delegations agreed on the approach to achieve a substantive harmonized reduction of tariffs, generally following the Swiss formula, they were still negotiating reciprocal adjustments in their initial offers involving improvements as well as exceptions.

Within the EC, France feared that the articles of the subsidy and countervailing measures code on the exportation of primary products could result in curbing farm exports which had an increasingly important role in improving its merchandise trade balance. France, with various degrees of support from the other member states, was not prepared to accept stricter discipline on domestic subsidies and in particular on a list of domestic subsidization measures that were likely to cause serious prejudice to the trade interest of other GATT parties. The British Labour government shared the French misgivings while Germany, though not reluctant to provide financial help to those industries that most suffered from the sluggish economic recovery, favoured a more flexible approach.

On the other side of the Atlantic, at a moment in which imports were by far exceeding exports, despite the ongoing devaluation of the dollar, Congress felt that concessions on countervailing measures should be subject to commitments to avoid any kind of subsidization, either domestic or export oriented, that could hinder US trade or impair American industries. In its view it seemed that other parties to the multilateral negotiations, nominally the EC, were dragging their feet on accepting a fair deal. A provision of the Trade Act of 1974 authorized the Secretary of the Treasury to waive the imposition of countervailing duties for a four-year period ending on 2 January 1979, one year prior to the expiration of the president's overall negotiating authority. Congress simply refused to renew this authority. The imports found to be subsidized amounted to about $600 million and were mostly agricultural products from the EC.

The move provoked a firm response from the EC side. Wilhelm Haferkamp, vice-president of the Commission, in a letter addressed to Robert Strauss in September made it clear that the imposition of countervailing duties on EC exports would precipitate a commercial war of considerable dimension that would prevent the Community from concluding the Tokyo Round.[32] Since the threat of pending countervailing measures was not removed, despite the good will pressure exerted by the US executive on Congress, the Commission's step was followed by an apparently more conciliatory public statement from the president of the Council of the Community announcing that 'in spite of the serious decision taken in Congress', the Community would continue the talks to prepare the way for the conclusion of the negotiations on the understanding, however, that 'the continued application of the waiver, even after 3 January 1979, is guaranteed'.[33] The US Special Representative managed to keep the negotiations on track. In November, in a series of visits to European capitals and meetings in Geneva, Strauss convinced his European counterparts that the US executive would introduce legislation in the opening days of the new Congress session and would take any appropriate measure to avoid the disruption of normal trade flow. The law temporarily extending the president's authority to waive countervailing duties was signed by Carter on 3 April 1979.

On safeguards, the EC could not overcome the opposition made by the developing countries to its proposal also because it failed to gain the backing of the United States and Japan. The former was not disposed to go beyond its compromise proposal as it was not willing to cause open confrontation with developing countries whose cooperation it aimed to gain or preserve and because the US believed that it already had more persuasive means than the selective imposition of safeguard measures to protect its industries. Japan, which in the final stages of the negotiations on safeguard measures maintained a low profile, was certainly not ready to support a proposal that could provide its

European partners, and prospectively the United States as well, with a powerful weapon against its exports. In April 1979, when the texts of the agreements reached in the negotiations were signed by the representatives of the participating governments, the GATT Secretariat submitted a working draft intended to serve as a basis for further consultations but by July it was clear that further efforts to find acceptable common ground were pointless.

In its report submitted to the Council of the Community in late December 1978, the Commission argued that the conditions for signing a comprehensive agreement on the various negotiating items had not yet been established.[34] Although most codes, including customs valuation and standards, could be signed and significant progress towards the EC position had been secured in the negotiations on subsidy and countervailing measures, further talks were needed in other areas. Apart from safeguards, where there was no prospective of a prompt deal, on government procurements there were still differences on both the government purchasing entities and the value level of contracts to be covered by the code. As regards the Aircraft Agreement, if a deal on zero import duties seemed near, the US desire for a series of additional clauses governing the degree of government involvement in the manufacture and sale of aircrafts was regarded with suspicion by the Commission.

As regards tariffs, the Commission related that progress had been made in securing possible improvements of US offers on textiles and chemicals, but that a full additional evaluation of the offers had not been completed and pending further discussions both parties had agreed that reaching a satisfactory overall balance was not yet possible. On the other hand, in the case of Japan, even though additional offers were forthcoming, they did not include significant concessions in areas of interest for the Community, such as textiles, leather goods and processed agricultural products. Since the additional offers were accompanied by a number of possible withdrawals, there was no prospect for real improvement at that stage.

It was only in a subsequent communication sent to the Council of Ministers at the end of February 1979 that the Commission claimed that conditions were ripe for a GATT agreement as, viewing the negotiating package as a whole, it was equitable and balanced and overall was advantageous for the EC.[35] According to the Commission, the agreement on tariffs would offer much greater access to new markets for EC producers, while the EC concessions were moderate and would be gradually introduced over a long span of years. As regards non-tariff barriers, a series of gains was to be achieved, from the repeal of the ASP and of the Wine Gallon Assessment method to the curtailment of the Buy American

Act in those sectors covered by the Government Procurement Agreement and to the acceptance of the 'material injury' principle in countervailing measures proceedings by the US authorities. After a delay of over a month, the Council gave the Tokyo Round agreements its green light in April.

The US executive, which in mid-December had reached a comprehensive understanding with Japan on issues under negotiation in the Tokyo Round, had to appease Congress on sensitive tariff issues. Indeed, if Congress was barred from introducing amendments on the agreements to be signed in Geneva, nevertheless it had the definitive word on any non-tariff agreement. If there was no hope for a comprehensive settlement on agriculture satisfying the expectations of the powerful farm lobby, and if the outcome of the negotiations on subsidies only partially met the expectations of key areas of American industry, no ground was to be given on tariff and quota protection for sectors threatened by foreign competition or on countervailing measures. The US government by the end of December felt that the balance of concessions and achievements negotiated in Geneva would not meet with opposition from the lawmakers and on 4 January notified Congress of its intention to enter into MTN agreements, according to the procedures envisaged by the Trade Act of 1974.[36] In the event, in the following three months the executive had to appease some interest groups with powerful lobbies in Congress, textiles and steel industries in particular. An agreement, made public on 15 February, was reached with the unions and employers of the textile industry in which the administration pledged to control disruptive import surges, to negotiate bilateral agreements with new emerging suppliers like China, and to continuously monitor textile imports on a global basis. Although no comparable overt arrangement was made with the steel industry, the administration had to be particularly attentive to the industry's insistence on a minimal injury test and on stricter rules on antidumping and countervailing proceedings. The executive had also to take heed of the chemical industry's call for more moderate tariff cuts on some of the products in the list negotiated in Geneva.

Results of the Tokyo Round

When at their annual meeting held in Geneva from 26 to 30 November 1979 the Contracting Parties to GATT approved the results of the negotiations by consensus, the conclusion of the Tokyo Round was hailed with satisfaction by both the US and the EC which claimed that significant advantages had been achieved by the whole International Community and, in particular, by each of them. The snag was that, in many areas and with a view to papering over their differences, the main actors sacrificed effective opening of markets to preservation of established policies.

Industrial tariffs

The tariff reductions negotiated in the Tokyo Round were apparently impressive. According to GATT estimates, the schedules of concessions annexed to two protocols signed in the second half of 1979 affected a total value of trade of over US$155 billion measured on MFN imports in 1977.[37] Concessions by the EC, the United States, Canada, Japan and five EFTA members covered imports for US$141 billion. Those agreed on industrial products covered about US$127 billion, 90 per cent of the industrial trade among the major developed countries in 1977. The weighted average tariff on manufactured products of the industrialized countries was bound to decline from 7 per cent to 4.7 per cent, amounting to a third of tariff collection. The adoption of the Swiss formula as a general criterion to establish reduction rates meant that the deepest cuts were mostly made on the highest tariffs. Most of the tariff reductions were scheduled to begin on 1 January 1980, to continue with equal annual cuts until 1987.

The average US tariff on total industrial products (dutiable plus duty-free), excluding petroleum, was cut by 32 per cent from 6.2 per cent to 4.2 per cent.[38] The US applied the Swiss formula with the 14 per cent coefficient, subject to the 60 per cent maximum imposed by the Trade Act of 1974, as well as to a set of exceptions for individual products. This allowed the United States to reduce the duty on products exposed to foreign competition such as textiles and apparel or iron and steel by much less than the average 40 per cent trade-weighted cut rate under the Swiss formula. On the other hand, the number of duties exceeding 20 per cent was greatly reduced.

The tariff concessions of the EC were slightly less generous overall than those of its transatlantic partner. A report on the final results of the Tokyo Round somewhat candidly stated that 'the Community's aim was to keep the Common Customs Tariff at a significant level and, at the same time, to obtain a reduction of tariff from its main trading partners to increase the degree of harmonization'.[39] The EC along with the Scandinavian countries applied the Swiss formula, however, using a coefficient of 16 rather than 14 as in the US and Japan. As noted above, the smaller the coefficient the higher the tariff reduction.

The EC also made a substantial number of exceptions to the general formula to protect industries particularly sensitive to import competition, such as motor vehicles, television sets, fertilizers, shoes and cutlery.[40] Overall, the Common Customs Tariff on industrial goods, excluding duty-free imports, was reduced from an average of 9.8 per cent to an average of 7.5 per cent. Thus most of the EC duties lay in a range between 5 per cent and 10 per cent with the exception of only 180 duties exceeding 10 per cent and one (on lorries) exceeding 20 per cent.[41] Including duty-free imports, the average tariff was cut by 27 per cent from 6.3 per cent to 4.6 per cent. The areas where tariff reductions offered the greatest opportunities to Community exporters included chemicals, ceramics and mechanical engineering, while the areas opened to increased competition from foreign producers were paper, plastics and non-ferrous metals.[42] The customs reductions were spread out over a period of eight years from 1980 to 1987, but the Community reserved the right to review the situation after the first five years before deciding whether to proceed to the final three stages of reduction.

The concessions made by the US and the EC to each other exceeded their average level of reduction as they made a depth of cuts of about 35 per cent on their reciprocal trade. The United States obtained gains on certain chemical items, certain paper items, printing machinery, electrical machinery, scientific instruments and photographic equipment, while it made important concessions to its trading partner in certain textile, leather, glassware, chemical and machinery items. The tariff concessions benefiting US products also made it possible to narrow the gap with the EFTA countries and those Mediterranean and former colonies which had preferential arrangements with the Community that allowed most industrial and some agricultural items to enter the European Common Market duty free.

The impact of tariff reductions was, however, watered down from the outset by the concessions already made in the previous rounds. For instance, a 30 per cent reduction on tariffs not exceeding 10 per cent would result, at most, in a 3 per cent cut. The cut, perhaps, could have been significant under fixed exchange rates but it was easily offset by currency movements in a floating exchange regime. Besides, as the tariff cut was to be completed in eight years, it would amount to a reduction in import prices of one-half of one percentage point a year, not to mention the fact that the tariff concessions agreed in the Tokyo Round might be nullified by antidumping or countervailing duties imposed on imported items and, as we shall see, the Tokyo Round codes did not prevent such measures from being adopted more and more frequently as a weapon against competing products which were performing too well.

Customs valuation

On the other hand, the modest impact of the tariff reductions agreed at the end of the round was balanced by the harmonization of the systems designed to assess the import value for the imposition of ad valorem duties and by the consequent elimination of assessment methods that unfairly distorted such a value. The Customs Valuation code established five valuation methods – applicable on either an f.o.b. or a c.i.f. basis – ranked in hierarchical order. The first and primary method referred to the transaction value as expressed by the invoice price. The second and third methods relied on the transaction value of identical or similar goods exported to the same country. Under the fourth method the resale price of the imported goods was used as the starting point for calculation. The fifth value was based on the computed value of the imported goods which comprised material and manufacturing costs plus general expenses and profits. If none of the above listed methods could be applied, the customs value was to be determined using any reasonable means consistent with the principles and general provisions of the code and of ArticleVII of the GATT. The methods provided by the code largely reflected the US practice, but the code also meant the abrogation of the American Selling Price (ASP) system as well as the special valuation system for what were known as Final List products which together accounted for about 20 per cent of customs entries. On the other hand, the United States secured agreement on higher tariff binding for some of the products protected by the eliminated systems, such as benzenoid chemicals and rubber-soled footwear. There was thus a trade-off between concessions in different, though related, areas of negotiations which left the actual tariff protection for some specific sectors almost unchanged, in spite of the fact that the US executive, whether under a Republican or a Democratic president, favoured the abrogation of these systems viewed as an irritant in the negotiations with foreign exporters.

Subsidies, countervailing measures and antidumping duties

The Subsidies and Countervailing Measures (SCM) code reinforced the ban on export subsidies on non-primary products and the prohibition was supported by an illustrative list of prohibited export subsidies. The code also introduced a four stage dispute settlement procedure providing for consultation, conciliation by a newly established committee on subsidies and countervailing measures, investigation by a panel and countermeasures. This procedure applied both to export subsidies and domestic subsidies, allegedly causing or threatening to cause serious prejudice to other contracting parties. The foregoing met the US goal of achieving stricter discipline on subsidies. However, there was no definition of what constitutes an export subsidy, even less a subsidy, and as regards domestic subsidization a compromise was reached between the United States and the EC which was aimed to satisfy everybody but was not destined to be very effective. Indeed, the code set out by claiming that non-export subsidies can be a means for achieving desirable social and economic policies, such as eliminating regional disadvantages, restructuring particular sectors, encouraging research and development and maintaining employment and encouraging retraining. But it added that domestic subsidies may cause adverse effects to the interest of other signatories in several forms: injury to the domestic industry of another signatory; nullification or impairment of previous benefits; and serious prejudice or threat of serious prejudice in the export market. The question was where to draw the line between commendable goals in the domestic market and adverse effects on other signatories. In particular, there was no clear definition of what could cause serious prejudice. Nor, contrary to the hopes of the United States and unlike export subsidies, was there a list of domestic measures likely to cause prejudice. Thus, the United States claimed that the code resulted in 'an explicit recognition of the needs for limits on domestic subsidies', while its transatlantic counterpart argued that 'the Community's freedom of action in the matter of internal subsidies (regional ones for instance) will not be fundamentally affected'.[43] If, as claimed by the United States, the code introduced stricter discipline also for domestic subsidies, there was more ground for confrontation than conciliation.

On the countervailing duty side, the code embodied the principle of material injury but here too it failed to provide a definition of what the term actually meant. Thus, the effectiveness of the code in preventing protectionist abuse would depend on the implementing legislation of the countries adhering to it. In ratifying the code the US Congress was likely to adopt a restrictive interpretation as prospects for industries like steel, facing competition from abroad and capable of conducting effective lobbies, were getting increasingly bleak.[44]

Substantially analogous rules were agreed on antidumping. Therefore, here too, particularly with regard to implementation in the United States, the question of what was meant by 'material injury' remained hovering and the code failed to prevent or at least effectively restrict the use of antidumping duties as a protectionist tool for import competing industries.

Public Procurement

The Government Procurement (GPR) code, which entered into force in 1981, contained detailed rules on the way in which tenders for government purchasing contracts should be invited and awarded to ensure they did not protect domestic products or suppliers or discriminate against foreign products and suppliers. The agreement applied to contracts worth more than 150,000 Special Drawing Rights (SDRs), equivalent to about US$197,000. In line with US hopes and contrary to the EC's wishes, the agreed minimum amount was below the threshold set by the EC Directive on good procurement within the Community. On the other hand, the SDR 150,000 threshold eliminated access to many smaller contracts frequent in the developing countries. In any case, the code had some relevant limitations. In the first place, its scope was not abreast with the widening areas of government procurement at the end of the 1970s. It did not apply to the purchase of services. This was in line with the purview of the General Agreement which referred only to trade in goods, but did not take into account the growing demand for the supply of services from public authorities. Neither did the agreement apply to construction contracts or to defence related purchases. Secondly, procurements by states and local governments (with or without federal funds) and by important government entities were not covered. The United States, for instance, excluded the Department of Transportation and the Department of Energy and certain quasi-governmental organizations. This entailed that, although the Buy American Act could no longer apply to some federal procurements, buy-American or buy-local law proliferated among states and local governments within the US.

Aircraft

The Aircraft Agreement abolished customs duties and similar charges not only on complete aircrafts but also on engines and components as well as on their maintenance and rebuilding. It also prohibited import and export restrictions unless justifiable under the provisions of the GATT and, with a sentence which sounds quite vague, provided that no obligation or unreasonable pressure should be imposed to persuade prospective aircraft buyers to choose from a particular source. As regards subsidies, the signatories noted that the code on subsidies and countervailing duties also applied to civil aircraft but qualified the statement by stressing that special factors applying to the aircraft sector, and in particular the widespread governmental support in this area, had to be taken into account. Thus domestic subsidies were left aside but even in the export subsidies area, export credit subsidization, one of the major instruments in promoting civil aircraft sales, was not covered by the agreement. Certain agreements on export credits were concluded under the aegis of the OECD, but at that time they did not prove very effective. The fact that just over 12 years later the United States and the EC would sign a bilateral agreement with the specific goal of solving a dispute by regulating their respective industry support measures is clear indication that the Tokyo Round Agreement on civil aircraft was far from establishing an environment free from state interference as was claimed at that time.

Agriculture

In keeping with the request and offer process agreed in mid-1977, both the United States and the EC made and obtained some important concessions on agricultural export. The United States obtained concessions on tariff reductions and quota liberalization on products representing about 16 per cent of its farm exports. The trade coverage of the concessions received from the EC, measured on a 1976 basis, was about $1 billion. The major concessions by the Community involved beef, tobacco, rice, poultry and certain fresh and canned fruits.[45] The most significant US concessions to its transatlantic partner concerned the increase of the quota allocation for cheese, the removal of certain retaliatory duties imposed as a result of the chicken war of the 1960s and the elimination of the so-called 'wine gallon' method of duty assessment.[46] This system assessed taxes and duties on all bottles containing less than one gallon as if they were 100 per cent proof. Instead domestic producers generally only paid excise tax on the proof gallon method, i.e. the actual alcoholic equivalent of one gallon of spirits at 100 per cent proof. The different method of assessment resulted in a classic non-tariff barrier penalizing foreign alcoholic beverages as they entered US customs already bottled.[47] In return for the removal of this system of assessment, the US received various concessions from other countries, including a pledge from the EC to ensure that its member states would eliminate any measures resulting in discrimination against US distilled spirits.

As regards the regulation of particular commodity markets, the round produced an International Dairy Arrangement (IDA) which provided for minimum export prices for butter, powdered milk and certain cheeses, and established a mechanism for information exchange and policy consultations. However, the agreement had neither enforcement mechanisms nor provisions for stock and production adjustments. The Bovine Meat Arrangement created a council with the task of monitoring the sector and a mechanism of consultation and settlement of differences, but had no economic or regulatory provisions. As regards wheat the only result, after the failure of the IWA Conference, was a decision to extend the 1971 International Wheat Agreement which contained no economic provisions.

Regarding farm export subsidies, limited progress was achieved by the code on Subsidies and Countervailing Measures whose Article 10 referred to primary products. The code provided a more precise interpretation of the expression 'equitable share of world export trade' and extended the ban to export subsidies that resulted in the acquisition of a non-equitable share 'in a particular market' and in cut price competition in that market.[48] However, these precisions proved to be ineffective when applied to actual cases of export support. Nor did the code provide any effective discipline on domestic mechanisms of farm price or income support. Thus Finn Olav Gundelach, vice-president of the Commission with special responsibility for agriculture, could claim with justified relief, at least for the time being, that the Uruguay Round agreements meant the acceptance 'of the principles and mechanisms of the Community's common agricultural policy' and 'had brought an end to the "trench warfare" and "religious wars" that had so often characterized discussion of agriculture in the past'.[49]

Safeguards

The most conspicuous absentee among the agreements signed at the end of the round was the code on Safeguards. Not only was it impossible to bridge the gap between the EC and the developing countries, whatever their industrialization progress, but differences remained in the negotiating stance of the main industrial participants: the call from the EC for unilaterally actionable safeguard measures was received with caution by the United States and with suspicion by Japan.

Failure to reach an agreement on the safeguard issue calls for a reflection that could be extended to areas where an agreement was signed. On the one hand, selectivity limited the impact of emergency measures to the actual origin of the problem, avoiding the obstruction of exports from third countries, and therefore was less disruptive to trade. On the other hand, the idea of selective safeguards was opposed to the principle of non-discrimination which was the cornerstone of the GATT system and in its implementation would be bound to penalize, contrary to the economic precept, those exporters that were in the best position to make inroads in the importing country's market, that is to say, the most efficient.[50] Moreover, the EC proposal presented a fundamental strategic difficulty: it impinged on the network of voluntary export restraints agreed outside the discipline of the GATT, which were in fact selective safeguards adopted with the, sometimes quite reluctant, countenance of the exporting country. If a radical reform of GATT Article XIX had been agreed extending the power of Western industrialized countries to curtail, though temporarily, the inflow of products from the NICs or other emerging countries, not to mention Japan, then it was to be expected that the vast array of so-called 'grey-area actions' was to be dismantled or at least conducted within the scope of the GATT.

Developing countries

In line with the stated objectives of the Tokyo Round, formal steps were made towards more favourable treatment to developing countries. In particular, the so-called 'enabling clause' provided that notwithstanding the MFN provision of GATT Article I, 'contracting parties may accord differential and more favourable treatment to developing countries without according such treatment to other contracting parties' with regard to both preferential tariffs and non-tariff measures. However, in keeping with the policies adopted by the United States and the EC during the decade, the provisions in favour of the developing countries contained a 'graduation clause' which made it clear that their capacity to accept obligation under the GATT and to benefit from preferential treatment would respectively increase and decrease according to their economic development. In short, countries like Hong Kong, Taiwan and South Korea and many other newly industrialized countries could not expect to be entitled to special treatment and had to play by the rules, which were prevalently established by the industrialized members of the General Agreement.

Did the agreements secure a freer and fairer trade environment and to what extent?

The Special Representative for Trade Negotiations, Robert Strauss, commenting upon the results of the Tokyo Round with specific reference to NTB codes said that 'we should be realistic about the significance of these agreements, neither overstating nor understating their importance. They are no more and no less than the first new chapters on a new book of rules for international trade'.[51] Strauss's prudently toned-down judgment can be extended to the whole package that emerged at the end of the negotiations.

In every trade negotiation, representatives must reconcile the call for trade liberalization by industries hoping to expand their trade with the call for protection by industries that feel the heat of foreign competition, often accused, rightly or wrongly, of not abiding by level playing field rules. As there were two major actors in the Tokyo Round, the US and the EC, the curves within which negotiators had to find a point of equilibrium were multiplied by two. Besides, the main parties felt it incumbent upon them to avoid the failure of the negotiations just when they had committed to cooperate in order to achieve a better economic environment while the recovery was shaky and new strains were looming on the world economy. Thus what many commentators have rechristened as the 'Strauss Round' was to be a success, but to achieve this goal it was necessary to paper over many differences that re-emerged when the agreements had to be implemented.

As was foreseeable, the round provided a good occasion to cut tariff rates but the results were not impressive, especially because the impact of tariff cuts had been pre-empted by concessions in previous rounds and also because, as was to be expected, import competing sectors managed to obtain greater tariff protection than the average.

Examining the performance of the Tokyo Round NTB codes in the 1980s, Grieco points out that there was significant variation in the effectiveness achieved by the codes and that their fate was a reflection of the level of US–EC cooperation or discord within the relevant committees of signatories.[52] Codes which were technical in nature like those on customs valuation and standards were brought into force with minimum difficulties, while the implementation of the SCM code, especially with reference to subsidizing measures, was marked by disputes and by attempts not to comply with transparency requirements. An intermediate level of success in implementation and extension of its purview was attained by the GPR code. It must be noted that the various code committees had not only the task of ascertaining the correct implementation of the codes and of solving disputes, but also acted as a forum wherein the contracting parties could discuss amendments and negotiate enlargements of the scope of the agreements.

Actually, the performance of the NTB codes in the 1980s reflected the balance of converging or conflicting interests between the main negotiators that had been achieved, with different levels of difficulty, in the previous decade, taking into account that the Tokyo Round agreements were as notable for what they excluded as for what they included.

For instance, on the one hand, the SCM code did not define what constituted 'material injury', thus allowing the United States to avoid significantly altering its administrative practice on countervailing proceedings. On the other hand, the EC resisted any extensive interpretation of obligations concerning subsidies and, ignoring US complaints, for a long time failed to notify its subsidy programmes and some EC member states never notified their industrial support measures. The unwillingness to notify lay in the fact that notification of subsidy programmes was likely to be taken as evidence that the programmes were affecting trade, thus harming the trading interests of other partners; therefore, it entailed the risk of becoming the target of countervailing measures or dispute settlement actions in the GATT.[53]

Likewise, the US attempt to extend the GPR provisions to government purchasing entities not covered by the code, but over which governments had direct or substantial control, such as government-owned companies, was resisted by the EC and analogous resistance met the attempt to extend GPR rules to the provision of services, a sector of growing interest for the United States but also one of the areas on which the EC executive focused to enhance integration within the Common Market. Finally, for over five years, the EC resisted the US call for a reduction of the threshold level above which public purchases were subject to the GPR code. It was only in 1986 that the threshold level was reduced by SDR 20,000, but this was done on a two year experimental basis. As noted above, the EC Directive on public procurements in the member states had set a much higher minimum threshold of approximately $250,000 than that agreed in the GATT and, therefore, the EC authorities had to introduce a new Directive addressing procurements covered by the GATT code. Unsurprisingly, the EC tried to dodge the Tokyo Round agreement arguing that bidding value should be determined excluding Value Added Tax. The United States lodged a complaint and a GATT panel in 1984 found that the EC practice was not in conformity with the GPR code.[54] The Community did not accept the panel's report and only three years later a compromise was laboriously worked out by which the Community accepted a further cut of the threshold of code covered purchases in the EC member states while continuing not to take VAT into account.

In short, in many areas the United States in particular felt that there was room for 'further' liberalization – no matter if it was really willing to offer corresponding concessions affecting the interests of American industries – but within the framework set by the NTB codes it was difficult to go beyond the terms agreed at the end of the Tokyo Round negotiations, which nevertheless were a step in that direction.

As regards agriculture, when in the early 1980s US exports plunged and EC competition became increasingly dangerous, the United States called for a reshaping of the rules but it had to wait for over ten years till the end of the Uruguay Round wherein agriculture turned out to be the stumbling block in the negotiations.

There were no reported clashes in the enforcement of the Antidumping code or calls for amendments to the 1979 agreement which either codified the practices of the two main parties in its negotiations or caused no serious obstacle to their maintenance, although, as already noted, such practices might be directed to protectionist ends. Indeed, exploitability for protectionist goals helps explain why antidumping proceedings became widely adopted not only in other industrial countries like Canada and Australia but also in some fast growing developing countries. As illustrated by the reports of the Committee on Anti-Dumping Practices, in 1980 the United States was by far the main user of antidumping measures, with 37 proceedings initiated between July 1979 and June 1980, and 19 provisional measures and 9 definitive duties applied in the same period.[55] The US was followed closely by Canada and the EC. Between July 1982 and June 1984 the US started 65 proceedings and applied 61 provisional measures and 42 definitive duties. The EC initiated 59 proceedings and applied 28 provisional measures and 18 definitive duties. However, both were outshone by Australia which, in spite of its much smaller economy, boasted 141 new proceedings, 55 provisional measures and 71 definitive duties.[56]

6

The end of the 1970s and the Dawn of a New Decade: The Second Oil Shock and the Aftermath of the Tokyo Round Negotiations

The second oil shock and its impact on the US and EC economies

Impact of the second oil shock on the OECD countries

The 1979–80 biennium ushered in a period of turmoil in the industrial economies characterized by rising inflation, worsening of trade and current account balances, although with the relevant exception of the United States, a generalized, but not uniform, slowdown and a renewed increase in unemployment. As had been the case five years earlier, the main culprit was seen to be the hike in the oil price. On 31 December 1978 the oil price was $12.70 per barrel. By 1 July 1980 it was around $30 and was approaching $35 at the close of the year. The volatility of the political situation in the Middle East led to widespread fears of an upcoming oil shortage for the Western world and this situation led to pressure on the market price for oil, which in turn allowed the OPEC countries to set higher prices. What was originally believed to be a looming supply crisis soon turned out to be a price crisis. No effective response to stop the rise came from the consuming countries. The IEA had been established in 1974 to deal with oil shortages but it was not equipped to coordinate the reaction to soaring prices.

As in the previous oil crisis, the new price rise had a double impact on the oil importing countries: direct and indirect inflationary consequences, and a curtailment of domestic demand as the so-called 'OPEC tax' reduced consumer spending power, which was not offset by a prompt increase in the oil exporting countries' demand for imported products. The gap between the transfer of resources to the OPEC countries and their capacity to absorb imports, in turn, caused strains on the ability of the international monetary system to recycle an increasingly huge volume of funds. However, the cyclical swings during the second oil crisis were less severe than those accompanying the first one. Whereas in the years preceding the first shock there had been a synchronized boom in the major industrial countries, in the late 1970s the upswing was weaker and less heavily synchronized. Likewise, the impact of the oil shock was not uniform and, in spite of the widespread adoption of restrictive monetary policies, in most industrialized countries there were offsetting factors which helped delay, with different lags, the constraints imposed on domestic demand.

The economic policy of the major industrial countries reflected these new, or more exactly, renewed challenges. The Tokyo and Venice G7 Declarations, in June 1979 and June 1980 respectively, focused on two priorities: inflation, whose reduction was regarded as the immediate top priority, replaced unemployment as the main target for the United States and the major EC member states, along with Japan; the need to counter the threat of narrower room for manoeuvre in running the economy caused by rising oil prices, aggravated by the possibility of supply shortages.

The first goal was pursued through a prudent fiscal policy and above all through a restrictive stance in monetary policy in the main industrial countries which, following a method implemented by the Bundesbank in 1973, set targets for the growth of monetary aggregates. The downward trend of such growth targets during the biennium was accompanied by repeated increases in official discount rates and in several industrialized countries by direct control of certain monetary aggregates.

As regards the second priority, the industrial countries adopted two sets of measures, starting with the reduction of oil consumption. Already in June 1979, at the Tokyo Summit, the EC declared its commitment to restrict 1979 oil consumption to 500 million tons and to maintain oil imports between 1980–5 at an annual level not higher than in 1978. As a goal for 1985, the United States adopted import levels not exceeding either the level of 1977 or of the 1979 target of 8.5 million barrels per day. The achievement of this policy objective relied on two instruments. First, curbing energy consumption in the production process; secondly, the shift to alternative sources of energy like coal and nuclear power. In the second instance, the industrial countries looked at sources other than the OPEC producers for their oil import needs. The consumption of the OECD members, measured in millions of oil barrels per day, fell from 40.5 million in 1979 to 35.4 million (–12%) in 1981 and stabilized at around 34 million in the next four years. Net exports from OPEC countries declined from 28.2 million in 1979 to 20.9 million (–26%) in 1981 and 14.1 million (–50%) in 1985.[1]

The United States

In the United States the long-awaited recession did not occur in 1979 but, in the words of Campagna, 'some of the old problems continued, and some new ones were added'.[2] The oil drag was estimated to reduce consumer spending power by about 3 per cent of after-tax income in 1979, wearing away 2 per cent of GNP by the end of 1980. Relative to the size of the US economy, the new oil price increase was larger than the 1973–4 rise. During the first shock the world price of oil tripled from about \$4 to about \$12 per barrel, adding about \$18 billion to the US bill for imported oil, roughly 1.4 per cent of the gross national product. In percentage terms the 1979–80 hike was definitely more modest (about 170 per cent), but in absolute terms it meant a rise of over \$20 per barrel, adding about \$50 billion to the oil cost. Its impact on GDP was, however, offset in the short-run by a drop in the personal saving rate which resulted in an increase in private spending. In 1979 unemployment remained below the average of the decade, even though it was above the average of the 1960s, but inflation accelerated (Tables 21–4). Consumer prices soared by 3.6 points above the already high 1978 rate and wholesale prices for manufactured goods rose by 5 points. As noted by the Economic Report of the President for 1980, the 1979–80 oil price shock worsened a ratchet-like inflationary process that had characterized the American economy since the mid-1960s, accelerating from the beginning of the following decade. In this process the inflation rate only partially decreased when the cause of the previous jump in price stabilized. In particular, after the hike of the first half of the 1970s, in spite of the subsequent recession, inflationary expectations remained high and were built into demand for higher wages by employees and price setting by firms. Monetary and fiscal restraint could, therefore, curb national income growth and with it employment, without significantly curtailing inflation.

To fight inflation the Carter administration adopted a more restrained fiscal policy, while the FED embraced a restrictive monetary policy directed at curbing the growth of the monetary aggregates. The Federal Reserve fixed low target ranges for M1 and M2 growth in 1979 allowing the federal funds rate to increase. However, the management of interest rate did not hit the target, and monetary aggregates exceeded their desired growth range. In October 1979 the FED, led by the new chairman Paul Volcker, announced a policy shift by direct control of bank reserves. Under the new approach, open market operations had to supply the volume of bank reserves consistently with the desired rate of monetary growth.[3] As the growth of monetary aggregates went on surging despite the new policy announcement, in March 1980 the FED imposed comprehensive credit controls, but in June adopted a more relaxed policy. The uncertainty caused by the persistence of inflation and the expectation of a restrictive stance from the monetary authorities resulted in skyrocketing interest rates which became positive in real terms too.

It was predicted that such measures would cause a recession with real GNP falling by 1 per cent. Actually, for the whole year GNP declined by only 0.3 per cent (Table 1) but in a way that did not favour the incumbent president in the run-up to the November elections. After rising in the first quarter, real GNP plummeted by almost 10 per cent, the sharpest decline in the post war period, although it quickly recovered in the second half of the year. Unemployment jumped to 7.1 per cent (Table 21), while inflation, rather than declining, went on growing, as the CPI rose by 13.5 per cent and the WPI by 14 per cent (Tables 22–3). The decline in consumption, under the strain of rising inflation in the wake of increasingly high oil prices, was accompanied by a contraction in housing and business investments. Although the current account balance markedly improved, the merchandise trade deficit remained high (Table 2). The private business sector's productivity growth rate, already negative in 1978, worsened in the two following years. In the presidential campaign Carter tried to keep his distance from the Federal Reserve's stance, stressing its independence from the executive under American law. The president even declared that 'the strictly monetary approach to the Fed's decision on the discount rate and other banking policies is ill-advised', adding that 'the Federal Reserve Bank Board ought to look at other factors and balance them with the supply of money'.[4] The voters did not pay much attention to his remarks.

The EC

The direct burden imposed on the Community's trade balance by the oil rise in 1979–80 was almost $70 billion compared with some $31 billion in 1974. Expressed as a percentage of the import bill in the years preceding the oil shocks, if exchange rate changes are ignored, the costs to the trade balance were quite similar: 13.4 per cent and 13 per cent respectively.[5] As a percentage of GDP they amounted to 3.4 per cent in the 1979–80 price rise and 2.9 per cent in the previous rise. However, during the second oil shock the dollar price rise was eased by the appreciation of the ECU, i.e. the basket of the EC member states' currencies, whereas during the first oil crisis the dollar price rise was amplified by the 1974 depreciation of the ECU vis-à-vis the dollar after the hike of the previous year. As a percentage of GDP the oil-price rises in ECU were respectively 3 per cent for the second oil shock and 3.1 per cent for the first.[6] Obviously, the exchange rate factor varied with reference to the various currencies included in the basket: for instance in 1979 and much of 1980 the Deutschmark went on appreciating vis-à-vis the dollar, while the Italian lira continued its downward trend (Figure 1).

However, the oil drag did not bring about a slowdown in the Community during 1979 and the first months of 1980. In partial contrast to the United States, the economic activity that had shown gradual improvements in 1978 strengthened in 1979 also benefiting from the stimulus package decided by the Bremen European Council in July 1978, which had assigned the 'locomotive' role to the Federal Republic. In 1979, GDP for the whole of the Community rose by 3.3 per cent and industrial production grew by 4.5 per cent (Tables 10 and 20). Consumer spending grew by the same rate as the GDP, while gross fixed capital formation increased by 3.8 per cent, the highest rate since the early 1970s. On the other hand, there was no reduction in the unemployment rate relative to 1978 and, as was to be expected, inflation remained high. The second quarter of 1980 marked the beginning of a severe slowdown. In the Community the GDP growth rate declined to 1.4 per cent reflecting the levelling off of domestic demand. Consumption slackened under the pressure of accelerating inflation triggered by the rising oil bill. Capital formation declined in the second half of the year in the face of high interest rates and the tightening of financial conditions. Real interest rates became positive in most EC member states and membership of the European Monetary System (EMS) prevented the countries participating in the new scheme from viewing depreciation of their currencies as an easy way to boost their exports.

The new EC currency system, which was established by the Brussels European Council on 5 December 1978, and entered into force on 13 March 1979, was mainly the result of a Franco–German initiative directed at tackling the drawbacks of the floating exchange for a highly integrated area like the EC. The new system, which replaced the unsuccessful Snake, was also based on a parity grid and compliance with bilateral margins of fluctuation (set at +2.25% and –2.25%, with the exception of the Italian lira which was allowed a wider 6% margin). However, the new regime provided for correctives aimed at guaranteeing greater flexibility, at more rapid forms of action when strains emerged and at avoiding that the burden of readjustment prevalently fell on the weaker currency, that is, on the currency at the bottom of the fluctuation range. The base of the EMS was the European Currency Unit (ECU), a basket of the currencies participating in the system, each of which was assigned a different weight. Each EC currency had an ECU related central rate – with the exception of the pound, excluded at the time from the exchange rate mechanism – which was used to establish the parity grill. When the margins of fluctuations were reached unlimited intervention on the exchanges became compulsory, usually in the currencies of the participating countries. However, the SME also adopted a preventive intervention mechanism, the 'divergence indicator', which established a requirement to take action by the authorities responsible for the currency whose rate exceeded certain limits fixed in terms of ECU, limits which, being narrower than those demarcating the bilateral margin, would be reached before it. These limits were particularly narrow for the Deutschmark while they were much larger for the weak currencies, the Italian lira in particular. The SME also provided for a substantial increase in the volume and the duration of credits to support the weakest currencies. These support mechanisms and the fact that greater responsibility for acting was cast on the authorities managing the stronger currencies could not free any SME member from bearing in mind that most of their partners wanted to keep a tight rein on the growth of monetary aggregates and were not willing to import inflation.

The trend was far from being uniform within the EC. Among the main member countries a distinction can be drawn between France and Germany, whose trend broadly coincided with the EC's average, and peripheral countries like the UK and especially Italy whose performance diverged.

In 1979, West Germany's GDP grew at a 4.3 per cent rate, the best result after the 1976 recovery, due mainly to a substantial increase in fixed investments and to the steady growth of export (Table 10). Imports, however, moved ahead more rapidly than exports and for the first time in the 1970s the current account balance was in the red. In 1980 the GDP growth rate fell to 2 per cent, the industrial production shrank and the value of imports almost caught up with that of exports. The current account deficit reached $17.5 billion. The 5.3 per cent consumer price growth rate was above the average of the years prior to the first oil shock, although it remained well below the average of the other EC members in 1980 (Table 22). In short, the continuous high value of the Deutschmark, in particular relative to the greenback, prevented the oil hike from stocking domestic inflation, but eroded the competitiveness of German industry.[7] Nevertheless, at the close of the year, under the impact of the deterioration of the current account balance, the German currency started to decline vis-à-vis the dollar.

In spite of the oil drag the French gross domestic product went on growing in 1979, although at a moderate 3 per cent rate (Table 10). The expectation of an accelerating inflation engendered speculative demand both in stocks and investments, while private consumption did not contract significantly because French consumers reacted by curbing their saving rate.[8] In 1980 the GDP growth rate fell to 1.3 per cent and industrial production declined. The inflation caused by the oil bill started to affect consumer spending power, while French firms' profit margin underwent the impact of an acceleration of salary expenditures, higher prices of intermediary products, oil in particular, and this impact could not be fully transferred to final consumers because of price competition from foreign products.

The Italian economy presented some peculiar characteristics compared to most of the major members of the Community. The rate of unemployment was higher than the EC average, reaching 7.5 per cent and 8 per cent in 1979 and 1980 respectively as the labour force grew faster than employment due to demographic reasons and a higher female participation rate (Table 21). The fiscal deficit, which since the late 1960s had been constantly higher than the EC average, amounted to 9.4 per cent of GDP in 1979 and 8.4 per cent of GDP in 1980 (Table 19). The inflation rate was especially high (Tables 22 and 23). The CPI, after slightly subsiding from its 19.2 peak in 1974, started to accelerate again during the second oil crisis reaching 21.2 per cent in 1980. Likewise, the wholesale price growth rate for industrial goods soared from 8.1 per cent in 1978 to 15.5 per cent in 1979 and 20 per cent in 1980. Faced with the alternatives of fighting inflation and defending the currency value in the exchange market or preventing the deterioration of the economy, since 1975 the monetary authorities had been playing the card of successive heavy depreciations of the lira.[9] Although entry into the EMS in 1979 forced Italy to adopt a rather less free management of the currency, the depreciation of the lira helped to preserve the competitiveness of Italian products in spite of high inflation and soaring unit labour costs on a national currency basis (Figure 3). The GDP growth rate from a 1.9 per cent low in 1977 jumped to 4.9 per cent in 1979 and 4 per cent in 1980, well above the EC average (Table 10). Also the rate of industrial production was much higher than the EC average in the period and the most dynamic factor was exports, which, in turn, helped bolster consumer spending and stimulate a recovery in investments. However, because of the deterioration of the terms of trade, imports grew faster than exports and increased the trade deficit in 1979 by over 1,100 per cent relative to the previous year (Tables 11 and 12) . The gap went on growing in 1980 as imports soared under the continuous pressure of the oil price rise while exports slackened because of the weaker competitiveness of Italian products caused by the inflation differential and the slowdown in foreign demand brought about by the worsening of the international economic environment. The trade deficit jumped to ECU 15.7 billion, with a 278 per cent increase over 1979.

At least at first sight, during the second oil crisis the United Kingdom shared most of the Italian problems without enjoying the main advantage of the southern EC member, nominally its fast income growth. In the years following the first oil crisis, the GDP growth rate of the United Kingdom was only once, in 1978, not below the EC average (Table 10). However, unemployment and fiscal deficit remained high and the trade gap showed no sign of shrinking (Tables 11, 12 and 21). The year 1979 witnessed an acceleration of inflation, as the CPI jumped to 13.4 under the combined pressure of a wage explosion consequent on the refusal of the Trades Union Congress (TUC) to further endorse the social contract at the centre of the Labour Government income policy, the increase in Value Added Tax decided by the incoming Conservative government and the impact of the oil bill (Table 22). The latter, however, was not as strong as in most other EC members, as North Sea oil came on stream in 1976 and by 1980 the direct contribution of domestic oil and gas to GDP reached 4.4 per cent. The Thatcher Government, which came into office in May 1979, made fighting inflation its main priority, duly stressing its commitment to the issue, whereas the previous administration had shown a commitment to both tackling unemployment and price stability.[10] And in the words of the Iron Lady, 'inflation was a monetary phenomenon which it would require monetary discipline to curb'.[11] In keeping with its declared monetarist approach, the new Conservative Government's strategy was to reduce the growth of monetary supply. Already in 1979, the first moves were taken to curb the demand for bank credit by raising interest rates. To lend more credibility to its monetarist policy, in 1980 the Thatcher administration introduced a medium-term financial strategy, establishing targets for periods of up to four years for both monetary growth and Public Sector Borrowing Requirement, the latter no longer seen as an instrument of demand control but as a source of monetary base and hence as an inflationary factor. In the short-run the new policy was not very successful as inflation continued to rise, reaching 18 per cent in 1980. On the other hand, the squeeze resulted in a marked GDP slowdown in 1979 which turned into a slump the following year, pushing the unemployment rate up. In contrast to Italy, the deficit of Britain's trade balance did not result in a steady depreciation of the pound. After the downfall of 1976, the UK currency went on rising from the following year, also in real terms.[12] Various factors explain this trend. If the trade balance was constantly in deficit, the current account, including the invisible balance, turned positive in 1978, and after a negative figure in 1979 yielded a surplus a year later. The sharp rise of interest rates in the first years of the Thatcher government attracted capitals from abroad because of the rate differential and also because the rise indicated the willingness of the new administration to curb inflation and consequently to avoid the weakening of the currency in the exchange rate market. After the widening of the gap in 1979 the trade deficit shrank in 1980 as demand for imports was curtailed by the recession; and North Sea oil replaced imports from the OPEC and other developing countries. On the other hand, the strength of the pound made it difficult to cushion the rising unit labour cost of manufactured products. By 1980 the differential between the unit cost increase measured on a dollar basis and on the national currency basis, allowed by the slide of the pound in 1976, petered out (Figure 3).

The trade balance

The foregoing shows that the years 1979–80 saw a generalized slowdown in most of the OECD countries that turned into a slump in the United States and in the UK. Among the other EC member states only Denmark had a negative growth rate in 1980. The slackening of the economy was accompanied by a price hike. In other words, the term 'stagflation' fits this period even more than the previous triennium. And there is no doubt that this unstable economic environment could foster protectionist policies, even though, in a world keen to abide by economic precepts, fighting inflation, an unreservedly shared priority, might encourage governments not to hinder the entry of cheap foreign products. This, however, does not offer proof that protectionism made actual progress, nor does it shed any light on the factors, if any, that stimulated protectionist measures, or on the form they took and on the sectors of the economy which were affected by such measures. To address these issues a first task should be to identify the weak industries in the US and the EC domestic economies and the measures eventually taken to boost them. It should be remembered, on the other hand, that if one gives, as did the Americans in particular, a wider meaning to the term 'protectionism', those areas whose competitiveness is enhanced by subsidization or other forms of support from public authorities might be regarded as protected sectors. Secondly, since this research focuses special attention on the relationship between the great transatlantic partners, the inquiry should consider the weight of the principal products in the trade balance between the US and the EC and between these two areas and the rest of the world.

The surplus sectors in the US merchandise trade balance were agriculture, high technology manufacture and crude materials and fuels except crude oil. The deficit sectors, apart from oil, which was the main factor of deficit, were low-technology manufacture, consumer goods and automotive products. As regards the EC, apart from raw materials and fuels, the sectors undergoing the main difficulties were chemicals and textiles and above all iron and steel products and the shipbuilding industry.

The United States managed to reduce its merchandise trade deficit from a $34 billion peak in 1978 to a more modest $27.6 billion the following year (–19%) and to $25.5 billion in 1980 (–25%). The US current account was almost in balance in 1979 after two years of large deficits, above all as a result of the increase in investment income from abroad, and it turned into a small surplus in 1980. The reduction of the deficit (Table 2) reflected the slowdown in import growth due to the fall of the GDP growth rate and with it of the domestic demand of which imports represented a pArticle Obviously the value of imports would have reduced further in the absence of the oil bill and actually in 1980 imports slightly declined in real terms (Table 1). The acceleration of the export growth was largely the result of the depreciation of the dollar from 1977 (Figure 2). However, the trade balance and the performance of the US currency showed a different trend according to its trading partners across the Atlantic and the Pacific.

The total trade deficit of the nine EC member states towards the United States swelled in 1979 and 1980 (Tables 4, 13 and 14). EC exports grew much more slowly than imports. Even Germany's positive gap shrank (or even turned into a deficit in 1980 according to the ECU data). The US surplus in agriculture grew from $1.4 billion in 1971 to $6.8 billion in 1980 (388%), but imports from the EC went on growing, increasing from a modest $423 million to $2 billion (391%); for manufactures the US deficit of $1.5 billion in 1971 turned into a surplus of $5.7 billion nine years later (485%).[13] In 1980, the main US export products were office machinery and computers, electrical machinery apparatus and chemicals and soybeans, while imports from the EC were concentrated in passenger cars, special purpose machinery, iron, steel and other ferrous metals, chemicals and, quite surprisingly, crude petroleum.[14] This trend reflects the depreciation of the dollar vis-à-vis the currency of its main EC partners except Italy, in particular after 1976 (Figure 1), and with it the increased competitiveness of the US. Indeed, as shown by Figure 3, under the pressure of inflation, incorporated in turn in the trade unions' demand for higher wages, which were not offset by sufficient productivity increase, the unit labour cost, grew in most

EC member states at a rate not lower than in the United States. However, the unit labour cost in the Community measured on a US dollar basis grew much faster than the equivalent cost in the United States, obviously with the exception of Italy and, to a lesser extent, the UK.

Both trade areas were suffering from the successful competition of Japan and a number of NICs. The US positive balance with the EC countries was dwarfed by the deficit with the OPEC and other oil exporting countries, which from $16.3 billion in 1978 soared to $31.9 billion two years later, and with Japan. The trade deficit with Japan, which in 1975 amounted to $1.9 billion, jumped to $11.6 billion three years later, averaging between $8.7 billion and $10 billion in the next two years (Table 4). The unit labour cost in yen grew at a higher rate than in the United States but starting from a much lower basis, while the yen appreciated vis-à-vis the greenback. Yet, the appreciation of the yen was definitely more limited than that of the Deutschmark in spite of the wider trade gap with the US. Besides, the upwards trend turned into a slight decline from 1979 under the strain of the second oil shock (Figures 1 and 3). Thus, the competitiveness of Japanese products in terms of costs was not reversed in the years under review.

In 1980, the principal US products out of a total $20.8 billion exports to Japan consisted of unmilled corn, logs and lumber, bituminous coal, soybeans, metal ores and metal scrap – worryingly reminiscent to those of a developing country rich in natural resources – while out of a $30.7 billion bill the main imports from Japan included passenger cars totalling $8.4 billion, telecommunications, sound recording and reproducing apparatus totalling $3.1 billion, iron and steel mill products totalling $2.8 billion and office machinery and automatic data processing machines totalling $1.2 billion.[15] It must be noted that Japanese exports of passenger cars and iron and steel products to the United States exceeded by 102 per cent and 67 per cent respectively those originating in the Community. The EC deficit on bilateral trade with Japan rose from $1.3 billion in 1973 to $7.1 billion in 1979, reaching about $10 billion in 1980.[16] Japan's exports concentrated on products such as cars, television sets and electronic goods and machine tools, while the Community failed to secure offsetting outlets for its manufactures.

The implementation of the Tokyo Round codes

Before analysing the crises that hit several sectors of the economy in the US and in the EC and the means adopted to cope with them, it is appropriate to examine the way in which both areas acceded to the codes signed at the end of the Tokyo Round and applied them to their domestic legislation.

The EC approved the codes in November 1979 and subsequently conformed the legislation of the Community and its member states to the international rules, in most cases reproducing their wording. Things were more complex in the case of the United States whose Congress was called by the 1974 Trade Act at the same time to approve, without passing any amendment, the multilateral NTB agreements signed in Geneva and to implement them by amending and, if necessary, establishing the relevant US statutes.

As noted in the previous chapter, before entering into the Geneva agreements, the US executive had to strike a deal with the powerful textiles and steel lobbies. In particular, the Carter administration gave assurances that the steel industry's call for a minimal injury test and the tightening of trade laws would be fully taken into account. The main expert on the Tokyo Round negotiations, Gilbert Winham, argued that in passing the Trade Act of 1974 'Congress removed itself from a major role in writing legislation or representing constituencies in connection with the MTN'.[17] This may be true as regards the course of the negotiation, but it does not imply that Congress was ready or willing to cut itself off from the dialogue between lobbies and administration in the final stages of the round. The dialogue was trilateral as Congress was empowered to approve or to reject the agreements worked out in Geneva and above all to preside over the consequent adaptation of domestic law. As in 1979, the traditional supporters of trade liberalization, such as electronics, had become increasingly concerned with foreign competition, their sway was not strong enough to offset the call from other sectors of the economy for rules against 'unfair' foreign competition that were more effective and less conditional on the executive's willingness to apply them, and Congress was bound to acknowledge the growing demand for protection. Thus, if Congress was certainly not prepared to scupper the international deals in which it had had a role, it was far from willing to allow such agreements to entail the weakening of the domestic system of defence against foreign competition it had inherited or had itself built over the last few years. On the contrary, the Trade Agreements Act of 1979 turned out to be an opportunity to render the domestic rules stricter and exploitable for protectionist ends.[18]

Thus, the Act approved the Tokyo Round codes, stressing, however, that no provision of any trade agreement would take precedence over domestic law in the event of a conflict. The Act also provided that the NTB agreements would not come into force in the US until each major industrial country also completed its domestic implementation procedure. The president, however, could accept a particular agreement if only one industrial country had not accepted it and acceptance by that country was not considered essential. As stated in the Senate Report, the intent of the provision was 'to assure that the United States would not commit itself to new international rules that could only be effective and beneficial to the United States if accepted by all major Western industrial countries'.[19]

As regards measures directed to counter so-called unfair trade practices, i.e. subsidies and dumping, the Act further shortened the investigation period and imposed more severe obligations on importers of subsidized or dumped products. In antidumping proceedings the 1979 Act allowed the Customs service six months to assess the duty and during the assessment period importers had to pay estimated antidumping duties. In countervailing procedures importers were forced to deposit bonds or cash in less than three months if a preliminary investigation should find that imports were subsidized.

As regards countervailing measures in particular, the Trade Agreements Act tightened the reins relative to the preceding statutes in two ways. First, by codifying a practice dating back to the Michelin case, the Act made it clear that countervailable subsidies included not only export subsidies, prohibited by the MTN code, but also a number of domestic subsidies, which, unsurprisingly, coincided with the list of domestic subsidies allegedly causing serious prejudice to other trading partners proposed by the American negotiators during the Tokyo Round but not accepted by the other parties. Secondly, it was a long established rule that US countervailing duties should be applied to so-called 'net subsidies' and a somewhat open-ended set of factors could be considered in arriving at their value. 'Gross subsidy' was the value of the subsidy provided, while 'net subsidy' was assessed by deducting from the gross subsidy one or more offsetting costs. The 1979 Act limited the allowed deductions to three: payments made to qualify for the subsidy; losses in the value of the subsidy resulting from its late receipt; and charges levied on the export of the merchandise specifically intended to offset the subsidy received. As the Senate Report on the Trade Agreements Act of 1979 pointed out, the reform wanted 'to place clear limits on offsets from a gross subsidy'.[20] Therefore, it was no longer recognized that subsidies are often granted to offset certain negative effects that government measures can have on an industry, such as interference in the location of new plants, closure of old installations in the context of industrial sector restructuring, or policies to buoy up employment and prevent lay-offs. All these policies were widely followed within the EC. The combination of the statutory extension of countervailing duties to domestic subsidies and the marked curtailment of allowed reductions in assessing net subsidies helps explain why the American steel firms, after prevalently relying on antidumping duties until the beginning of the 1980s, in 1982 shifted the emphasis of their attacks to the countervailing duty provisions of the Trade Agreements Act of 1979 so as to coerce their European counterparts into a comprehensive pact to regulate production and exports.[21]

The Trade Agreements Act, in keeping with the Tokyo Round codes, made the imposition of both antidumping and countervailing duties conditional on proof of material injury or threat of it to an industry in the US or material retardation to the establishment of such an industry. Before the Trade Agreements Act of 1979, the US law provided for an injury test in antidumping cases and the American authorities claimed that their assessment of injury, based on the occurrence of more than 'de minimis' injury, was consistent with GATT Article VI and with the Kennedy Round code on subsidy, both of which required the injury to be 'material'. No injury test was provided for countervailing measures except in the case of duty-free imports. The new provision, however, was much less innovative than could appear at first sight. In the first place, the material injury requirement applied only to countries that had enacted the two Tokyo Round codes and to countries that had assumed substantially equivalent obligations. Even more important was the fact that both the statute and the executive's Statement of Administrative Action defined 'material injury' as 'injury which is not inconsequential, immaterial or unimportant'. The term 'material' is commonly considered equivalent to important, substantial and significant. Certainly, the definition of 'material injury' adopted by the US lawmakers might be in line with the ordinary meaning of the term, but it could also mean something less and it was for the US administrative authorities and subsequently for the US trade courts to decide where to draw the line.

Thus, on the one hand, the Trade Agreements Act of 1979 marked the approval by the US of a multilateral regime aimed at better preventing trade distortion and improving the environment for solving potential dispute. On the other hand, with regard to domestic rules directed at countering imports of allegedly dumped or subsidized products, the Act meant not only the confirmation of practices that could carry protectionist effects, like the imposition of antidumping duties even though the export price was not lower than the price of like products in the exporting countries, but made new legal instruments exploitable for protectionist ends available to import competing firms. Many importers expressed their misgivings on the stricter antidumping and countervailing regimes. The representative of the Automobile Importers of America, John Rehm, was quoted as saying that he deplored 'the fact that as the product of an international effort to liberalize trade, we now see these two statutes turned into protectionist measure'.[22] As the Act did not have to implement any Safeguard code, given the failure to reach an agreement on this subject at the close of the Uruguay Round, no amendment was made to the previous US law. It was, therefore, natural that American firms threatened by foreign competition, irrespective of whether it was fair or unfair, looked at antidumping and countervailing proceedings as the only effective method to keep imports at bay. Indeed, as noted by Finger, Halland and Nelson, though the 'legal objective' of antidumping and countervailing duties was distinct from that of safeguards, their 'economic objective', that is, protection from foreign competition through import restrictions, was the same.[23]

In other sectors too the Trade Agreements Act of 1979 did not involve the opening of the American market that the ratification of the Tokyo Round codes could have allowed. For instance, the implementation of the Customs Valuation code meant the repeal of the ASP system, but converted ASP rates of duty into tariffs estimated to afford the same level of protection provided under the abrogated valuation method. Contrary to the hopes of the EC, the implementation of the Government Procurement code was far from bringing about a significant curtailment of the preference given to American firms by existing federal and state laws. The president was given power to waive certain Buy American Act restrictions, but the Act was not repealed. According to the Senate Report, the procurements subject to presidential waiver accounted for about 15 per cent of federal government procurement. Apart from the $190,000 threshold agreed in the Uruguay Round, several US agencies, among which the Departments of Transportation and Energy, were excluded. So too were State and local government purchases, existing preferences for small and minority businesses, strategic goods, and purchases for farm support and foodstuffs for the indigent.

At the same time the Carter administration carried out a reorganization of the trade programmes. The trade reorganization plan enhanced the role of the trade negotiator creating a permanent Office of the US Trade Representative (USTR). The assessment of both the existence and amount of dumping and subsidization was withdrawn from the Department of Treasury, considered not responsive enough to the interests of domestic industries, and transferred to he Department of Commerce.

Sectors calling for financial aid and protection from foreign competition

The Chrysler bail out and the crisis of the US automotive industry

The difficulties experienced by the US automobile industry in the period under review were certainly aggravated by the second oil shock which highlighted the industry's failure to adapt production to growing demand for fuel-efficient cars, but were also the result of other long-standing factors. The first trade deficit dated back to 1968, becoming, however, 13 times as high ten years later and over 14 times in 1980 (Table 3). The (higher) price assurances given by foreign manufacturers from Europe, Canada and Japan, to obtain the discontinuance of a mega antidumping investigation opened in 1976, only entailed a weak and short respite.

The first firm to run into trouble was Chrysler, the smallest of the 'Big Three' US automakers, after Ford and General Motors. The company closed 1978 with a net loss of $204.6 million and its deficit grew by $53.8 million in just the first quarter of 1979, which made the corporation's bankruptcy and massive redundancies for its 130,000 workers in the US alone a likelihood, if not a certainty. Realizing that the company would go out of business if it did not receive a significant amount of money to continue and enhance its activities, Chrysler's president and CEO, Lee Iacocca, called for public aid. Iacocca received support from the powerful automobile workers union, UAW, which lobbied for the approval of a financial package in Congress and convinced the company's employees to accept financial sacrifices in order to save their jobs.[24] After a difficult process, Congress, with the backing of the executive, gave its approval to a $3.5 billion aid package. Public aid did not come directly as a loan but as a $1.5 billion loan guarantee, conditional on the company's coming up with a matching $2 billion in help from creditors, dealers and workers. The latter had to give up over $580 million in pay rises over the next three years. Obviously the loan guarantee, authorized by a law signed by Carter the following January, was the key for the company to obtain the credits necessary for its survival. In his memoirs Lee Iacocca expressed the unreserved view that Chrysler was lucky to have 'appealed to a Democratic administration that put people ahead of ideology' and that it was quite likely that a Republican administration would not have endorsed the rescue package for ideological reasons.[25] Indeed, the way Reagan coped with the widespread crisis in the US automotive industry partially differed from his predecessor's. Yet, the rescue of one of the 'Big Three' deserves some critical remarks in light of the issue of the strengthening of protectionist tendencies in both the US and the EC. Apparently the rescue package was just a domestic measure without impact on international trade and there were no government outlays. However, according to the proposal tabled by the US negotiators during the Tokyo Round, the provision of loan guarantees on terms inconsistent with commercial considerations would be an index of serious prejudice to the interests of other trading partners caused by domestic subsidization, and there is no doubt that very few, if any, American or foreign financial institutions would have been willing to provide credit to the ailing company without the security of governmental money in case of default. And it is easy to guess that the fact that one of the 'Big Three' went on producing meant that fewer Japanese or European cars could enter into the US market while Chrysler could go on competing in the world market. It is then arguable that, under the circumstances, it was a piece of luck for the US itself that its call for more stringent rules on domestic subsidies was not reproduced in the final text of the Tokyo Round code on subsidies and countervailing duties. Besides, as noted above, according to the US statute loan guarantees inconsistent with commercial considerations were sanctioned with countervailing measures. This could give support to the accusation of a double standard: practices subject to penalties by the US administrative authority, if adopted by foreign states, were no longer condemnable but became instead a sensible intervention to redress the economy if the decision was taken by US lawmakers and implemented by the US government.

However, the Chrysler bail-out did not put an end to the sector crisis, rather it was its herald. Things started to get worse for the whole industry in 1980 when a steadily rising oil price accelerated consumer demand for a switch to smaller cars. Production plummeted to a 19-year low while unemployment in the car industry and in its suppliers surged to 40 per cent of a work force of 2.5 million persons. The domestic production downturn was mirrored by a surge in imports, the Japanese share of which went on growing.[26] Passenger car imports, excluding Canada, rose from 2,192 thousands of units in 1978 to 2,522 in 1980 (+15%) and Japanese cars, which in 1973 accounted for 40 per cent of total imports, amounted to 71 per cent of imports five years later, reaching 79 per cent in 1980. Exports declined from 164 thousands of units in 1978 to 105 thousand in 1980.

The plight of the US industry and the rise in imports resulted in the introduction of several bills in Congress to raise trade barriers on automobiles. However, the response of the administration was cautious and could not be classified as protectionist. In March 1980 an administration panel, composed of the USTR, the Council of Economic Advisers and the Departments of Commerce, Transportation and Energy, testified against new import barriers, arguing that the crisis was due to a cyclical depression in the market exacerbated by the slow response of the US industry to the change of demand to smaller and more fuel-efficient cars which was met by foreign, prevalently Japanese, models. However, the panel pointed out that the decline in overall demand far exceeded the number of purchases of imported cars. The administration also stressed that if the industry believed that imports were the cause of its worsening economic conditions, it should pursue the remedies provided by section 201 of the Trade Act of 1974, i.e. adoption of safeguard measures. However, when a petition for import relief was filed by the United Automobile Workers in June 1980 and by the Ford Motor Company in July, the US International Trade Commission determined that car imports had not increased in the medium-term to such an extent as to constitute a cause of serious injury to the domestic industry in the United States. The executive, therefore, preferred to rely on special assistance programmes for the domestic auto industry and advances to the Japanese government to achieve further liberalization of the trade in automotive parts. In July 1980, Carter announced a set of support initiatives including a special $50 million Community Assistance programme, a special Small Business Administration loan programme for auto dealers and measures to reduce the economic impact of safety, fuel economy and emission standards to the automobile industry.[27] In May 1980, in response to the US requests, the Japanese government announced the elimination of duties on most automobile parts to facilitate American manufacturers' access to the Japanese replacement market.[28] In short, Carter, rather than adopting tariff and quota restrictions to solve the problems of the ailing motorcar industry, opted for domestic aid, quite akin to subsidization, and efforts to reduce the obstacles to American exports. Reagan did not overturn his predecessor's approach but somewhat changed its emphasis, modifying adjustment assistance procedures and lifting some antitrust provisions to allow for consolidation of American firms. Also the Republican administration opposed proposals in Congress to introduce quotas on car imports. In April 1981, however, a US delegation, headed by the new

United States Trade Representative (USTR), William Brock, flew to Tokyo for talks with Japanese officials. A month later the Japanese government announced a voluntary restraint of automobile exports to the United States. The good news was soon followed by an upsurge of over 130 per cent in Japanese direct investments in the United States during the following two years, in large part directed to the automobile sector.

Import penetration of Japanese automobiles, i.e. the share of domestic consumption covered by import products from Japan, also grew rapidly in many EC member states during the 1970s.[29] By 1977 Japanese exports accounted for about ten per cent of the British and German markets. However, the import penetration of Japanese cars in the French market remained constantly below the 5 per cent threshold and the Italian market remained almost impermeable. Only the Dutch and Belgian markets experienced level of imports penetration higher than the US market, even exceeding the 20 per cent threshold at the end of the decade.

The steel industry crisis across the Atlantic

The contraction in US motor vehicle production and the resulting fall in the demand for car input was one of the causes of the downturn that hit the steel industry on both sides of the Atlantic.

In the United States the decline in steel demand during 1980 was the outcome of the downturn in domestic automotive manufacture along with the impact of high interest rates on inventories and machinery and construction markets. Domestic shipments plunged to 83.9 million tons, which represented a 16.4 per cent decline from 1979 and the lowest level since 1975. From June to August more than 40 per cent of the domestic industry's production capability was rendered idle and by August the industry employed only 264,000 workers, the lowest number since 1933. As 1980 was a recession year, steel imports declined too (−11.5%), but since they fell less sharply than domestic shipments, import penetration grew magnifying the effects of an already depressed market.[30]

In March 1980, a volley of antidumping petitions was fired against EC steel exports. The US Steel Corporation filed 28 petitions covering five categories of steel products for a trade value totalling $147 million from seven EC member states. Soon after the United States suspended its TPM applied on steel imports, arguing that it had to devote its limited resources to the investigations provoked by the petition. As noted in Chapter 4, the TPM was a somewhat biased means of ascertaining likelihood of dumping based on the presupposition, subject to contrary proof, that sales in the US at prices below the steelmaking cost of the most efficient producer, Japan, were evidence of dumping.[31] However, European products usually stood up to this test. Apparently the Carter administration had tried to dissuade US Steel from filing the antidumping complaints, fearing that it would make cooperation with the Community more difficult, but antidumping investigations were based on quasi-judicial proceedings with no room for interference from the executive. The EC complained that the threat posed by the antidumping investigations was not consistent with the 1977 OECD consensus on steel, obstructing EC exports when domestic and world demand was plummeting. Only in September did the petitioner withdraw its complaint, but the Department of Commerce, reinstating the Trigger Price Mechanism, had to introduce a series of amendments which portended new troubles for the EC steel industry in the near future. The most significant amendments were the monitoring of surges of unfairly priced imports and the extension of the TPM to subsidization. Under the modified mechanism, whenever imports captured more than 15.2 per cent of the US domestic market and when the US steel industry was operating at less than 87 per cent of its productive capacity, the Department of Commerce was to initiate a 90 day review to determine whether the surge in imports appeared to be the result of dumping or subsidization practices. In the affirmative case the Department could either initiate an autonomous investigation or provide non-confidential material to interested parties in the US who might file complaints on their own behalf. Unfortunately for the EC steel industry, there was no denying that it benefited from a host of domestic subsidies.

In the EC the steel industry was affected from the early summer of 1980 by a sharp decline of demand from the internal and world markets, leading to an overall drop in production, in turn resulting in an unprecedented fall in the rate of capacity utilization which by the autumn fell to around 50 per cent. The fall in demand entailed a lowering of prices which by early autumn declined by 13 per cent compared to the beginning of the year. Input prices, in particular ores, fuel, coke, electricity, labour and overheads, went up on average by about 5 per cent. Consequently, most firms were no longer able to cover depreciation costs as well as a part of variable costs. The decline in profitability led most EC steel firms, struggling for their survival, to dodge the straightjacket of the voluntary discipline agreed in 1977 to stabilize the market. The so-called 'Bresciani firms', which had tried to exceed the market share assigned by the 1977 agreement because they were able to increase production efficiently, that is to say securing a good profit margin, were followed by a growing number of firms that, in order to avoid going out of business, were willing to sell at prices that did not cover their total production costs. In this difficult context the Commission submitted a request to the Council for the compulsory establishment of a system of production quotas on the basis of Article 58 of the ECSC Treaty.[32] The quotas were to be imposed for a maximum period until June 1981 on all undertakings with a steel production of over 1,000 tonnes per month, with the exception of companies producing only liquid steel for casting. The Commission's request was opposed by West Germany which had a particularly high number of efficient producers and, therefore, felt it had little to gain from a compulsory curtailment of production. It was only at the end of October 1980, after the exception was extended to certain special steels, which the whole EC Council of Ministers, including the Federal Republic, gave its assent to the measures proposed by the Community's executive. The measures, the first of this kind to be applied since the coming into force of the ECSC Treaty, concerned crude steel and four groups of rolled products. Thus from October 1980 steel production in the EC member countries was officially regulated from the top. The measures were meant to be repealed in the short-term but were subsequently extended several times as the EC steel industry found it difficult to recover from its plight. Obviously the new system was not supposed to be disrupted by inflows of cheaper foreign products. No import quotas could be applied as GATT Article XI prevented their imposition, but new base prices for iron and steel imports from non-Community countries were soon adopted in antidumping proceedings and the monitoring regime based on import licences was made stricter. New Orderly Marketing Agreements were negotiated for 1981 allowing lower import volumes.

Troubles and Frictions in other industrial sectors

The 1979–80 biennium did not turn the tide for the EC member states' ailing textile industry. The EC had traditionally posted a substantial surplus in textile and apparel trade with the US, but from 1977 the United States started to close the gap as its exports to the EC more than doubled while its imports started to level off. In 1979 the EC industry showed a deficit that widened to almost $1.4 billion the following year. The British industry was particularly affected by foreign competition and in February 1980 the EC instituted a safeguard action under GATT Article XIX on imports of certain synthetic yarns into the UK for the whole of 1980. The United States contested the selective nature of the safeguard action as the bulk of imports came from the US and threatened the retaliatory withdrawal of tariff concessions on imports of certain wool apparel items, mostly supplied by the UK. Finally, at the end of the year, the EC lifted the quotas on synthetic yarns while the US accepted as compensation the Community's offer of accelerated implementation of Tokyo Round tariff concessions on certain chemical products. As is usual in such cases, the Community also resorted to the antidumping lever imposing duties on imports of acrylic and polyester fibres from the United States.

In the petrochemical sector, where the US had a trade surplus with the EC, the latter had been complaining in the GATT since 1979 that growing US synthetic fibre exports to the Community were the result of indirect subsidization allowed by price control regulation on oil and natural gas combined with export controls on petroleum and naphtha, which gave American exporters a cost advantage over European producers. The United States rejoined that the rise in synthetic fibre exports was instead brought about by US competitive advantage combined with current EC structural problems in the sector and the depreciation of the dollar relative to EC currencies. In 1980 the two parties agreed to establish a bilateral government-industry group to explore on the one hand the impact of US energy controls on petrochemicals and on the other the general causes of the chemical industry difficulties in the EC. Did the controversy evidence a further covert form of domestic subsidization, to which the US claimed to be the enemy, or did it demonstrate an attempt by the EC to protect with legal sophistry a vulnerable sector battered by foreign competition? There is no documentary evidence in either direction since the dispute did not result in a GATT complaint or the adoption of countervailing measures. The conflict on petrochemicals subsided in 1982 when the recession dampened EC demand for these products and the appreciation of the dollar curbed the US cost advantage.

Increasing government support in the agricultural sector and troubles in the offing

The year 1980 was one of turmoil in world agriculture as it witnessed the strengthening of a long-standing interventionist trend and foreboded the looming problems that afflicted agriculture throughout the decade.

To protest against the December 1979 Soviet invasion of Afghanistan, on 4 January 1980 Jimmy Carter announced a grain embargo on exports to the Soviet Union, suspending delivery of all US grain sales in excess of the eight million tons guaranteed by a 1975 bilateral agreement. The USSR had made plans to import a record 35 million tons, mostly from the United States, as its grain harvest had fallen short of production targets by over 20 per cent. Whatever the political and economic effectiveness of the embargo, it was bound to cause serious problems to US exporting companies and farmers. The Commodity Credit Corporation (CCC), the financial branch of the Department of Agriculture, covered the contractual obligations of the exporters for undelivered embargo grains, at a cost to the government of two billion dollars, and subsequently managed to gradually retender the bulk of the grains it had acquired. To relieve farmers from the potential price depression caused by the recycling of grains, the loan rate – that is, the amount of credit for bushels of produce covered by government programmes – was increased with further costs to the taxpayer.[33] As for the Chrysler bail out, here too it is quite likely that the lavish amount of financial support provided to ease the pain of the 1980 grain embargo could have fallen under a subsidization ban had a code on agriculture been signed in the Tokyo Round. But this was not the case.

Despite the executive's financial efforts, farmers were highly critical of Carter's policy and the Republican platform for the November 1980 elections vowed to end the embargo immediately. Actually, the embargo did not entail any slowdown in farm exports as the fall in exports to the Soviet Union was offset by an upsurge in demand from other countries, prominent among which was China (Figure 4). Likewise, farmers' gross income rose significantly thanks to governmental price support, growing demand from countries other than the USSR, along with the effect on prices of a severe drought (Figure 4). What fell was net income as farmers were hit by soaring input costs and rocketing interest rates. In defence of the Carter administration, it must be said that things certainly went no better for farmers in the Reagan years when export declined because of the appreciation of the greenback (Figure 2), the downturn in world demand and increasingly aggressive competition from the EC member states, while interest rates went on rising in the US.[34] On the other hand, the embargo led to a rapid backlash for American producers as other main grain exporting countries like Argentina, Australia, Canada and France were ready to fill the gap in the Soviet market, not because they had the short-run capacity to expand production but simply by drawing down their surplus stock.[35]

France, the main grain producer in the EC, was able to tap into its stock because it had long since achieved self-sufficiency. By the end of the 1970s the Community had reached self-sufficiency in grains and exceeded it in wheat, and the surplus was even higher in sectors like sugar and butter (Figure 5). For these products, as pointed out by the European Commission, the most urgent problem for the EC was how to balance demand with supply rather than security of supply.[36] Indeed, the management of surpluses was becoming increasingly burdensome for the EC budget since it prevented funds from being destined to other programmes, interest in which was growing as the slump approached. The Commission proposed two sets of measures to cope with the problem. First, to curb supply the Commission deemed it necessary to replace guaranteed prices or aid levels for unlimited quantities with producer co-responsibility, thus obliging farmers to bear the whole or part of the expense to absorb supply beyond a certain ceiling.[37] Secondly, the Commission proposed to take actions on agricultural trade with regard to both import and export. In particular, the Commission called for more vigilance over the import of certain feeding stuff, most of which was provided by the US, and for the implementation of instruments similar to those already adopted by other major exporters like the US, Australia and Canada, chiefly the ability to conclude long-term agreements with foreign importers.[38] However, a series of factors, whose analysis is beyond the scope of this research, prevented a significant reorientation of the Common Agricultural Policy to coherently address the supply-demand disequilibrium problem and it was only in 1992 that a substantial reform of the CAP was implemented.

Overview of the development in the 1970s from the perspective of the following decade

At the onset of the new decade the United States share of world exports, which had amounted to over 14.5 per cent 16 years earlier, was slightly below 11 per cent (Figure 7). The US share of world exports in manufactures that was above 15 per cent in 1965 slightly declined to 14 per cent in 1980 and was exceeded by the share of West Germany which had become the main exporter of manufactured goods by the early 1970s, though its quota began to decline a little from the beginning of the first oil crisis (Figure 8). Japan was the third exporting country, having outpaced the United Kingdom. Yet, the loss of a few percentage points in the 1970s was far less conspicuous than the decline that characterized the period from the end of the Korean War to the mid-1960s when the US share of exports in manufactures had fallen from over 29 per cent to just over 15 per cent. However, the above sketched decline was not an unpredictable event but was the natural outcome of the rapid end of the exceptional circumstances that had put the United States on top of the world trade map in the aftermath of World War Two. The European countries, both in Western and Eastern Europe, as well as Japan, not only were able to rapidly reconstruct their production capacity affected, with different degrees of severity, by the wartime events, but soon began to catch-up with the American giant, demonstrating in the process that they were endowed with higher productivity.

The share of world exports of the whole EC reached its highest level in 1970, declining slightly over the next decade (Figure 7). The EC share of manufacturing exports reached its peak in 1974 and remained almost unchanged in the following six years (Figure 8). Nonetheless, by the early 1970s the dynamic of the EC countries in outpacing their transatlantic partner in world trade showed signs of slowing down (Table 25). In the period going from 1955 to the mid-1960s, the rate of export growth of the EC member states outshone that of the United States in most manufactured products ranked approximately in order of their knowledge content, but especially in those falling in group 1 and group 2. Group 1 consisted of high research-intensive products; group 2 of medium research-intensive products; group 3 of low research-intensive products. It must be observed that Table 25 has its drawbacks, which stem from the fact that it lacks sophistication, i.e. it provides the export value in current US dollars without the corrections necessary to take into account that from the beginning of the 1970s trade estimates were subject to a wide margin of error caused by inflation and by the fluctuation of exchange rates. Notwithstanding this, it appears that the United States was able to recover and to close the gap with the EC member states in both group 1 and group 2 exports from 1970 onwards.

The troubles that increasingly plagued the two transatlantic partners in the years following the start of the first oil crisis did not concern the whole economy or the whole trade balance. They predominantly affected particular sectors of the manufacturing industry on both sides of the Atlantic, including textiles, apparel, steel, motor vehicles and shipbuilding. All these sectors were characterized by shrinking demand from both the international and the domestic market and consequent falling production, worryingly accompanied by a steep contraction in employment. In short, these were the sectors that hindered full recovery and ushered in decline in the stagflation years. These sectors, which, non-technically, could be labelled as basic industries, weighed heavily in terms of production and employment on the American and European economies. The decline in output and employment was aggravated by the steady increase of the share of the domestic market captured by competing imports. As reported by American scholars, the import penetration ratios rose sharply in the second half of the 1970s in the US automobile, steel and textile industries and went on expanding, except for motor vehicles, in the first half of the 1980s.[39] Analogous trends marked the EC basic industries. The impact of import penetration was repeatedly cushioned, although without lasting effect, by measures directed at hampering imports, often culminating in the acceptance of VERs by the exporting countries[40].

Other sectors of the economy continued to grow in terms of domestic production and exports on both sides of the Atlantic. In the United States service exports grew in the decade under review by 260 per cent, reaching a recorded $36 billion, although estimates put them at around $60 billion.[41] Despite this, the United States complained that its service industry was experiencing a multifaceted variety of trade barriers. This kind of problem was not yet addressed in the GATT, which only dealt with trade in goods, though the Trade Act of 1974 gave the US executive a mandate for the negotiation of international agreements limiting non-tariff barriers to trade in services and section 301 of the Act authorized the president to retaliate against unfair foreign practices affecting both trade in goods and in services.

US exports of capital goods quintupled between 1970 and 1980, while the positive trade balance quadrupled (Table 3). Particularly dynamic was the high-technology sector where the US had a steadily growing positive balance with Western Europe, with the not particularly relevant exception of West Germany, and especially with the developing countries. From 1974 the US had, however, a trade deficit with Japan which concerned primarily consumer electronics. In 1982 the Republican administration complained that many countries had adopted a broad range of interventionist policy instruments to protect and foster technology-intensive industries which were steadily becoming the focus of national industrial policies. State intervention in support of such industries was particularly active in Japan and in France but it was not absent in countries like West Germany that were less inclined to have a strong role in the choices of the industrial sector. Yet, the picture was not completely different for the United States where the electronic revolution, especially in integrated circuits and software, benefited from the high level of federal government involvement both through massive procurement, although the administration was primarily motivated by defence objectives rather than by the goal of boosting the US industry, and as a funder of R&D.

On the eve of the 1982 GATT Ministerial Meeting, the United States suggested that the parties should assess possible trade distortions caused by the various forms of high-technology industry support and ascertain whether or not they could be addressed by existing trade agreements and, in the negative case, which further steps were needed to deal with the trade problems of the advanced technology sector.[42] On the other hand, the United States maintained that specific problems with individual nations should be dealt with by bilateral negotiations.[43] Prominent among the countries with which negotiations were needed was Japan, but no mention was made of the EC and its member states. In other words, the United States was not convinced that the instruments provided by the Tokyo Round, signed just three years earlier, were suitable for the more complex environment of high-tech industry. Indeed, as illustrated by this study, the Tokyo Round, although making progress in creating a better environment for international trade, codified or at least did not upset the law and the administrative practice that had been building up on both sides of the Atlantic. Two strands of interests, sometimes interwoven, are present in trade relations. On the one hand, there is the interest of those industries with a comparative or competitive advantage that aim at removing access barriers to foreign markets. On the other, there is the voice of the import competing industries. Even though during the run-up to the launching of the Tokyo Round negotiations there was a chance for the first strand to have a particularly visible role, the worsening conditions of a growing number of so-called basic industries in the United States and in the EC member states meant that particular attention was given to their claims. Conversely, no effective agreement was made on regulating, if not curtailing, the various forms of government support provided to national industries, either to buoy up declining industries or, as was the case of aircraft and high-tech industries, to protect them during their initial stage and later to foster their operations in the international trade arena.

Outward and inward foreign investments soared on both sides of the Atlantic in the 1970s. Despite the efforts of the government to promote exports directly from the United States, American FDIs grew almost seven times between 1951 and 1970. In nominal terms, that is, without taking into account the acceleration in the inflation rate, they were almost three times as high in 1980 but starting from a much higher basis and in a far shorter period (Table 5). The share of investments directed to Europe grew from 33.5 per cent in 1970 to almost 45 per cent ten years later. In manufacturing the European share of American FDIs grew five times (Table 6). Foreign investments in the United States grew by 3.6 times between 1951 and 1970, but became five times as great in the next ten years, two-thirds of them originating from Europe which were also stimulated by the depreciation of the dollar vis-à-vis many European currencies and in particular the Deutschmark. The growing presence of MNCs in the world economy meant that a growing share of trade flow was becoming intra-firm flow and this meant potentially growing support for the dismantlement of tariff and non-tariff barriers. In particular, the US multinational corporations turned out to be more successful in exporting than the American industries as a whole. The world market shares of the United States and its multinationals were about equal in 1966, but the share of the United States declined in the following 16 years while that of the multinational corporations remained almost unchanged.[44] This implies that increasingly larger portions of the world market outside the US were supplied by production outside the country. The comparative advantage of US multinationals was in the same industries as the United States as a country but to a larger degree. In particular, MNCs were stronger than other US firms in chemicals, electrical and non-electrical machineries and especially in transport equipments.

It must be stressed, however, that taking for granted that the 1970s western economy could be divided between export and foreign investment oriented industries, on the one hand, and import competing industries whose activity was mostly focused on the domestic market on the other, would be misleading. Likewise, to assume that, at least in the 1970s and in the following decade, the first group of industries favoured free trade while the second group was protectionist and dependent on governmental support is a farfetched generalization. Proof can be found in the policy of the automobile and electronics industries. [45]

Between 1973 and 1980 the ratio of cars produced in Latin America to those produced in the United States grew from 3.5 per cent to 7 per cent in the case of the General Motors, from 8 per cent to 22 per cent for Ford and from 7 per cent to 16 per cent for Chrysler.[46] By 1980, 37.2 per cent of total motor vehicle production was located abroad.[47] In 1967 Ford reorganized its European operations, previously separately managed in the UK, Germany and Belgium, into a transnationally integrated operation. Thus the production of the Ford Escort involved 16 countries of which 13 were European. GM's European operations were based on two separate subsidiaries which were controlled by the American giant long before the 1970s and whose production responsibilities were redrawn in 1979. Therefore, the US motor vehicle industry had a double, apparently conflicting, feature. On the one hand, it developed highly integrated regional and international strategies. On the other hand, within the US it was an industry which was outcompeted by foreign car manufacturers, especially Japanese, and successfully called first for government financial help and later in the early 1980s for the imposition of import quotas. This, in turn, prompted the biggest

Japanese firms to change their strategy of exporting from their national market or from East Asia and to invest heavily in the countries where they wanted to strengthen their trade hold.

Unlike the US giants, the operations of EC motor vehicle companies remained mostly concentrated within the Community boundaries and quite often, as was the case of the Italian FIAT within national boundaries.

US electronics industries started to move some of their activities abroad in the early 1960s. For semiconductors the push factor towards offshore assembly was growing competition within the United States itself and the acceleration of domestic production costs. For consumer electronics, television manufacture in particular, the push factor towards offshore assembly came from intensifying competition from low cost overseas producers, nominally the Japanese. The dominant motivation for investing in the European market was market access, though American MNCs were also heedful to select the lowest cost production sites, including those where government incentives operated. Although the main EC producers of electronics were slower in establishing offshore facilities across the Atlantic and were not able to establish affiliates or branches in Japan, firms such as Philips, Siemens and Thomson, created a production network in East and South East Asia as well as in many Mediterranean countries. Thomson, the French national champion, was not the only one to benefit from various kinds of governmental support.

As a matter of fact the major objectives of the companies engaged in foreign direct investments not always coincided with trade as was understood by the drafters of the General Agreement on Tariffs and Trade and consequently in the multilateral negotiating rounds, including the Tokyo Round, that is, trade among nations. FDIs were motivated by the desire to overcome tariff and non-tariff barriers by getting into a foreign customs area, or to avoid the burdens imposed by the national economy by moving production facilities to countries offering lower costs. Firms making FDIs certainly were not hostile to public support. Many multinational corporations, the Europeans in particular, were 'national champions' and received various kinds of governmental support. Most MNCs establishing branches or subsidiaries overseas benefited from a gamut of incentives directed at attracting foreign investments which were provided by national governments or, especially in the case of developed countries, by local authorities. They were opposed, however, to the imposition of export or local content requirements on their affiliates by some governments, especially in the developing countries, as the price for the continued operation in the host country, since such requirements were viewed as undue interference in the management of their global operations. On the other hand, as borne out by the quotas imposed by the US on colour TV receivers from Japan, Korea and Taiwan in the late 1970s, even high-tech industries would call for import restrictions whenever they felt threatened by foreign competition.[48]

In parallel, in the 1970s the attitude of many countries, including certain OECD members, towards foreign investments was ambivalent. On the one hand, they believed that foreign control could hamper the development of important sectors of the national economy. Therefore, developed and developing countries banned or limited foreign investments in a number of industries, or limited foreign participation in domestic firms. On the other hand, they started to claim that obstacles to foreign investments imposed by potentially recipient countries were preventing their companies from getting a foothold in those markets. Some countries, especially the developing ones, tried to attract foreign investments but made access and prospective benefits conditional on requirements impinging on trade choices. A further concern, in particular for both the United States and the EC, was to prevent foreign production facilities from being just assembly plants and quite often the two transatlantic trading partners made free circulation within their markets of the products of foreign corporations' affiliates conditional on a high content of domestic added value.

In spite of the initial efforts of the EC and of its member states, France in particular, the Tokyo Round shed no light on the relationship between trade and exchange rate fluctuations. It appears that, from the beginning of the 1970s, the United States exploited the depreciation of its currency to contain the damages caused to its trade balance by other factors like the discrepancy between the US demand and that of its trading partners or the non-competitive costs of some of its industries (Figures 1 and 2). The main targets were Japan and in particular West Germany. The Carter administration was often accused of exploiting the downwards trend of the dollar to improve the US trade and current account balances.

The foregoing issues, which did not attract overt attention in the 1970s and were not tackled by the Tokyo Round, from the beginning of the following decade became pressing and along with the more traditional bones of contention, including agriculture, were the subject of heated negotiations and disputes when important changes took place in the economic and political environment in which the main trading partners were acting.

Conclusion

Some methodological clarifications and a comprehensive assessment

A proper answer to the question regarding which conclusions can be drawn from a detailed analysis of not directly linked up facts presupposes an understanding of the parameters that underpin the analysis itself.

Do the foregoing chapters allow us to conclude that the 1970s were marked by protectionism? Such a straightforward approach presents many difficulties. First, it would posit a definition of protectionism, which risks ending up in an alley of vague generalizations. Even if a common denominator could be agreed upon – for instance viewing protectionism as the complex of trade barriers or of those trade barriers intentionally directed at sheltering domestic industries from foreign competition – it would be necessary to prove that the measures in question actually had a protectionist bias or a protectionist intent. As was indeed the case, it could be re-joined that measures deemed protectionist actually were the necessary answer to trade-distorting practices by foreign competitors and were allowed by long-established international rules. Above all, this approach does not meet the rules of historical analysis: 'protectionist' compared to which period and to what extent? Leaving aside tariff barriers, which till the Kennedy Round could hinder imports effectively, the sheer fact that after the mentioned round the GATT parties spent about ten years debating and negotiating on non-tariff barriers means that there was plenty of choice and that quite a few of the measures in question could shelter domestic industries from foreign competition. Analogous difficulties would meet the rather simplistic statement that in the 1970s world trade was distorted by an upsurge of policies aimed at financially supporting the declining economies of some or most OECD countries.

Thus, even though this research, in dealing with the narrow period of the 1970s, does not cast aside the use of the term protectionism, it has focused on more specific questions the answer to which lends itself to a longer-term analysis: which kind of trade barriers were at play? Which factors contributed to strengthen the alleged grip of protectionism and government interventionism?

Which were the sectors affected, their possible number ranging from a few industries to the whole economy? Did protectionist pressures grow proportionally or progressively when the economic environment became harsher? That is, were the same kind of measures simply applied to a growing number of sectors or was there a qualitative leap like a change in the law or in the administrative practice that made such measures more biting and hence more effective in discouraging the inflow of foreign products? Which were the counteracting agents and to what extent were they effective? Finally, what kind of relationship can be detected between protectionist measures and the new attention given to fair trade? Was there a constant contraposition or were some protectionist measures able to exploit the room for manoeuvre offered by the drive to establish fair trade? It must be emphasized that this research has focused on the United States and the European Community, only dealing with the policies of other trading partners in passing.

A commonly accepted premise is that until the second half of the 1960s the spotlight was on two kinds of trade barriers: tariffs, and in particular high tariffs, and quantitative restrictions. Tariffs were regarded as legitimate but were on a path of steady reduction, although with strong variations according to the sectors concerned, thanks to a series of GATT rounds. On the other hand, quotas, viewed by definition as a straightforward constraint to trade flow, were banned (GATT Article XI) although allowed in a limited range of cases (nominally, exceptions for primary product programmes and balance of payments safeguard). Notwithstanding the general ban, many states managed to preserve existing quantitative restrictions on imports. For instance, the GATT Contracting Parties allowed the United States to maintain quotas on some farm imports although such restrictions actually fell outside the exceptions envisaged by Article XI. At the margin of the picture there was a set of policies whose implementation was regarded as falling within the economic sovereignty of the states but, being viewed as exploitable for protectionist ends, were at the same time, quite loosely, regulated by the General Agreement. This would apply to GATT ArticleVI on antidumping and countervailing duties, and GATT Article VII on valuation for customs purposes. Other measures that could have a protectionist bias, such as preferences granted to domestic producers in public procurement, were left outside the picture.

This having been said, it is common knowledge that the post World War Two trend was in the first two decades definitely toward trade liberalization, being marked by tariff reduction and dismantlement of quotas. Yet, at least from the outset of the 1960s an opposite drift was detectable under the main trend. The

Long Term Arrangement Regarding International Trade in Cotton Textiles (LTA) was an example, establishing, under the aegis of the GATT, a network of bilateral agreements limiting the amount of imports. The LTA regime had a certain amount of flexibility and took into account production growth in the exporting countries, but at the end of the day it boiled down to a series of quotas. From 1962, the year in which the Trade Expansion Act sailed through Congress leading to the Kennedy Round, the number of US industrial imports subject to restrictions, including voluntary restraints, rose almost tenfold. In the 1960s the EC Common Agricultural policy took final shape which, under the banner of community preference, established a variable levy system whose effects were even more severe than the imposition of quotas.

Thus, applying the criteria set out above, this research only demonstrates that the 1970s merely witnessed the strengthening of protectionist tendencies which were fostered by the less stable economic climate. The number of protected sectors increased along with the number of VERs and OMAs negotiated with overly dynamic exporting countries, which were a covert form of imposition of import quotas. Although such so-called grey-area measures were particularly frequent in the textile and steel sectors, they were used whenever the need arose to protect declining sectors from import competition, ranging from footwear to consumer electronics.

The introduction of rules and administrative practices which made the tools to protect domestic industries against foreign competition more aggressive was of greater importance. As illustrated in chapters 3 and 4, the Trade Act of 1974, while granting negotiating authority to the US executive, rendered more severe, more rapid and thus more effective the antidumping and countervailing regime; this allowed the US trade authorities to close the net around practices that probably did not deserve this destiny and indeed would not have been subjected to extra duties under the previous regime. On the other side of the Atlantic the answer to the steel crisis was an aggressive antidumping policy that either forced foreign exporters to review their export prices or compelled their states to accept 'voluntary' export restraints. It follows that on a large range of merchandise trade the progress toward liberalization of the preceding decades was impaired or nullified. The ban on quotas was dodged through negotiated VERs and OMAs. Tariff concessions were eroded or eliminated through the imposition of antidumping and countervailing duties.

On the other hand, the 1970s witnessed a growing drive among many trading partners to support struggling industries as well as those sectors that for political or economic reasons were viewed as worthy of support, whether to boost their competitive capacity in the international market or irrespective of the impact of such measures on international trade. As shown in the previous chapters, the measures in question could take several forms, including: price support, direct transfer of funds, provision of goods and services at prices lower than market prices and tax cuts. These policies, despite the claim of the United States, were present, perhaps with different weight, on both sides of the Atlantic. It is suggested that the term 'special protection' can be used as an umbrella to encompass both directly protectionist policies and measures directed at supporting domestic industries, whether declining or expanding, in the battle with foreign competitors.

The conclusion that during the 1970s international trade fell under the grip of protectionism as a result of the recession also calls for several caveats. Although international trade slowed down, it went on growing. In particular, the internationalization of the American economy showed a strong acceleration, even though it remained below the values of its OECD trading partners, which is explained by the different weight of domestic demand in the two areas. In the EC countries exports and imports went on growing, except regarding the latter during the 1975 recession. It is likely that the depression that followed the first oil shock induced the US lawmakers to seek a strict trade-off between the granting of trade authority and the safeguard of domestic industry from foreign competition. However, the actual implementation of trade restrictive measures took place mostly during a phase of general recovery of the US economy which showed a growth rate not lower than that of the previous decade. Although the unemployment rate strongly increased from the first oil crisis onwards, in the EC member countries, on average, the second half of the 1970s recorded a slow down in the growth of the economy but not a recession. On both sides of the Atlantic industrial production went on growing for the whole decade except during the 1975 slump. This implies that the difficulties of import competing industries were offset by the progress of other manufacturing industries along with the growth of the service sector. This research, however, does not venture to suggest that, in contrast to the declining sectors of the economy, the service and high-tech industries in the OECD countries were completely free from state interference and trade barriers.

If there was a quantitative and qualitative leap in protectionist and other trade-distorting policies, the 1970s also witnessed the successful conclusion of a GATT round directed at achieving fair and freer trade. The success was prevalently political. Looking back at its achievements, it is arguable that progress did not come up to initial expectations. Yet, some trade barriers were successfully tackled while in others the round provided the basis for future negotiations. On the other hand, the Tokyo Round in its effort to achieve an agreement failed to effectively discipline governmental support to domestic industries, from agriculture and import-competing industries to high-tech industries, while allowing each GATT Party to continue to apply countermeasures without the constraint of any effective multilateral supervision. Hence the accusation of unilateralism in the 1970s and in the following decade. Sectors like services of growing weight in international trade remained outside the scope of the negotiations.

In short, in the decade there was neither the outset nor the dominance of protectionism. What marked the 1970s was the growth in number and sophistication of measures directed at sheltering domestic industry from foreign competition. Correspondingly, the decade witnessed, in spite of the ambitious programmes of the Tokyo Round, a deceleration in the progress towards free trade. Whereas the previous decades saw the erosion of tariff barriers in successive rounds and the partial elimination of quotas, during the decade the main trading partners were able to find ways to re-establish under different names and in allegedly legitimate ways these kinds of barriers, although their actual application concerned limited sectors of the economy, while overall no significant progress was achieved in removing other trade obstacles. Thus, the legacy of the 1970s to the next decade could only be mixed and uncertain. As happens in these cases, the greatest part of the outcome depended on the receiver of the legacy. Factors like the general trend of the economy, the unemployment rate, the condition of industries having a particular economic or political importance and the attitudes of executive and lawmakers in the countries concerned all had their weight. As can be inferred from the last chapter, the conditions overall were not favourable to cooperation between the two sides of the Atlantic and to the curbing of policies aimed at protecting their industries.

of 1972 US dollars)

1 Year	2 GNP	3 % Year change	4 GDP	5 % Year change	6 Exports	7 Imports	8 Net Exports	9 Exps+ Imps	10 6/2%	11 9/2%
1950	534.8		531.8		23.6	17.7	5.9	41.3	4.4	7.7
1951	579.4	8.3	575.7	8.3	28.6	18.5	10.1	47.1	4.9	8.1
1952	600.8	3.7	596.9	3.7	27.9	20	7.9	47.9	4.6	8
1953	623.6	3.8	619.9	3.9	26.6	21.8	4.8	48.4	4.3	7.8
1954	616.1	−1.2	612.1	−1.3	27.8	20.9	6.9	48.7	4.5	7.9
1955	657.5	6.7	653	6.7	30.7	23.4	7.3	54.1	4.7	8.2
1956	671.6	2.1	666.5	2.1	35.3	25.2	10.1	60.5	5.3	9
1957	683.8	1.8	678.3	1.8	38	26.1	11.9	64.1	5.6	9.4
1958	680.9	−0.4	676.3	−0.3	33.2	27.6	5.6	60.8	4.9	8.9
1959	721.7	6	716.8	6	33.8	31.1	2.7	64.9	4.7	9
1960	737.2	2.1	732	2.1	38.4	30.7	7.7	69.1	5.2	9.4
1961	756.6	2.6	750.9	2.6	39.3	30.9	8.4	70.2	5.2	9.3
1962	800.3	5.8	793.8	5.7	41.8	34.3	7.5	76.1	5.2	9.5
1963	832.5	4	825.6	4	44.8	35.4	9.4	80.2	5.4	9.6
1964	876.4	5.3	868.9	5.2	50.3	37.5	12.8	87.8	5.7	10
1965	929.3	6	921.4	6	51.7	41.6	10.1	93.3	5.6	10
1966	984.8	6	977.4	6.1	54.4	47.9	6.5	102.3	5.5	10.4
1967	1011.4	2.7	1003.9	2.7	56.7	51.3	5.4	108	5.6	10.7
1968	1058.1	4.6	1049.9	4.6	61.2	59.3	1.9	120.5	5.8	11.4
1969	1087.6	2.8	1079.7	2.8	65	64.1	0.9	129.1	6	11.9
1970	1085.6	−0.2	1077.6	−0.2	70.5	66.6	3.9	137.1	6.5	12.6
1971	1122.4	3.4	1112.9	3.3	71	69.3	1.7	140.3	6.3	12.5
1972	1185.9	5.7	1175	5.6	77.5	76.7	0.8	154.2	6.5	13
1973	1254.3	5.8	1239.2	5.5	97.3	81.8	15.5	179.1	7.8	14.3
1974	1246.3	−0.6	1229	−0.8	108.5	80.7	27.8	189.2	8.7	15.2
1975	1231.6	−1.2	1217.8	−0.9	103.5	71.4	32.2	174.9	8.4	14.2
1976	1298.2	5.4	1282.6	5.3	110.1	84.7	25.4	194.8	8.5	15
1977	1369.7	5.5	1352.8	5.5	112.9	90.9	22	203.8	8.2	14.9
1978	1438.6	5	1418.7	4.9	126.7	102.7	24	229.4	8.8	15.9
1979	1479.4	2.8	1453.2	2.4	146.2	109	37.2	255.2	9.9	17.3
1980	1475	−0.3	1449.3	−0.3	159.1	108.8	50.3	267.9	10.8	18.2

Source: Economic Report of the President, February 1985: Table B–2, Table B–9; auhor's calculations

Table 2 Trade Balance and Current Account Balance of the United States, 1950–80 (Millions of US dollars)*

Year	Merchandise Trade Balance			Balance on Goods and Services	Balance on Current Account
	Exports	Imports	Net		
1950	10,203	9,081	1,122	2,177	-1,840
1951	14,243	11,176	3,067	4,399	884
1952	13,449	10,838	2,611	3,145	614
1953	12,412	10,975	1,437	1,195	-1,286
1954	12,929	10,353	2,576	2,499	219
1955	14,424	11,527	2,897	2,928	430
1956	17,556	12,803	4,753	5,153	2,730
1957	19,562	13,291	6,271	7,107	4,762
1958	16,414	12,952	3,462	3,145	784
1959	16,458	15,310	1,148	1,166	-1,282
1960	19,650	14,758	4,892	5,132	2,824
1961	20,108	14,537	5,571	6,346	3,822
1962	20,781	16,260	4,521	6,025	3,387
1963	22,272	17,048	5,224	7,167	4,414
1964	25,501	18,700	6,801	9,604	6,823
1965	26,461	21,510	4,951	8,285	5,432
1966	29,310	25,493	3,817	5,963	3,031
1967	30,666	26,866	3,800	5,708	2,583
1968	33,626	32,991	635	3,563	611
1969	36,414	35,807	607	3,393	399
1970	42,469	39,866	2,603	5,625	2,331
1971	43,319	45,579	-2,260	2,269	-1,433
1972	49,381	55,797	-6,416	-1,941	-5,795
1973	71,410	70,499	911	11,021	7,140
1974	98,306	103,811	-5,505	9,147	1,962
1975	107,088	98,185	8,903	22,729	18,116
1976	114,745	124,228	-9,483	9,205	4,207
1977	120,816	151,907	-31,091	-9,894	-14,511
1978	142,054	176,020	-33,966	-10,340	-15,446
1979	184,473	212,028	-27,555	4,686	-964
1980	224,269	249,781	-25,512	8,975	1,888

* Excluding military

Source: Economic Report of the President, February 1984: Table B–98, Table B–99

	Foods, Feeds and Beverages			Industrial Supplies and Materials			Capital Goods, except Automotives			Automotive Vehicles, Parts and Engines			Consumer Goods (nonfood), except Automotives		
Year	Exports	Imports	Balance	Exports	Imports	Balance	Exports	Imports	Balance	Exports	Imports	Balance	Exports	Imports	Balance
1951	2,433	3,087	-654	6,190	6,952	-762	2,526	170	2,356	1,218	38	1,180	1,111	666	445
1952	2,201	3,156	-955	5,553	6,537	-984	2,812	227	2,585	1,024	56	968	1,015	663	352
1953	1,838	3,282	-1,444	4,826	6,456	-1,630	2,929	224	2,705	998	53	945	1,086	757	329
1954	1,713	3,317	-1,604	5,479	5,764	-285	2,919	220	2,699	1,072	53	1,019	1,097	787	310
1955	2,119	3,108	-989	6,065	6,843	-778	3,071	254	2,817	1,276	85	1,191	1,134	991	143
1956	2,807	3,190	-383	7,383	7,674	-291	3,834	364	3,470	1,395	145	1,250	1,246	1,133	113
1957	2,781	3,306	-525	8,669	7,595	1,074	4,487	400	4,087	1,349	339	1,010	1,336	1,210	126
1958	2,590	3,472	-882	6,436	5,944	492	4,752	460	4,292	1,123	555	568	1,314	1,195	119
1959	2,871	3,445	-574	6,146	8,343	-2,197	4,617	591	4,026	1,187	844	343	1,371	1,632	-261
1960	3,170	3,286	-116	7,924	7,887	37	5,511	562	4,949	1,266	633	633	1,396	1,901	-505
1961	3,418	3,331	87	7,705	7,714	-9	5,910	693	5,217	1,188	383	805	1,441	1,889	-448
1962	3,829	3,573	256	7,132	8,573	-1,441	6,443	758	5,685	1,301	521	780	1,455	2,276	-821
1963	4,282	3,753	529	7,822	8,874	-1,052	6,604	823	5,781	1,468	586	882	1,558	2,389	-831
1964	4,849	3,915	934	9,185	9,563	-378	7,463	1,039	6,424	1,729	767	962	1,751	2,694	-943
1965	4,928	3,946	982	8,917	11,024	-2,107	8,039	1,458	6,581	1,929	939	990	1,799	3,305	-1,506
1966	5,489	4,499	990	9,613	12,162	-2,549	8,892	2,136	6,756	2,354	1,910	444	2,035	3,912	-1,877
1967	4,998	4,586	412	9,971	11,856	-1,885	9,913	2,382	7,531	2,784	2,634	150	2,111	4,213	-2,102
1968	4,813	5,271	-458	11,006	14,159	-3,153	11,072	2,825	8,247	3,453	4,295	-842	2,334	5,330	-2,996
1969	4,687	5,239	-552	11,758	14,163	-2,405	12,322	3,331	8,991	3,888	5,346	-1,458	2,596	6,503	-3,907
1970	5,874	6,147	-273	13,795	15,343	-1,548	14,659	3,978	10,681	3,870	5,515	-1,645	2,798	7,403	-4,605
1971	6,110	6,364	-254	12,703	17,444	-4,741	15,372	4,334	11,038	4,698	7,358	-2,660	2,913	8,388	-5,475
1972	7,504	7,258	246	13,966	20,958	-6,992	16,914	5,919	10,995	5,484	8,685	-3,201	3,583	11,104	-7,521
1973	15,199	9,119	6,080	19,862	28,049	-8,187	21,999	8,263	13,736	6,878	10,257	-3,379	4,800	12,892	-8,092
1974	18,638	10,568	8,070	30,129	54,428	-24,299	30,878	9,819	21,059	8,678	12,028	-3,350	6,399	14,380	-7,981
1975	19,234	9,642	9,592	29,945	51,030	-21,085	36,639	10,166	26,473	8,625	11,693	-3,068	6,560	13,211	-6,651
1976	19,800	11,500	8,300	32,000	63,700	-31,700	39,100	12,300	26,800	12,200	16,800	-4,600	8,000	17,200	-9,200
1977	19,700	14,000	5,700	34,300	79,900	-45,600	39,800	14,000	25,800	13,500	19,400	-5,900	8,900	21,800	-12,900
1978	25,200	15,400	9,800	39,000	83,600	-44,600	46,500	19,700	26,800	15,700	25,000	-9,300	10,400	28,900	-18,500
1979	30,000	17,400	12,600	58,100	109,000	-50,900	58,800	25,000	33,800	18,400	26,400	-8,000	12,800	30,600	-17,800
1980	35,700	18,100	35,600	71,900	133,300	-61,400	74,200	31,200	43,000	17,500	27,900	-10,400	16,600	34,400	-17,800

Source: Historical Statistics of the United States Colonial Times to 1970 – Part 2: Series U 249–263; Statistical Abstract of the United States: Exports and Imports – Value by Broad End-Use Class, various issues; author's calculations

Table 4 US Exports and Imports by Areas and Selected Countries of Destination and Origin, 1951–80 (Millions of US dollars)

	Americas				Europe								Asia				Austr. and Oc.		Africa	
	Total		Canada		Total		France		Germany		UK		Total		Japan		Total		Total	
Year	Exps.	Imps.	Exps.	Imps.	Exps.	Imps.	Exps.	Imps.	Exps.	Imps.	Exps.	Imps.	Exps.	Imps.	Exps.	Imps.	Exps.	Imps.	Exps.	Imps.
1951	6607	5826	2693	2275	5121	2119	843	263	523	233	1000	466	2410	1983	601	205	270	451	624	589
1952	6682	6025	3003	2386	5089	2029	1013	167	459	212	787	485	2541	1813	633	229	267	243	621	607
1953	6514	6117	3197	2462	5711	2335	1236	186	363	277	826	546	2783	1626	686	262	203	201	563	593
1954	6520	5896	2966	2377	5118	2083	783	157	505	278	808	501	2577	1467	693	279	264	165	630	605
1955	6903	6262	3404	2653	5126	2453	536	202	607	366	1006	616	2581	1876	683	432	295	174	642	619
1956	8243	6856	4149	2894	6434	2963	829	236	943	494	982	726	3417	1996	998	558	265	203	731	597
1957	9001	7048	4041	2907	6838	3147	708	256	1330	607	1162	766	3961	1985	1319	601	295	216	755	587
1958	7999	6703	3539	2674	5566	3340	570	308	887	629	905	864	3411	1983	987	666	282	208	652	557
1959	7692	7071	3825	3042	5554	4607	483	462	878	920	1097	1137	3284	2603	1079	1029	376	338	728	589
1960	7684	6864	3810	2901	7398	4268	699	396	1272	897	1487	993	4186	2721	1447	1149	514	266	793	534
1961	7673	6995	3826	3270	7370	4141	704	435	1343	856	1206	898	4652	2583	1837	1055	445	320	859	672
1962	7724	7591	4045	3660	7758	4621	735	428	1581	962	1128	1005	4676	2960	1574	1358	519	440	1023	754
1963	7944	7850	4251	3829	8338	4811	813	431	1582	1003	1213	1079	5448	3192	1844	1498	565	502	1054	777
1964	9207	8390	4915	4239	9436	5307	990	495	1606	1171	1532	1143	5802	3620	2009	1768	803	440	1259	917
1965	9908	9203	5642	4833	9365	6292	971	615	1649	1341	1615	1405	6012	4528	2080	2414	956	453	1229	878
1966	11429	10829	6661	6125	10003	7857	1007	698	1674	1796	1737	1786	6733	5276	2364	2963	805	593	1349	979
1967	11883	11741	7165	7107	10297	8227	1025	690	1706	1955	1960	1710	7146	5348	2695	2999	1017	581	1182	906
1968	13411	14148	8072	9005	11347	10337	1095	842	1709	2721	2289	2058	7582	6911	2954	4054	1026	696	1269	1122
1969	14713	15547	9137	10384	12641	10334	1195	842	2142	2603	2335	2120	8261	8274	3490	4888	998	828	1392	1046
1970	15612	16928	9079	11092	14817	11395	1483	942	2741	3127	2536	2194	10027	9621	4652	5875	1189	871	1580	1113
1971	16850	18730	10365	12692	14562	12881	1373	1088	2831	3651	2369	2499	9588	11780	4055	7259	1168	895	1694	1236
1972	19690	21911	12415	14907	16180	15744	1609	1369	2808	4250	2658	2987	11297	15117	4963	9064	1034	1145	1577	1595
1973	25033	27322	15104	17715	23161	19812	2263	1732	3756	5345	3564	3657	18419	18156	8313	9676	1744	1562	2306	2583
1974	35745	40710	19936	22286	30070	24625	2942	2305	4985	6429	4574	4023	25785	27522	10697	12456	2697	1505	3659	6621
1975	38843	38209	21744	22151	32732	22789	3031	2164	5194	5410	4527	3773	28223	27252	9563	11425	2340	1508	4949	8299
1976	41074	43356	24106	26237	35900	29892	3446	2509	5731	5592	4801	4254	29729	39367	10145	15504	2690	1671	5206	12644
1977	43751	50697	25788	29599	37304	27669	3503	3032	5989	7238	5951	5141	31436	49312	10529	18550	2877	1728	5546	17121
1978	50394	56473	28374	33525	43608	36483	4166	4051	6957	9962	7116	6514	39630	58264	12885	24458	3464	2350	5887	16898
1979	61555	68509	33096	38046	60026	41681	5587	4768	8478	10955	10635	8028	48771	66739	17581	26248	4319	3072	6299	24382
1980	74114	78489	35395	41459	71371	46602	7485	5265	10960	11693	12694	9842	60168	80299	20790	30714	4876	3392	9060	34410

Table 5 US Direct Investments in Foreign Countries by Areas, 1951–80 (Percentage shares)

Year	TOTAL Millions of US dollars	Canada %	Europe %	Latin American and Caribbean %	Asia and Pacific %	Africa, M. East International %
1951	12,979	30.6	15.3	38.1	5.3	10.7
1952	14,721	31.5	14.6	37.5	5.6	10.8
1953	16,253	32.9	14.6	35.5	5.5	11.4
1954	17,631	34.3	15	33.6	5.8	11.3
1955	19,395	34.9	15.5	32.2	6.2	11.3
1956	22,505	34.6	15.8	32.4	6	11.1
1957	25,394	34.5	16.3	31.7	6.2	11.2
1958	27,409	34.6	16.7	30.9	6.3	11.5
1959	29,827	34.6	17.8	29.8	6.4	11.4
1960	31,865	35.1	21	26.3	6.7	10.9
1961	34,717	33.4	22.3	26.6	6.8	10.9
1962	37,276	32.5	24	25.5	6.9	11
1963	40,736	32	25.4	24.4	7.3	12.4
1964	44,480	31.1	27.3	23.1	7.6	10.9
1965	49,474	31	28.3	22	7.8	11
1966	51,792	30.3	31.6	18.8	7.7	11.5
1967	56,560	29.5	32.2	18.2	8.4	11.7
1968	61,907	29	32.1	18.3	8.7	11.9
1969	68,093	28.8	32,7	17.7	9	11.9
1970	75,480	27.8	33.5	17.2	9.3	12.2
1971	82,760	26.4	34.6	16.9	10.1	12
1972	89,878	25.6	35.3	16.6	10.7	11.8
1973	101,313	25.1	37.8	16.3	10.9	9.8
1974	110,078	25.8	40.6	17.7	11.7	4.2
1975	124,050	25	39.7	17.9	12.3	5.7
1976	136,809	24.7	40.3	17.5	11.4	6.1
1977	145,990	24	42.8	18.8	11.2	3.1
1978	162,727	22.4	43.4	19.5	11.4	3.3
1979	187,858	24.2	49.5	21	12.7	4.6
1980	215,578	20.9	44.8	18	10.6	5.7

Source: Historical Statistics of the United States Colonial Times to 1970 – Part 2: Series U 41–46; Statistical Abstract of the United States: US Direct Investment Position Abroad and Income, by Country and by Selected Industries, various issues; own calculations

TABLE 6 Share and Growth Rate of Canada and Western Europe in US Foreign Direct Investments in Manufacturing (1951–80). [Total FDI in 1951 = US$4,348 Mill.]

	Total	Canada		Western Europe		R.O.W	
Year	Index N.	%	Index N.	%	Index N.	%	Index N.
1951	100	46.2	100	24.7	100	29.1	100
1952	114.2	46.4	114.6	24	111.2	29.6	116.2
1953	122.8	47.6	126.4	24.5	122	27.9	117.8
1954	135.7	47	138.2	25.1	137.6	27.9	130
1955	152.3	46.7	154	25.4	156.9	27.9	145.8
1956	173.9	46.6	175.5	25.8	181.8	27.5	164.7
1957	184.2	49	195.3	27.4	204.4	23.6	149.4
1958	199.5	48	207.3	28.6	230.4	23.5	160.8
1959	223.3	47	227.2	30.4	274.4	22.6	173.5
1960	254.2	43.7	240.3	34.4	354.2	21.9	191.3
1961	275.9	42.3	252.7	35.5	396.2	22.2	210.8
1962	304.7	40.1	264.4	36.9	454.7	23.1	241.5
1963	343.5	38.6	286.8	37.7	524.6	23.7	280
1964	389.5	36,6	308.5	38.9	613.3	24.5	328.1
1965	444.8	35.5	342.1	39.3	708.2	25.1	384.3
1966	477	32.3	333.3	42.9	829.2	24.8	406.1
1967	524.4	31	351.4	43.3	918.7	25.8	464.6
1968	578.7	30	375.1	43.4	1018.6	26.6	528.5
1969	651.6	29.6	418.3	43.7	1152	26.7	597.3
1970	714.1	28.9	446.5	44.5	1286.7	26.6	652.9
1971	790.2	27.7	473.1	45.5	1455.1	26.9	729.4
1972	881.4	27.4	522.2	45.7	1632.1	26.9	814.6
1973	1020.5	26.5	585.1	46.8	1934.5	26.7	935.8
1974	1176.9	26.3	669.5	46.9	2233.7	26.8	1085.5
1975	1285.3	26.3	731.3	46.5	2422.1	27.2	1200.2
1976	1406.6	26.1	794.7	47.1	2680,	26.9	1297.1
1977	1426.4	23.9	736.4	49.1	2837.1	27	1324.4
1978	1602.3	22.6	783.3	49.7	3226.7	27.7	1524
1979	1817.5	22.2	872.6	50.1	3688.9	27.7	1728.3
1980	2053.6	21.3	947.1	50.7	4216.7	28	1974.3

Source: Calculations based on Historical Statistics of the United States Colonial Times to 1970 – Part 2: Series U41–6; Historical Statistics of the United States Millennial Edition Vol. 5: Table Ee 72–131

Year	All Areas				Canada				Europe			
	Total	Petroleum	Manufact.	Finace and Insurance	Total	Petroleum	Manufact.	Finance and Insurance	Total	Petroleum	Manufact.	Finance and Insurance
1951	3658	466	1274	1105	1109	62	525	150	2410	404	747	912
1952	3945	552	1377	1170	1218	90	592	149	2575	462	782	977
1953	4251	706	1451	1219	1350	168	611	162	2751	538	836	1014
1954	4633	776	1582	1371	1427	192	651	168	3049	584	925	1158
1955	5076	853	1759	1499	1542	196	711	179	3369	657	1040	1272
1956	5459	937	1940	1534	1690	200	775	196	3598	737	1155	1289
1957	5710	1043	2083	1496	1773	211	816	208	3753	832	1248	1238
1958	6115	1099	2232	1660	1835	214	863	222	4070	885	1332	1384
1959	6604	1184	2471	1734	1896	207	907	227	4452	972	1501	1451
1960	6910	1238	2611	1810	1934	203	932	246	4707	1028	1611	1504
1961	7392	1325	2754	2025	1989	194	975	274	5129	1125	1708	1690
1962	7612	1419	2885	1943	2064	212	1015	269	5245	1203	1797	1611
1963	7944	1513	3018	2045	2183	213	1063	337	5491	1306	1881	1640
1964	8363	1612	3213	2181	2284	205	1129	382	5819	1404	2005	1723
1965	8797	1710	3478	2169	2388	208	1219	370	6076	1481	2167	1724
1966	9054	1740	3789	2072	2439	98	1342	386	6273	1620	2335	1611
1967	9923	1885	4181	2193	2575	99	1397	354	7005	1772	2669	1758
1968	10815	2261	4475	2305	2659	100	1413	376	7750	2146	2941	1855
1969	11818	2493	5344	2189	2834	132	1644	325	8510	2322	3530	1766
1970	13270	2992	6140	2256	3117	190	1836	324	9554	2777	4091	1805
1971	13914	3139	6722	2553	3335	207	2013	330	10336	2893	4455	2048
1972	14868	3272	7262	2911	3466	243	2201	353	11087	3012	4836	2336
1973	20556	4792	8231	3415	4203	426	2319	376	13937	4079	4790	2174
1974	25144	5614	10387	3530	5136	547	2905	425	16756	4714	6109	1954
1975	27662	6213	11386	3928	5352	596	3061	451	18584	5478	6673	2218
1976	30770	5921	12620	4741	5907	676	3386	541	20162	4999	7426	2815
1977	34595	6573	14030	5398	5650	710	3077	464	23754	5523	9267	3273
1978	42471	7762	17202	6392	6180	734	3213	540	29180	6569	11717	3905
1979	54462	9906	20876	9395	7154	943	3615	839	37403	8010	13952	6080
1980	68351	12363	25159	10365	10074	1308	5199	852	45731	9766	16064	7606

Source: Historical Statistics of the United States Colonial Times to 1970 – Part 2: Series U 47–74; Statistical Abstract of the United States: Foreign Direct Investment in the US – Value, by Area and Industry, various issues

Table 8 Annual Percentage Changes in Productivity and Related Data in the US, 1950–80

	Output per hour of all persons		Compensation per hour		Unit Labour Cost	
Year	Private business sector	Nonfarm business sector	Private business sector	Nonfarm business sector	Private business sector	Nonfarm business sector
1950	7.9	6	7.1	5.8	−0.8	−0.2
1951	2.8	1.7	9.8	8.8	6.9	6.9
1952	3.2	2.3	6.4	5.5	3	3.1
1953	3.2	1.7	6.4	5.6	3.1	3.9
1954	1.6	1.4	3.2	3.2	1.6	1.7
1955	4	3.9	2.5	3.6	−1.4	−0.3
1956	1	−0.3	6.5	6	5.5	5.7
1957	2.5	1.7	6.5	5.7	3.9	3.9
1958	3.1	2.4	4.4	3.8	1.3	1.4
1959	3.2	3.4	4.3	4	1	0.6
1960	1.5	−0.8	4.2	4.3	2.7	3.5
1961	3.3	2.9	3.8	3.2	0.5	0.3
1962	3.8	3.6	4.6	4	0.7	0.4
1963	3.7	3.2	3.7	3.5	0	0.2
1964	4.3	3	5.2	4.5	0.8	0.6
1965	3.5	3.1	3.9	3.4	0.3	0.3
1966	3.1	2.5	7	6	3.8	3.5
1967	2.2	1.9	5.3	5.5	3	3.5
1968	3.3	3.3	7.8	7.5	4.4	4.1
1969	0.2	−0.3	7	6.5	6.7	6.8
1970	0.9	0.3	7.4	7	6.4	6.6
1971	3.6	3.3	6.6	6.6	2.9	3.1
1972	3.5	3.7	6.5	6.7	2.9	2.8
1973	2.7	2.5	8	7.6	5.2	4.9
1974	−2.3	−2.4	9.4	9.4	11.9	12.1
1975	2.3	2.1	9.6	9.6	7.2	7.4
1976	3.3	3.2	8.6	8.1	5.1	4.7
1977	2.1	2	7.7	7.6	5.5	5.5
1978	−0.2	−0.2	8.4	8.5	8.6	8.7
1979	−0.3	−0.7	10.1	9.7	10.4	10.4
1980	−0.2	−0.3	10.2	9.9	10.4	10.4

Year	Federal Government				Total Government			
	Receipts	Expenditures	Surplus or Deficit	Surplus-Deficit as % of GDP	Receipts	Expenditures	Surplus or Deficit	Surplus-Deficit as % of GDP
1950	50	40.8	9.2	3.2	69	61	8	2.8
1951	64.3	57.8	6.5	2	85.2	79.2	6.1	1.9
1952	67.3	71.1	-3.7	-1.1	90.1	93.9	-3.8	-1.1
1953	70	77.1	-7.1	-1.9	94.6	101.6	-6.9	-1.9
1954	63.7	69.8	-6	-1.6	89.9	97	-7.1	-1.9
1955	72.6	68.1	4.4	1.1	101.1	98	3.1	0.8
1956	78	71.9	6.1	1.5	109.7	104.5	5.2	1.2
1957	81.9	79.6	2.3	0.5	116.2	115.2	0.9	0.2
1958	78.7	88.9	-10.3	-2.3	115	127.6	-12.6	-2.8
1959	89.8	91	-1.1	-0.2	129.4	131	-1.6	-0.4
1960	96.1	93.1	3	0.6	139.5	136.4	3.1	0.6
1961	98.1	101.9	-3.9	-0.7	144.8	149.1	-4.3	-0.8
1962	106.2	110.4	-4.2	-0.7	156.7	160.5	-3.8	-0.7
1963	114.4	114.2	0.3	0.1	168.5	167.8	0.7	0.1
1964	114.9	118.2	-3.3	-0.5	174	176.3	-2.3	-0.4
1965	124.3	123.8	0.5	0.1	188.3	187.8	0.5	0.1
1966	141.8	143.6	-1.8	-0.2	212.3	213.6	-1.3	-0.2
1967	150.5	163.7	-13.2	-1.7	228.2	242.4	-14.2	-1.8
1968	174.4	180.5	-6	-0.7	263.1	269.1	-6	-0.7
1969	196.9	188.4	8.4	0.9	296.7	286.8	9.9	1.1
1970	191.9	204.3	-12.4	-1.3	302.8	313.4	-10.6	-1.1
1971	198.6	220.6	-22	-2.1	322.6	342	-19.4	-1.8
1972	227.5	244.3	-16.8	-1.4	368.3	371.6	-3.3	-0.3
1973	258.6	264.2	-5.6	-0.4	413.1	405.3	7.8	0.6
1974	287.8	299.3	-11.5	-0.8	455.2	460	-4.7	-0.3
1975	287.3	356.6	-69.3	-4.5	470.5	534.3	-63.8	-4.2
1976	331.8	384.8	-53.1	-3.1	538.4	574.9	-36.5	-2.2
1977	375.2	421.1	-45.9	-2.4	605.4	623.3	-17.8	-0.9
1978	431.6	461	-29.5	-1.4	681.9	681.1	0.8	0
1979	493.6	509.7	-16.1	-0.7	765.1	750.8	14.3	0.6
1980	540.9	602.1	-61.2	-2.4	838.3	869	-30.7	-1.2

Source: Economic Report of the President, February 1985: Table B–74; own calculations

Table 10 GDP Growth Rate in EC Member States, 1960–80 (1975 prices)

Year	Belgium	Denmark	France	Germany	Ireland	Italy	Luxemb.	Netherl.	UK	EC
1960	5.8	6.6	7.2	10.5	5.8	6.7	5.6	9.9	5	7.6
1961	5	6.4	5.5	5.1	5	8.2	4.4	2.9	3.3	5.2
1962	5.2	5.7	6.7	4.6	3.2	6.2	1.4	4.3	1	4.3
1963	4.3	0.6	5.3	3.2	4.8	5.6	2.6	3.3	3.9	4.3
1964	6.9	9.3	6.5	6.5	3.8	2.8	7.5	8.6	5.2	5.7
1965	3.6	4.6	4.8	5.6	1.9	3.3	1.7	5.3	2.3	4.2
1966	3.2	6.4	5.2	2.6	0.9	6	1.7	2.7	2	3.7
1967	3.9	3.7	4.7	0	5.8	7.2	1.6	5.3	2.6	3.4
1968	4.2	3.8	4.3	6.1	8.2	6.5	4.2	6.4	4.1	5.1
1969	5.9	6.5	7	7.8	5.9	6.1	8.9	6.4	1.5	5.7
1970	6.2	2.3	5.7	6	2.7	5.3	2.2	6.7	2.2	4.9
1971	3.9	2.4	5.4	3.3	3.5	1.6	4.3	4.3	2.7	4.4
1972	5.3	5.4	5.9	3.7	6.5	3.2	6.3	3.4	2.2	4
1973	6.2	3.8	5.4	5	4.6	7	10.7	5.7	7.5	6.1
1974	4.5	-0.7	3.2	0.7	4.2	4.1	3.6	3.5	-1	1.7
1975	-1.9	-1	0.2	-1.6	2	-3.6	-6.1	-1	-0.6	-1.2
1976	5.3	6.9	4.9	5.1	2.1	5.9	1.7	5.3	3.6	4.9
1977	1	1.9	3.1	3	6.9	1.9	0.8	2.4	1.3	2.4
1978	3.2	1.3	3.5	3.3	6.7	2.7	4.6	2.7	3.3	3.2
1979	2.3	3	3	4.3	2.4	4.9	4.1	1.8	1.4	3.3
1980	2.5	-0.2	1.3	2	1.9	4	0.7	0.6	-1.4	1.4

Source: Commission of the European Communities. European Economy, Number 14, Nov. 1982: Statistical Annex, Table 8

Table 11 EC Member States Total Exports, 1960–80 (Mill. ECU)

	1960	1965	1968	1970	1971	1972	1973	1974	1975	1976	1977	1978	1979	1980
Belgium – Lux.	3775	6382	8164	11609	12184	14404	18203	23703	23193	29340	32892	35203	41033	46459
France	6863	10048	12672	17739	19576	23042	28902	38469	41981	49915	55667	60120	71510	80151
Germany F.R.	11415	17892	24842	34189	39141	41633	54397	74753	72666	91155	103316	111332	125243	138787
Italy	3468	7200	10186	13206	14465	16583	18102	25557	28246	33507	39698	43978	52614	56116
Netherlands	4028	6393	8341	11767	13468	15045	19511	27745	28593	36149	38283	39290	46434	53184
EC – 6	**29549**	**47915**	**64205**	**88510**	**98834**	**110707**								
Denmark	1471	2273	2584	3290	3412	3869	5063	6464	7024	8139	8816	9224	10767	12195
Ireland	428	618	873	1120	1257	1441	1727	2226	2585	2992	3852	4460	5222	6101
UK	10349	13722	15365	19258	21423	21708	24795	32373	35288	41458	50276	56093	66038	82060
EC – 9							**170700**	**231290**	**239576**	**292655**	**332800**	**359700**	**418861**	**475053**

Source: Eurostat Review: Foreign Trade, 1970–1979; Eurostat, External Trade Statistical Yearbook, 1985; author's calculations

Table 12 EC Member States Total Imports, 1960–80 (Mill. ECU)

	1960	1965	1968	1970	1971	1972	1973	1974	1975	1976	1977	1978	1979	1980
Belgium – Lux.	3957	6374	8333	11362	12357	13812	17910	25015	24818	31714	35418	38093	44053	51612
France	6279	10336	13927	18922	20262	23818	30042	44293	43682	57646	61784	64217	77705	97102
Germany F.R.	10103	17472	20150	29184	34431	35827	44106	58046	60442	78912	88803	95398	116310	135243
Italy	4725	7378	10286	14970	15298	17217	22645	34438	31128	39489	42143	44313	56763	71813
Netherlands	4531	7464	9293	13393	14624	15466	19799	27847	28389	35832	39970	41530	49053	55368
EC – 6	**29595**	**49024**	**61989**	**87831**	**96972**	**106140**								
Denmark	1799	2811	3226	4388	4343	4513	6333	8331	8383	11093	11616	11422	13670	14106
Ireland	633	1041	1239	1624	1761	1877	2263	3193	3046	3764	4728	5592	7176	7998
UK	12714	16103	18936	21643	22915	24848	31562	45347	42905	50122	55522	61642	74745	85652
EC – 9							**174660**	**246510**	**242793**	**308572**	**339984**	**362207**	**439475**	**518894**

Source: Eurostat Review: Foreign Trade, 1970–1979; Eurostat, External Trade Statistical Yearbook, 1985; author's calculations

Table 13 EC Member States Exports to the US, 1960–80 (Mill. ECU)

	1960	**1965**	**1968**	**1970**	**1971**	**1972**	**1973**	**1974**	**1975**	**1976**	**1977**	**1978**	**1979**	**1980**
Belgium – Lux.	366	532	770	697	812	879	1021	1328	946	1044	1384	1454	1535	1556
France	396	594	765	954	1057	1232	1371	1879	1647	2260	2862	3353	3496	3544
Germany F.R.	897	1436	2707	3124	3780	3857	4605	5614	4311	5110	6872	7857	8268	8509
Italy	385	619	1090	1354	1419	1623	1552	1938	1840	2161	2648	3134	3402	2981
Netherlands	198	244	436	506	535	561	693	1096	778	1019	1312	1300	1302	1335
EC – 6	**2242**	**3425**	**5768**	**6635**	**7603**	**8152**	9242	11855	9522	11594	15078	17098	18003	17925
Denmark	103	159	216	263	270	316	364	378	370	475	511	527	526	569
Ireland	31	25	117	144	140	136	169	215	517	208	239	275	255	321
UK	968	1458	2185	2264	2556	2711	3026	3464	3152	3961	4671	5244	6262	7750
EC – 9							**12801**	**15912**	**13561**	**16238**	**20499**	**23144**	**25046**	**26565**

Source: Eurostat Review: Foreign Trade, 1970–9; Eurostat, External Trade Statistical Yearbook, 1985; author's calculations

Table 14 EC Member States Imports from the US, 1960–80 (Mill. ECU)

	1960	**1965**	**1968**	**1970**	**1971**	**1972**	**1973**	**1974**	**1975**	**1976**	**1977**	**1978**	**1979**	**1980**
Belgium – Lux.	392	550	689	995	790	778	1012	1627	1575	1939	2133	2200	2972	3982
France	745	1088	1319	1896	1730	1948	2516	3438	3290	4222	4289	4683	5254	6921
Germany F.R.	1423	2296	2173	3293	3553	3007	3725	4524	4665	6235	6080	6432	7611	9724
Italy	670	993	1197	1547	1379	1423	1875	2626	2710	3111	2930	2998	3850	4995
Netherlands	600	765	1014	1308	1397	1256	1732	2481	2800	3244	3409	3575	4130	4867
EC – 6	**3830**	**5692**	**6392**	**9039**	**8849**	**7156**	10860	14696	15040	18751	18841	19888	23817	30489
Denmark	177	240	274	326	364	321	425	504	508	571	665	604	705	914
Ireland	52	83	92	117	153	144	156	207	219	322	421	471	526	627
UK	1586	1882	2554	2817	2555	2628	3229	4935	4833	5698	5810	7315	8725	11437
EC – 9							**14670**	**20342**	**20600**	**25342**	**25737**	**28278**	**33773**	**43467**

Source: Eurostat Review: Foreign Trade, 1970–9; Eurostat, External Trade Statistical Yearbook, 1985; author's calculations

Table 15 Intra-EC Imports, 1960–80 (Mill. ECU)

	1960	1965	1968	1970	1971	1972	1973	1974	1975	1976	1977	1978	1979	1980
Belgium – Lux.	1894	3473	4576	6665	7811	7938	12658	16531	16688	21446	23958	26306	29625	32519
France	1848	4015	6617	9256	10141	11994	16657	21102	21337	28562	30521	33030	39065	44627
Germany F.R.	3024	6661	8358	13232	16129	17489	23032	27907	29923	38033	43509	47838	57378	63524
Italy	1309	2305	3723	6167	6498	7727	11068	14612	13375	17162	18167	19796	25082	31444
Netherlands	2076	3987	5146	7483	8011	8702	12082	15983	16152	19796	21920	23828	27664	29486
Denmark							2900	3788	3841	5233	5535	5675	6739	6918
Ireland							1623	2181	2109	2612	3220	3925	5411	5964
UK							10339	13604	13913	16137	21400	23394	30505	32897
Total EC	**10151**	**20441**	**28420**	**42803**	**48590**	**53850**	**90359**	**115708**	**117338**	**148981**	**168230**	**183792**	**221469**	**247379**

Source: Eurostat Review: Foreign Trade, 1970–9; Eurostat, External Trade Statistical Yearbook, 1985

Table 16 Percentage of Intra-EC imports over Member States' Total Imports, 1960–80

	1960	1965	1968	1970	1971	1972	1973	1974	1975	1976	1977	1978	1979	1980
Belgium – Lux.	47.9	54.5	54.9	58.7	63.2	63.2	70.7	66.1	67.2	67.6	67.5	69.1	67.2	63
France	29.4	38.8	47.5	48.9	50	50	55.4	47.6	48.8	49.6	49.4	51.4	50.3	46
Germany F.R.	29.9	38.1	41.5	45.3	46.9	46.8	52.2	48.1	49.5	48.2	49	50.1	49.3	47
Italy	27.7	31.2	36.2	41.2	42.5	42.5	48.9	42.4	43	43.5	43.1	44.7	44.2	43.8
Netherlands	45.8	53.4	55.4	55.9	54.8	54.8	61	57.4	56.9	55.2	54.8	57.4	56.4	53.2
Denmark							45.8	45.5	45.8	47.2	47.7	49.7	49.3	49
Ireland							71.7	68.3	69.2	69.4	68.1	70.2	75.4	74.6
UK							32.8	30	32.4	32.2	38.5	37.9	40.8	38.4
Total EC	**34.3**	**41.7**	**45.8**	**48.7**	**50.1**	**50.7**	**51.7**	**46.9**	**48.3**	**48.3**	**49.5**	**50.7**	**50.4**	**47.7**

Source: Calculations based on Eurostat Review: Foreign Trade, 1970–9 and Eurostat, External Trade Statistical Yearbook, 1985

Table 17 EC Trends in Trade by Commodity Groups: Exports, 1970–80 (Mill. ECU) (1970–2: EC–6; 1973–80: EC–9)

Commodity/Year	1970		1971		1972		1973		1974		1975		1976		1977		1978		1979		1980	
	M.ECU	%	M.ECU	%	M.ECU	%	M.ECU	%	M.ECU	%	M. ECU	%	M.ECU	%	M.ECU	%	M.ECU	%	M.ECU	%	M.ECU	%
Food, Beverages and Tobacco	8547	9.8	9576	10.1	11556	10.6	19225	11.4	22999	10.1	25808	11	30312	10.5	33961	10.4	37585	10.6	42349	10.3	48421	10.4
Fuel Products	3622	4.1	4249	4.5	4631	4.2	6761	4	12503	5.5	12706	5.4	16076	5.6	18786	5.8	19511	5.5	28918	7	38594	8.3
Raw Materials	3714	4.2	3646	3.9	4242	3.9	7080	4.2	9962	4.4	8454	3.6	10556	3.7	11532	3.5	12041	3.4	14644	3.6	16071	3.5
Chemicals	9136	10.5	9776	10.4	11397	10.4	18046	10.7	29711	13.1	26044	11.1	33352	11.6	37548	11.5	40734	11.5	49719	12.1	54976	11.8
Machinery and Transport Equip.	31402	35.9	34413	36.5	39950	36.5	59665	35.4	74227	32.7	86643	36.8	106456	37	120415	36.9	127442	36.1	141712	34.5	157899	33.9
Other Manufactured Goods	31040	35.5	32721	34.7	37580	34.4	57777	34.3	77713	34.2	75513	32.1	90771	31.6	104161	31.9	116137	32.9	133438	32.5	149441	32.1
Total EC	87461	100	94381	100.1	109356	100	168554	100	227115	100	235168	100	287523	100	326403	100	353450	100	410780	100	465402	100

Source: Eurostat Review: Foreign Trade, 1970–9; Eurostat Review: Foreign Trade, 1971–80; author's calculations

Table 18 EC Trends in Trade by Commodity Groups: Imports, 1970–80 (Mill. ECU) (1970–2: EC–6; 1973–80: EC–9)

Commodity/Year	1970		1971		1972		1973		1974		1975		1976		1977		1978		1979		1980	
	M.ECU	%	M.ECU	%	M.ECU	%	M.ECU	%	M.ECU	%	M. ECU	%	M.ECU	%	M.ECU	%	M.ECU	%	M.ECU	%	M.ECU	%
Food, Beverages and Tobacco	12946	14.8	13807	14.9	16188	15.4	27664	16	30897	12.8	34253	14.4	41362	13.6	47390	14.2	49203	13.8	53124	12.3	57057	11.3
Fuel Products	9505	10.9	11580	12.5	12459	11.9	20275	11.7	49797	20.5	46886	19.8	59654	19.7	61597	18.4	59128	16.6	81273	18.9	113767	22.4
Raw Materials	11479	13.1	10790	11.7	11652	11.1	20194	11.7	27972	11.5	22892	9.7	29341	9.7	30846	9.2	30092	8.5	37236	8.6	40703	8
Chemicals	6467	7.4	6930	7.5	7910	7.5	12797	7.4	20181	8.3	17850	7.5	23839	7.9	26439	7.9	28747	8.1	36848	8.6	40458	8
Machinery and Transport Equip.	19848	22.7	21567	23.3	24306	23.2	38581	22.3	44957	18.5	49718	21	64440	21.3	73742	22.1	83874	23.6	97133	22.5	109883	21.7
Other Manufactured Goods	27113	31.1	27834	30.1	32425	30.9	53352	30.9	68823	28.4	65678	27.7	84388	27.8	94052	28.2	104540	29.4	125352	29.1	145121	28.6
Total EC	87358	100	92508	100	104940	100	172863	100	242627	100	237277	100.1	303024	100	334066	100	355584	100	430966	100	506989	100

Source: Eurostat Review: Foreign Trade, 1970–9; Eurostat Review: Foreign Trade, 1971–80; author's calculations

Table 19 General Government Surplus and Deficit in EC Member States as % of GDP, 1960–80

Year	Belgium	Denmark	France	Germany	Ireland	Italy	Luxembourg	Netherlands	UK
1960	–2.9	2.6	0.9	3.1	–1.3	–0.8	3	0.8	–1
1961	–1.3	–0.7	1	2.9	–2.1	–0.7	4.5	0.1	–0.7
1962	–1.2	–0.4	–0.1	1.5	–2.6	–0.9	2.2	–0.6	0
1963	–2	1.3	–0.1	1	–2.6	–1	2.5	–1.3	–2.8
1964	–0.6	0.9	0.7	0.7	–3.2	–0.7	2.1	–1.5	–1.1
1965	–1.4	1.5	0.7	–0.6	–3.3	–3.6	2.8	–0.8	–2
1966	–0.8	1.6	0.6	–0.2	–1.8	–3.6	1.3	–0.9	0
1967	–1.2	–0.6	0	–1.4	–2.2	–2	–0.7	–1.3	–1
1968	–2.2	–0.1	–0.8	–0.8	–2.3	–2.6	–2.4	–0.9	–0.8
1969	–1.6	0.3	0.9	1.1	–3.1	–2.9	0.6	–0.5	–0.7
1970	–1.1	3	0.9	0.3	–4	–2.8	2.9	–0.8	2.6
1971	–2.1	3.6	0.7	–0.2	–3.8	–4.6	2.4	–0.5	1.2
1972	–3.3	4.6	0.8	–0.5	–3.5	–6.5	2.2	0	–1.9
1973	–2.7	5.9	0.9	1.2	–4.1	–5.8	3.5	1.1	–3.4
1974	–1.8	1.8	0.6	–1.4	–7.5	–5.4	5.1	–0.1	–4.1
1975	–4.1	–2	–2.2	–5.8	–11.6	–13.3	1.2	–2.7	–5
1976	–4.8	–0.8	–0.5	–3.6	–8.1	–9	1.6	–2.4	–5
1977	–4.9	–1.7	–1.3	–2.6	–7.6	–9	2.1	–1.5	–3.4
1978	–5.5	–2.2	–2.3	–2.8	–10.4	–10.5	3.3	–2.1	–4
1979	–6.9	–3.1	–0.8	–3	–11.9	–9.4	0.1	–2	–3.3
1980	–9.4	–5.9	0	–3.5	–12.8	–8.4	–1.8	–3.4	–3.5

Source: Commission of the European Communities. European Economy, Number 14, Nov. 1982: Statistical Annex, Table 46

Table 20 Industrial Production in Major Industrial Countries, 1960–80 (1967 = 100)

Year	United States	Canada	Japan	European Community	France	West Germany	Italy	United Kingdom
1960	66.2	63.1	43	74.7	70	78.4	59.2	83.9
1961	66.7	65.6	51.2	78.1	73	82.8	65.5	84.2
1962	72.2	71.2	55.4	81.3	78	86.1	71.9	85
1963	76.5	75.7	61.7	84.8	86	88.9	78.4	87.8
1964	81.7	82.6	71.4	91	90	96.6	79.2	95
1965	89.8	89.7	74.2	94.7	93	102.1	82.8	97.8
1966	97.8	96.2	83.8	98.4	98	103	93.3	99.3
1967	100	100	100	100	100	100	100	100
1968	106.3	106.4	115.2	107.4	104	109.2	106.4	107.6
1969	111.1	113.7	133.4	117.6	114	123.2	110.5	111.3
1970	107.8	115.3	151.8	123.3	120	131.1	117.6	111.8
1971	109.6	121.5	155.7	126.1	128	133.6	117.5	111.2
1972	119.7	130.7	167	131.7	135	138.7	122.7	113.2
1973	129.8	144.6	190.5	141.4	145	147.7	134.6	123.3
1974	129.3	149.2	183.1	142.3	148	145.1	140.6	120.8
1975	117.8	140.3	163.9	132.8	139	137.1	127.6	114.4
1976	130.5	148.5	182	142.6	149	149.1	143.5	118.1
1977	138.2	152.7	189.7	145.9	152	152	145.1	124.2
1978	146.1	157.8	201.1	149.7	155	154.1	147.9	127.8
1979	152.5	167.6	215.3	156.8	163	155.7	157.6	132.8
1980	147	165.1	225.2	155.8	161	152.3	166.5	124.1

Source: Economic Report of the President, February 1985: Table B–107

Table 21 Civilian Unemployment Rate in Major Industrial Countries, 1960–80

Year	United States	Canada	Japan	France	West Germany	Italy	United Kingdom
1960	5.5	6.5	1.7	0.7	0.7	7.2	1.6
1961	6.7	6.7	1.5	0.6	0.6	6.6	1.4
1962	5.5	5.5	1.3	0.7	0.7	5.5	1.9
1963	5.7	5.2	1.3	0.7	0.7	5.2	2.3
1964	5.2	4.4	1.2	0.6	0.6	5.2	1.6
1965	4.5	3.6	1.2	0.7	0.6	5.7	1.4
1966	3.8	3.4	1.4	0.7	0.6	5.5	1.4
1967	3.8	3.8	1.3	1	1.8	5	2.2
1968	3.6	4.5	1.2	1.3	1.3	4.7	2.3
1969	3.5	4.4	1.1	1.1	0.7	4.4	2.3
1970	4.9	5.7	1.2	1.3	0.6	4.4	2.5
1971	5.9	6.2	1.3	1.6	0.7	5.1	3.2
1972	5.6	6.2	1.4	1.8	0.9	5.2	3.5
1973	4.9	5.5	1.3	1.8	1	4.9	2.5
1974	5.6	5.3	1.4	2.3	2.2	4.8	2.4
1975	8.5	6.9	1.9	3.9	4.2	5.3	3.8
1976	7.7	7.1	2	4.3	4.1	5.6	5.3
1977	7.1	8.1	2	4.8	4	6.4	5.7
1978	6.1	8.3	2.3	5.2	3.9	7.1	5.7
1979	5.8	7.4	2.1	6	3.4	7.5	5.3
1980	7.1	7.5	2	6.4	3.4	8	6.9

Source: Economic Report of the President, February 1985: Table B–108; Commission of the European Community. European Economy – number 14, November 1982: Table 3

Table 22 Percent Annual Growth Rate in Consumer Prices in Major Industrial Countries

Year	United States	Canada	Japan	France	Germany	Italy	United Kingdom
1961–73	3.2	3.3	6.1	4.5	3.4	4.7	5.1
1973	6.2	7.5	11.8	7.3	6.9	10.7	9.1
1974	11	10.9	24.4	13.7	7	19.2	16
1975	9.1	10.8	11.8	11.8	6	17	24.2
1976	5.8	7.5	9.3	9.6	4.4	16.8	16.6
1977	6.5	8	8	9.4	3.7	17	15.8
1978	7.7	8.9	3.8	9	2.7	12.1	8.3
1979	11.3	9.1	3.6	10.8	4.2	14.8	13.4
1980	13.5	10.2	8	13.5	5.3	21.2	18

Source: Calculations based on Economic Report of the President, February 1985: Table B–107

Table 23 Percent Annual Growth Rate in Wholesale Prices (Manufactures) in Major Industrial Countries

Year	United States	Canada	Japan	France	Germany	Italy	United Kingdom
1960–73	2.7	2.7	2.1	3.8	2	3.8	4.2
1973	13.1	11.2	15.8	14.7	6.6	17.2	7.4
1974	18.8	19.1	31.4	29.1	13.4	40.8	22.6
1975	9.3	11.2	3	-5.7	4.7	8.5	22.2
1976	4.6	5.6	4.4	7.4	3.5	22.7	17.3
1977	6.2	8.7	1.7	5.6	2.7	16.4	19.8
1978	7.4	10	-1.6	4.3	1	8.1	9.1
1979	12.5	14.4	7.2	13.1	4.8	15.5	12.2
1980	14	13.4	17.7	8.8	7.5	20	16.2

Source: Twenty-Fifth Annual Report of the President of the United States on the Trade Agreements Program 1980–1: Table 27

Table 24 Percent Annual Growth Rate in Export Prices in Major Industrial Countries (Unit values in US$)

Year	United States	Canada	Japan	France	Germany	Italy	United Kingdom
1960–73	3.3	2.8	2.5	4	5.5	2.8	3.3
1973	16.7	13.2	20.2	24.7	25	16.9	8.3
1974	27	35.5	27.5	16.7	20	27	20.3
1975	11.9	6.5	-0.1	18.5	14.2	13	15.7
1976	3.6	5.6	-1.3	-2.1	1.6	-5.6	-1.9
1977	4	-1.2	10.2	6.9	9.6	13	14.1
1978	10.2	1.2	22.7	14.4	15.7	11.2	19.7
1979	16.5	17	6.9	15.8	12.4	20.1	22.9
1980	10.4	16.9	7.9	11.5	8.3	17.5	23

Source: Twenty-Fifth Annual Report of the President of the United States on the Trade Agreements Program 1980–1: Table 27

Table 25 Increase in Exports of Selected Products: United States and European Community, 1955–1980

	UNITED STATES					EUROPEAN ECONOMIC COMMUNITY				
	1955–60	1960–5	1965–70	1970–5	1975–80	1955–60	1960–5	1965–70	1970–5	1975–80
	1955 = 100	1960 = 100	1965 = 100	1970 = 100	1975 = 100	1955 = 100	1960 = 100	1965 = 100	1970 = 100	1975 = 100
Group 1										
Aircraft	169.2	88.7	144.8	230.5	208.5	820.2	264.5	192.8	382	311.8
Instruments	218.2	228	180.9	220.6	184.3	156.7	186.9	200.9	251.6	214.3
Agricultural machinery	433.1	119.5	99	335.1	148.5	377.4	185.9	174.8	306.3	214.3
Office machinery	192.7	226.6	330.7	171.9	317	259.5	222.6	219.1	175.8	218.3
Electrical machinery	138.5	155.2	182.6	256.2	222.8	188.2	194.7	194.6	182.4	202.4
Chemicals										
Drugs	119.3	94.2	165.1	207.6	232.3	186.5	169	209.4	239	222
Other chemicals	165.4	145.2	159.3	230.2	265	173.4	176.1	138.2	293.4	242.3
All Group 1	169.7	134.8	186.8	232.8	231.1	190.2	185.5	175.8	245.1	225.6
Group 2										
Motor Vehicles	91.9	158.9	180.8	282.3	144.1	253.6	171.6	154.1	247.7	218.3
Non-electrical machinery	121.6	158.8	167.4	90.4	163.7	190.4	174.2	90.8	247.5	184
Rubber products	121.8	105.3	22.6	292.4	142.6	155.8	168.5	192.1	263.4	203.3
Petroleum products	77.6	92	24.7	193.8	225.2	138.7	140	163.6	410.7	275.8
all Group 2	105.6	150	166.8	151.3	235.7	195.2	172.2	125.1	268.5	217.9
Group 3										
Fabricated metals	123.9	145.1	135.6	254.4	187.3	153.7	160.3	103.4	237.8	245.4
Primary metals										
Non-ferrous	248.1	108.3	175.8	144.5	380.2	149.5	172.4	168.4	161.1	339.6
Ferrous	98.3	94.9	202.7	194.7	127.1	180.6	119	177	274	157.8
Stone, clay and glass	102.1	138.9	182.5	199.9	242.9	155.8	153	157.7	230.6	318.8
Printing and publishing	149.6	160.8	162.5	169	198.6	183.6	190.1	182.6	306.1	210.4
Tobacco	155.7	126.1	135.4	186.7	191.4	211.9	279.8	123	223.8	213.1
Food and drink	137	98	111.8	351.1	177.3	140.8	188.7	176.5	281.7	207.8
Textiles and clothing	109.2	118.6	53.7	550.3	237.1	128	160.9	159.8	242.5	201.3
Lumber and wood products	117.3	132.1	229.3	209.5	58.4	193.7	174.8	187.8	227.2	365.2
Paper	129.2	152.6	160.8	232.4	196.1	162.2	181.2	80.3	259.1	234.4
All Group 3	126.2	118.5	131.1	275	188	153.9	134.9	158.1	253.1	215.6

Source: Calculations based on United Nations, Commodity Trade Statistics, various issues

Figure 1 US$ Cents per Unit of Foreign Currency, 1967–84 (Index: March 1973 = 100)

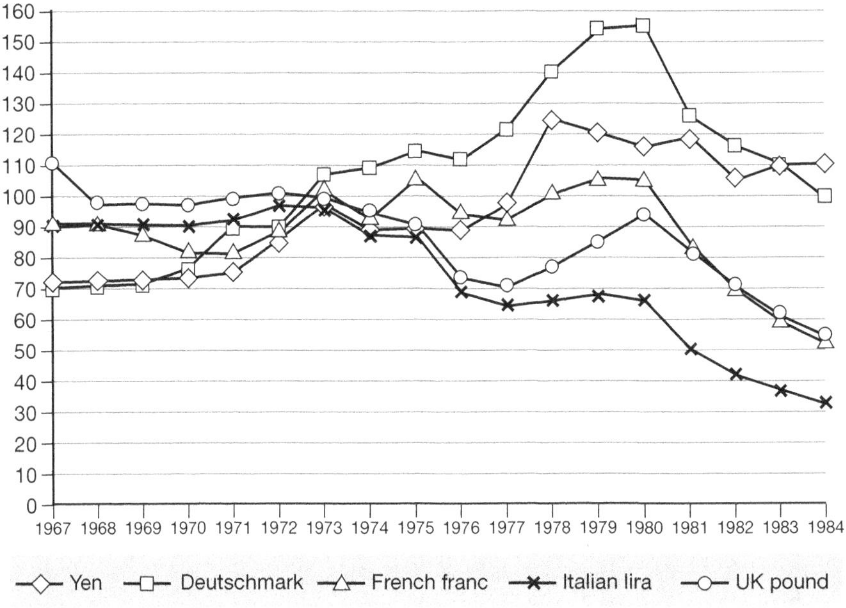

Source: Calculations based on Economic Report of the President, February 1985: Table B–104

Figure 2 Multilateral trade-weighted value of the US dollar, 1967–84 (Index: March 1973 = 100)

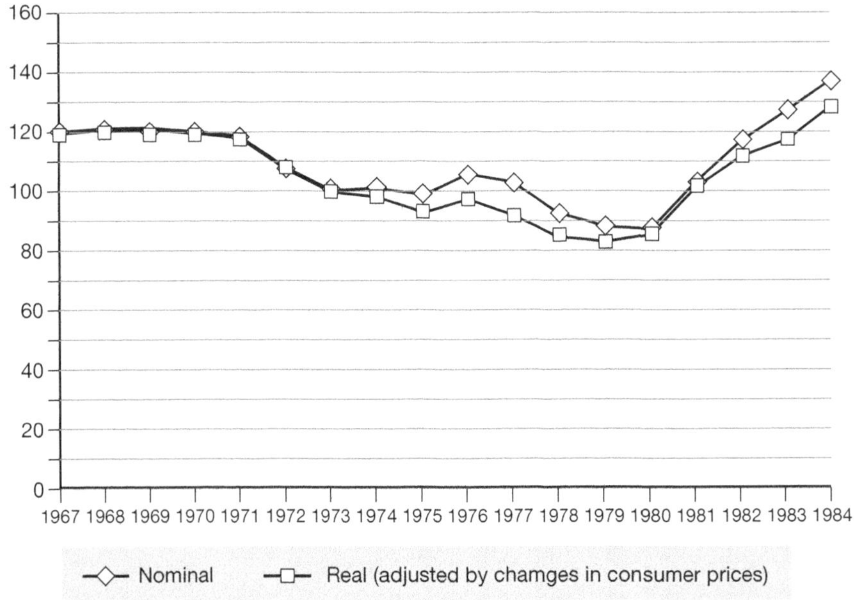

Source: Economic Report of the President, February 1985: Table B–104

Figure 3 Unit Labour Costs in Manufacturing, 1960–80 (national currency basis and US dollar basis) Index: 1970 = 100

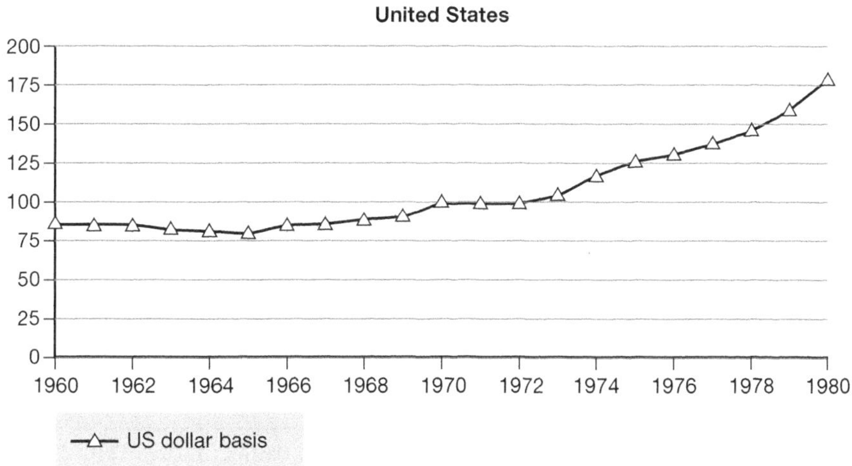

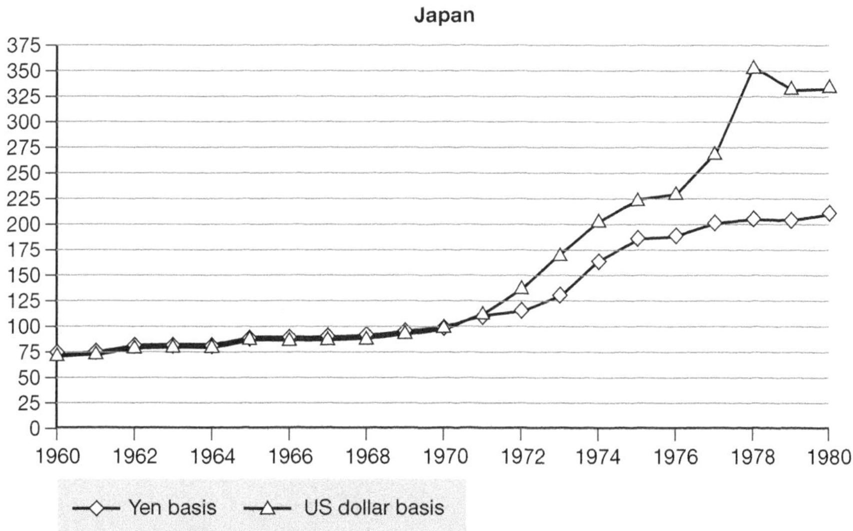

Figure 3 Unit Labour Costs in Manufacturing, 1960–80 (national currency basis and US dollar basis) Index: 1970 = 100

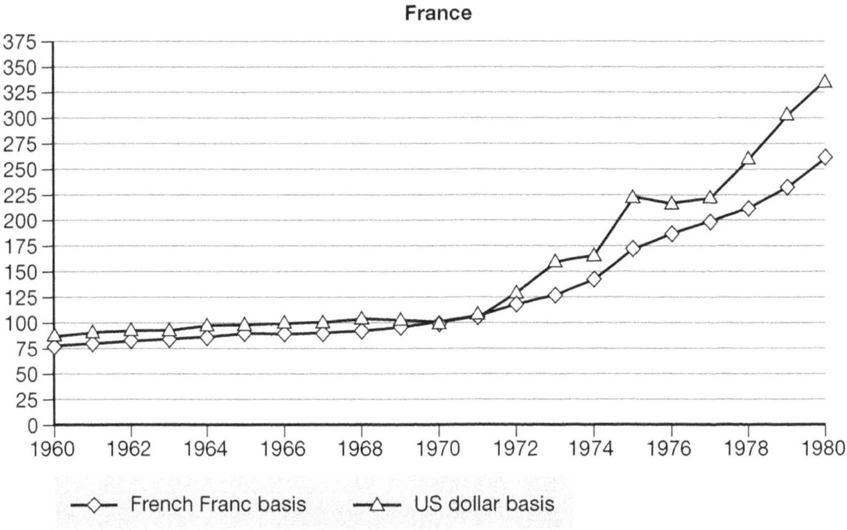

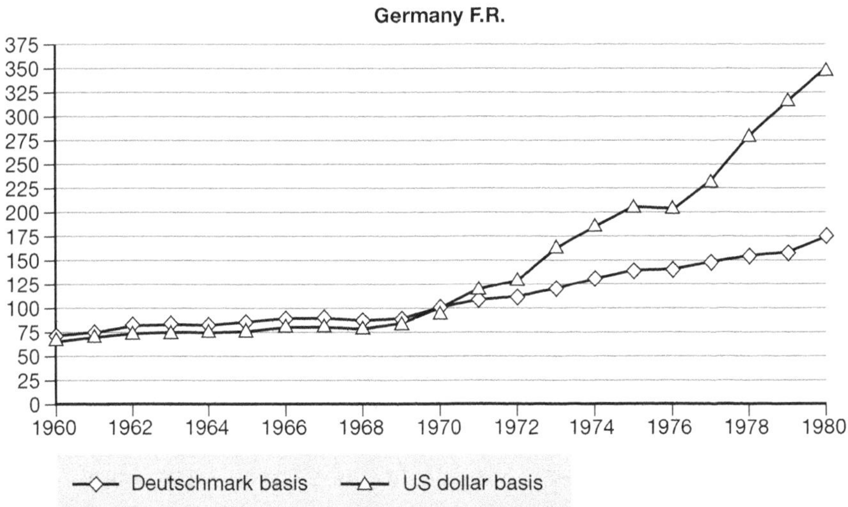

Figure 3 Unit Labour Costs in Manufacturing, 1960–80 (national currency basis and US dollar basis) Index: 1970 = 100

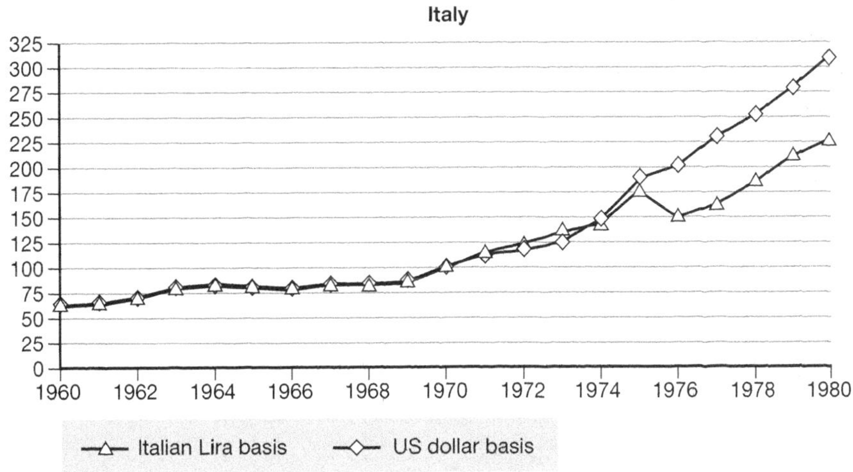

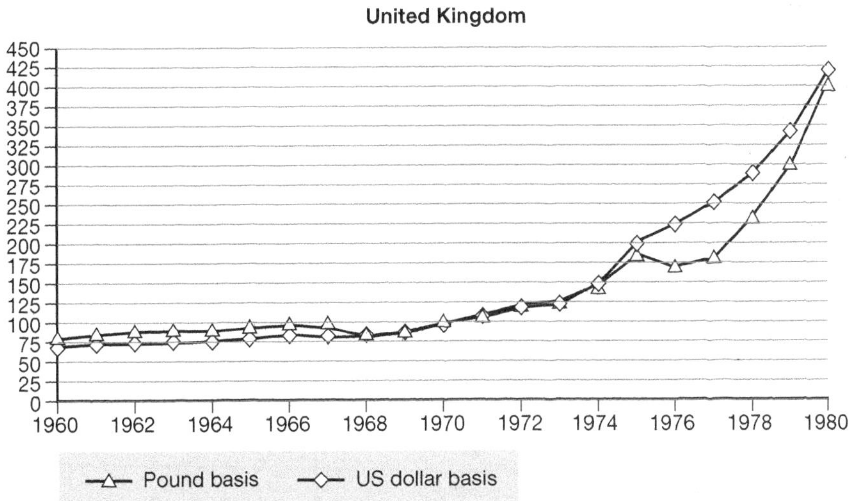

Source: US Department of Labor. Bureau of Labor Statistic. International Labor Comparisons. Supplementary Tables 1950–2003. Table 9.1 and Table 10.1

Figure 4 US Farm Trade and Income, 1965–80 (US$ Bill.)

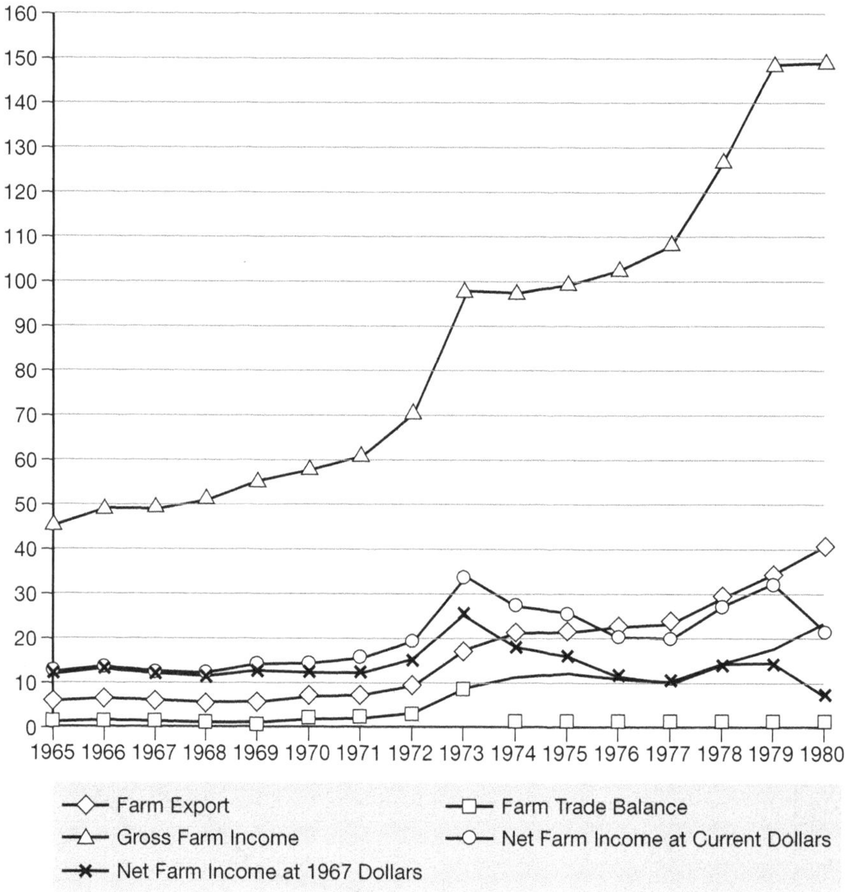

Source: ers.usda.gov.DATA/FATUS: value of US agricultural trade by calendar year; Economic Report of the President, February 1985: Table B-92

Figure 5 Degree of Farm Product Self-Sufficiency in the EC, 1973–79

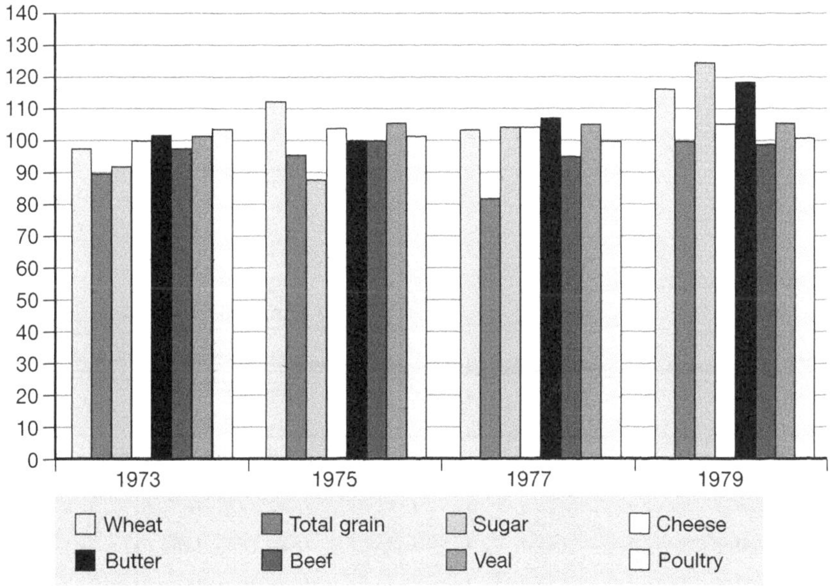

Source: EUROSTAT Basic Statistics of the Community: Agriculture, Forest, Fishery. Various Issues

Figure 6 Main Exporters of Farm Products, 1971–79 (US$ Mill.)

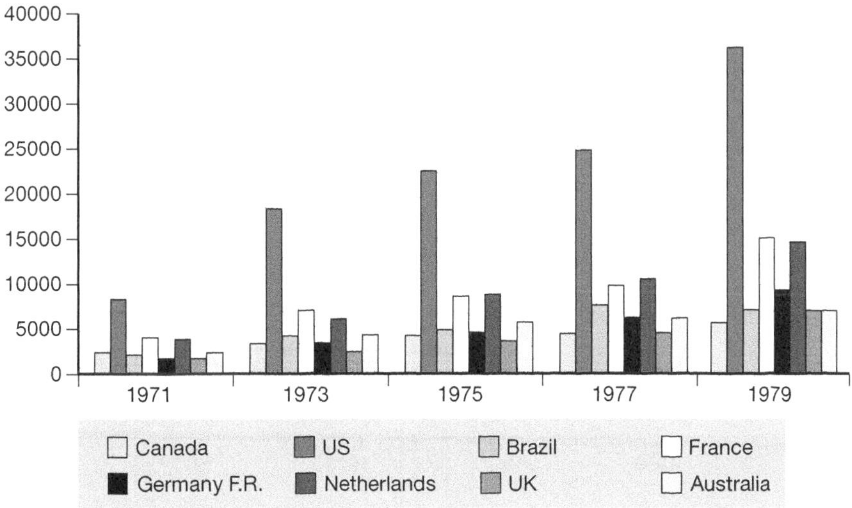

Source: FAO Trade Yearbook Vol. 30, 1976: Table 5; FAO Trade Yearbook Vol. 35, 1981: Table 6

Figure 7 World Export Share of the Main Exporting Countries, 1965–80

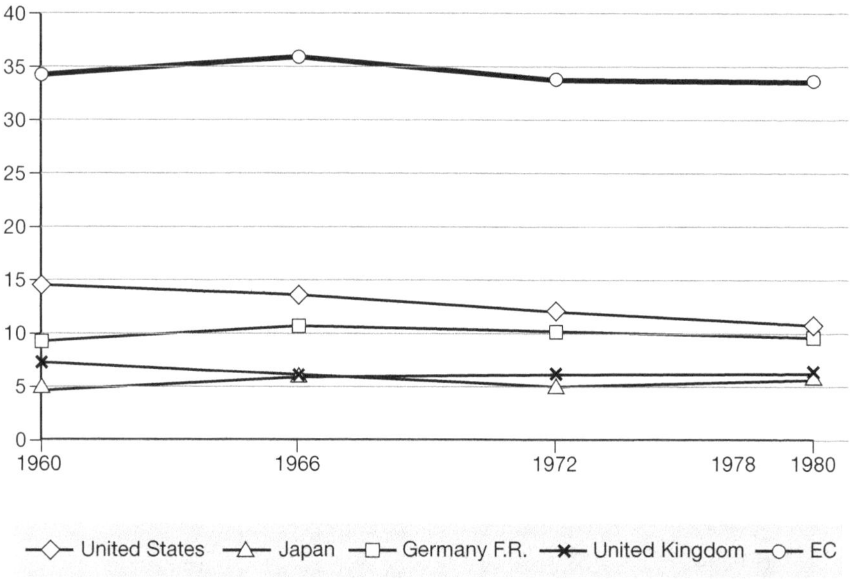

Source: Calculations based on theTwenty-Fifth Annual Report of the President of the United States on the Trade Agreements Program 1980–1: Table 27

Figure 8 World Manufactures Export Share of the Main Exporting Countries 1965–80

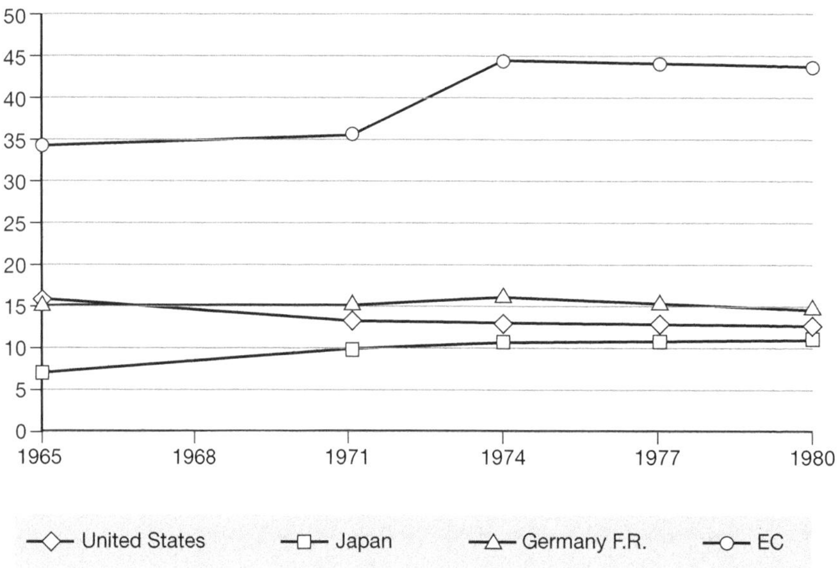

Source: Calculations based on US Department of Commerce Time Series Trade by Commodities; WTO Time Series Merchandise Trade by Commodities 1980

Notes

Introduction

1 Gianni Toniolo, 'Europe's golden age, 1950–1973: speculations from a long-run perspective', *Economic History Review*, 51 (1998), 252–66.
2 International Trade Agreement on Tariffs and Trade. International Trade 1972, p. 1; International Trade Agreement on Tariffs and Trade. International Trade 1980, Table 1.
3 Ibid.
4 Gilbert R. Winham, *International Trade and the Tokyo Round Negotiation* (Princeton: Princeton University Press, 1986).
5 William H. Branson et al., 'Trends in United States International Trade and Investment since World War II', in Martin Feldstein (ed.) *The American Economy in Transition* (Chicago and London: University of Chicago Press, 1980), p. 196, Table 3–13.

Chapter 1

1 U.S. Code Congressional and Administrative News. 93rd Congress Second Session 1974. Legislative History. *Trade Act of 1974*, p. 7189.
2 Harold G. Vatter, *The U.S. Economy in the 1950s. An Economic History* (New York: W. Norton & Company Inc., 1963), pp. 153 et seq.
3 Peter H. Lindert, 'U.S. Foreign Trade and Trade Policy in the Twentieth Century', in Stanley L. Engerman and Robert E. Gallman (eds) *The Cambridge Economic History of the United States, Volume III: The Twentieth Century* (Cambridge: Cambridge University Press, 2000), p. 426.
4 Ibid., p. 429
5 Ibid., p. 434.
6 Harold G. Vatter, *The US Economy*, p. 179, Table 6–4.
7 Angus Maddison, *The World Economy: A Long-Run Comparative View* (Oxford and New York: Oxford University Press, 1991), Appendix C, Table C–11.
8 Economic Report of the President (hereinafter E.R.P). Transmitted to the Congress January 1977, pp. 45 et seq.

9 William H. Branson et al., 'Trends in United States International Trade and Investment since World War II', in Martin Feldstein (ed) *The American Economy in Transition* (Chicago and London: University of Chicago Press, 1980), p. 196, Table 3–13.

10 John Llewellyn et al., 'Competitiveness and the Current Account', in Andrea Boltho (ed.) *The European Economy: Growth and Crisis* (Oxford: Oxford University Press, 1982), p. 144.

11 Antony S. Campagna, *U.S. National Economic Policy, 1917–1985* (New York and London: Praeger, 1987), p. 318.

12 Eric Owen Smith, *The German Economy* (London and New York: Routledge, 1994), p. 503; Hans-Joachim Braun. *The German Economy in the Twentieth Century. The German Reich and the Federal Republic* (London and New York: Routledge, 1990), p. 238.

13 Klaus Hinrich Hennings 'West Germany', in Andrea Boltho (ed.) *The European*, p. 487.

14 Ibid., p. 489.

15 Christian Sautter, 'France', in Andrea Boltho (ed.)*The European*, p. 461.

16 Guido Rey, 'Italy', in Andrea Boltho (ed.) *The European*, p. 520.

17 See Alec Cairncross, *The British Economy since 1945: Economic Policy and Performance,1945–55,* 2nd edn. (Oxford: Blackwell Publishers, 1995), Chap. IV; also J. Foreman-Peck, 'Trade and the Balance of Payments', in N. F. R. Grafts and W. C. Woodward (eds) *The British Economy since 1945* (Oxford: Clarendon Press, 1991), p. 168.

18 Jacob Viner, *The Customs Union Issue* (London: Stevens & Sons Limited, 1950), Chap. IV.

19 See Catherine R. Schenk, 'Foreign Trade and Payments in Western Europe', in Max-Stephan Schulze (ed.), *Western Europe Economic and Social Change since 1945* (London and New York: Longman, 1999), p. 111.

20 A. D. Morgan, 'Commercial Policy', in F. T. Blackaby (ed.) *British Economic Policy 1960–74* (Cambridge: Cambridge University Press, 1978), p. 555, Table 12.2.

21 Ernest Mandel, *Europe versus America?: Contradiction of Imperialism* (London: N.L.B., 1970), p. 63.

22 C. Fred Bergsten, *Toward a New International Economic Order. Selected Papers of C. Fred Bergsten 1972–1974* (Toronto: Lexington Books, 1975), p. 193.

23 Benyamin Bardan, 'The Cotton Textile Agreement 1962–1972', *Journal of World Trade Law*, 7 (1973), 9.

24 Ibid., 17.

25 The official name of the Arrangement was 'the Arrangement Regarding International Trade in Textiles'.

26 Hans-Helmut Taake et al., 'The World Textile Arrangement. The Exporter's

Viewpoint', *Journal of World Trade Law*, 8 (1974), 626 et seq.; Joseph Pelzman, 'The Multifiber Arrangement and Its Effect on the Profit Performance of the U.S. Textile Industry', in Robert Baldwin and Anne O. Krueger (eds) *The Structure and Evolution of Recent U.S. Trade Policy* (Chicago and London: University of Chicago Press, 1984), p. 114.

27 Luc Fauvel, 'The Common Agricultural Policy of the European Economic Community and North American Exports', in Charles P. Kindleberger and Andrew Shonfield (eds) *North American and Western European Economic Policies. Proceedings of a Conference Held by the International Economic Association* (London: MacMillan and Co. Ltd, 1971), p. 303.

28 Michael Tracy, *Agriculture in Western Europe: Challenge and Response 1880–1980* (London: Granada, 1982) p. 279.

29 Willard W. Cochrane, *The Development of American Agriculture. A Historical Analysis* (Minneapolis: University of Minnesota Press, 1979), p. 147.

30 Public Papers of the Presidents of the United States (hereinafter PPPUS) – John F. Kennedy, 1962. *Special Message to the Congress on Foreign Trade Policy*, 25 January 1962.

31 Ernest H. Preeg, *Traders and Diplomats. An Analysis of the Kennedy Round of Negotiations under the General Agreement on Tariffs and Trade* (Washington, DC: The Brooking Institute, 1970), p. 251.

32 Raymond Vernon, *Sovereignty at Bay: The Multinational Spread of U.S. Enterprises* (London: Longman Group LtD, 1971), pp. 65–7.

33 Charles P. Kindleberger, *American Business Abroad: Six Lectures on Direct Investment* (New Haven: Yale University Press, 1969), Lecture 1.

34 Frederick T. Knickerbocker, *Oligopolistic Reaction and Multinational Enterprises* (Boston: Harvard University Graduate School of Business Administration, 1973).

35 Peter Buckley et al., *The Future of the Multinational Enterprise* (London: MacMillan & Co Ltd, 1976).

36 John Dunning, *International Production and the Multinational Enterprise* (London: George Allen Unwin, 1981), Chapter 2.

37 Richard N. Cooper, *The Economic of Interdependence. Economic Policy in the Atlantic Community* (London: McGraw-Hill, 1968), pp. 89 et seq.

38 Robert Gilpin, *U.S. Power and the Multinational Corporation*, (New York: Basic Books Publishers, 1971), pp. 176 et seq.

39 John H. Dunning, 'United States Foreign Investments and the Technological Gap', in Charles P. Kindlberger and Andrew Shonfield (eds) *North American*, p. 398.

40 Jean-Jacques Servan-Schreiber, *The American Challenge* (London: Hamish-Hamilton, 1968), Chapter I–VI.

41 PPPUS – John F. Kennedy, 1962. *Message to the Congress Presenting the President's First Economic Report*, 22 January 1962.

Chapter 2

1 Ernest H. Preeg, *Traders and Diplomats*, p. 260.
2 Economic and Social Committee of the European Communities. *Avis du Comité économique et sociale sur la 'communication de la Commission au Conseil relative à l'élaboration d'une conception globale en vue des prochaines négociations multilatérales'*, 24 May 1973.
3 Gerard Curzon et al., *After the Kennedy Round: what trade policies now?* (London: Atlantic Trade Studies, 1968), p. 15.
4 General Agreement on Tariffs and Trade (hereinafter GATT). *Contracting Parties - Twenty-Fourth Session. Summary Record of the Nineteenth Meeting, Held on Friday 24 November 1967.* SR. 24/19, 12 December 1967.
5 T. H. Farrer, Bart, *Free Trade versus Fair Trade*, 2nd edn. (London: Cassell & Company Limited, 1885), p. 6.
6 PPPUS - Richard Nixon, 1969. *Special Message to the Congress on United States Trade Policy*, 18 November 1969.
7 PPPUS - Richard Nixon, 1970. *The President News Conference of July 20, 1970.*
8 Fred Bergsten, *Toward a New International Economic Order. Selected Papers of C. Fred Bergsten* (Toronto: Lexington Books, 1985), p. 196.
9 *United States International Economic Policy in an Interdependent World. Report to the President by the Commission on International Trade and Investment Policy (Williams Commission), July 1971* (Washington, DC: GPO, 1971).
10 Bulletin of the EC (hereinafter Bull. EC), January 1971, *Community - United States - Japan: Trade Policy - Problems and Outlooks. Address by Professor Dahrendorf, member of the Commission to the European Parliament, 19 January 1971.*
11 See Michael Bordo, 'The Bretton Woods International Monetary System: A Historical Overview', in Michael D. Bordo and Barry Eichengreen (eds) *A Retrospective on the Bretton Woods System. Lesson for International Monetary Reform* (Chicago and London: The University of Chicago Press, 1993), pp. 74 et seq.
12 In particular, Brian Tew, The *Evolution of the International Monetary System 1945-77*, 2nd edn. (London: Hutchinson, 1986), Chapter 9.
13 Ibid.
14 Samuel Rosemberg, *American Economic Development since 1945: Growth, Decline and Rejuvenation* (Houndmills: Palgrave MacMillan, 2003), p. 170.
15 Charles A. Coombs, *The Arena of International Finance* (New York: John Wiley & Sons, 1976), p. 189.
16 PPPUS - Richard Nixon, 1971. *Address to the Nation Outlining a New Economic Policy: The Challenge of Peace*, 15 August 1971.
17 Robert E. Hudec, *Enforcing International Trade Law. The Evolution of the Modern GATT Legal System* (Salem, NH: Butterworth Legal Publishers, 1993), p. 60.

18 ERP transmitted to the Congress January 1972, p. 67.
19 PPPUS - Richard Nixon, 1971. *Address to the Nation.*
20 Charles A. Coombs, *The Arena*, p. 196.
21 Henry Kissinger, *White House Years* (Boston: Little Brown and Company, 1979), p. 961.
22 Ibid.
23 West Germany 13.6 per cent, Japan 16.8 per cent, Belgium and the Netherlands 11.6 per cent, France and the UK 8.6 per cent, Italy and Sweden 7.5 per cent, while Canada went on floating.
24 *Telegram from Secretary of the Treasury Connally to the White House, Rome November 30, 1971.* Foreign Relations of the United States, 1969–1976. Vol. 3, Foreign Economic policy, 1969–1972; International Monetary Policy, p. 580.
25 See Bull. EC, 1971, *Preparation of trade negotiations between the Community and the United States.*
26 See Federico Caffè, *Lezioni di Politica Economica* (Torino: Boringhieri, 1981), p. 332.
27 Brian Tew, The *Evolution*, p. 160.
28 John Williamson, *The Failure of the World Monetary Reform* (Sunbury on Thames: Thomas Nelson and Son Ltd, 1977), p. 61.
29 Ibid., p. 84.
30 JHB. Tew, 'Policies aimed at improving the Balance of Payments', in F. T. Blachaby (ed.) *British Economic Policy*, p. 315.
31 John Llewellyn et al., 'Competitiveness', in Andrea Boltho (ed.) *The European* p. 145.
32 U.S. Code Congressional and Administrative News. 93rd Congress – First Session 1973. Legislative History. *Agriculture and Consumer Protection Act of 1973 (P.L. 93–86). Statement of the Honorable Earl L. Butz, Secretary of Agriculture*, p. 1801.
33 François Duchêne et al., *New Limits on European Agriculture. Politics and the New Agricultural Policy* (London: Croom Helm Ltd, 1985), p. 61.
34 See J. C. Nagle, *Agricultural Trade Policies* (Westhead: Saxon House, 1976), p. 53.
35 Timothy Josling, 'World Food Production, Consumption and International trade. Implications for U.S. Agriculture', in D. Gale Johnson (ed.) *Food and Agricultural Policy for the 1980s* (Washington, DC and London: American Enterprise Institute for Public Policy Research, 1981). pp. 87 et seq.
36 Michael Hudson, *Global Fracture. The New International Economic Order* (New York: Harper and Row Publishers, 1977), p. 71.
37 US Code Congressional and Administrative News. *Agriculture and Consumer*, pp. 1750–1800.
38 D. Gale Johnson, *World Agriculture in Disarray* (London: Fontana The Trade Policy Research Centre, 1973), p. 40.
39 US Code Congressional and Administrative News. *Agriculture and Consumer*, p. 1806.

40 ERP transmitted to Congress February 1974, p. 133.
41 The likelihood of such a reaction and its impact on the international trade was clearly anticipated by some top-rank members of the Nixon administration. See *Memorandum for the President's Deputy Assistant or National Security Affairs (Snowcroft) to Secretary of the Treasury Shulz.* Foreign Relations of the United States, 1969–76. Vol. 31, Trade Policy, 1973–76, p. 649.
42 Supplement 6/71 Annex to Bull. EC 9/10 – 1971. *Consequence for the Community of the present situation in the monetary and commercial field*, 15 September 1971.
43 General Agreements on Tariffs and Trade, Basic Instruments and Selected Documents (hereinafter BISD) 18th Suppl., *Report of the Working Party on the United States Temporary Import Surcharge* (L3573).
44 Bull. EC 2–1972, *Commission Memorandum to the Council on the results of the commercial negotiations with the United States.*
45 GATT. *Joint EC–United States Declaration – 11 February 1972.* L/3670, 11 February 1972.
46 Ibid.
47 GATT. *Joint Japan–United States Statement on International Economic Relations – 8 February 1972.* L/3669, 10 February 1972.
48 GATT. *Council 7 March 1972. Minutes of the Meeting.* C/M/76, 22 March 1972.
49 PPPUS. – Richard Nixon, 1973. *Special Message to the Congress Proposing Trade Reform Legislation*, 10 April 1973.
50 'House Passes Trade Act; USSR Denied Tariff Concessions', *1973 Congressional Quarterly Almanac*, pp. 833 et seq.
51 Commission of the European Communities. *Development of an overall approach to trade in view of the coming multilateral negotiations in GATT. Memorandum from the Commission to the Council, forwarded on 9 April and amended on 22 May 1973.* COM (73) 556; COM (73) 556/2.
52 Economic and Social Committee of the European Communities, Brussels 21 March 1973. *Exposé de M. Wallenstein, représentant de la Commission.*
53 GATT. *Multilateral Trade Negotiations. Statement by the European Economic Community.* L/3879, 4 July 1973.
54 Council of the European Communities. *Note de Transmission. Projet de rapport du Comité de préparation des négociations commerciales du GATT.* Brussels, 10 August 1973.
55 Ibid.; *Briefing Paper.* Foreign Relations of the United States, 1969–76. Vol. 31, Trade Policy, 1973–6, p. 681.
56 Economic and Social Committee of the European Communities. *Annexe au Procès Verbal de la 6ème réunion – Exposé de M. Phan Van Phi, 6 novembre 1973.*
57 GATT. *Ministerial Meeting – Tokyo. Declaration of Ministers approved at Tokyo on 14 September 1973.* Min (73)1, 14 September 1973.

58 Economic and Social Committee of the European Communities. *Annexe au Procès* Verbal de la 6ème *réunion.*

Chapter 3

1 ERP transmitted to Congress February 1975, Chapter 4.
2 Ibid.
3 See in particular Frank R. Wyant, *The United States, OPEC and Multinational Oil* (Lexington: Lexington Books, 1977), p. 130.
4 Fiona Venn, *Oil Diplomacy in the Twentieth Century* (Houndmills: MacMillan Education Limited, 1986), p. 143.
5 Frank R. Wyant, *The United States*, p. 133.
6 See Henry A. Kissinger, *Years of Upheaval* (Boston: Little, Brown and Company, 1982), pp. 905 et seq.
7 Albert L. Danielsen, 'Oil Price Regulations and the United States', *Journal of World Trade Law*, 13 (1979), 383.
8 Twenty-Fourth Annual Report of the President of the United States on the Trade Agreements Program 1979, p. 159, Tables 15 and 16.
9 Ibid.
10 Fiona Venn, *The Oil Crisis* (London and New York: Longman, 2002) p. 123
11 Ernest Mandel, *The Second Slump: A Marxist Analysis of Recession in the Seventies* (London: N.L.B., 1978), p. 22.
12 Derek H. Aldcroft, *The European Economy 1914–2000*, 4th edn. (London and New York: Routledge, 2002), p. 197.
13 ERP transmitted to Congress, February 1974, p. 49.
14 W. W. Rostow, *Getting from Here to There* (London: The MacMillan Press Ltd, 1979), p. 45.
15 Michel Hau, Histoire Économique de l'Allemagne XIXe–XXe siècles (Paris: ECONOMICA, 1994), p. 190.
16 Simon Bromley, *American Hegemony and World Oil: The Industry, the State System and the World Economy* (Cambridge: Polity Press, 1991), p. 146.
17 A. P. Thirlwall, 'The Balance of Payments Constraint as An Explanation of International Growth Rate Differences', *Banca Nazionale del Lavoro Quarterly Review*, 32 (1979), 45–53.
18 Ibid., p. 46.
19 Alex N. McLeod, 'The Fearsome Dilemma: Simultaneous Inflation and Unemployment', *Banca Nazionale del Lavoro Quarterly Review*, 32 (1979), 378.
20 Anthony S. Campagna, *U.S. National Economic Policy, 1917–1985* (New York and London: Praeger, 1987), p. 400.

21 Herbert Giersch et al., *The Fading Miracle. Four decades of market economy in Germany* (Cambridge: Cambridge University Press, 1982), p. 187.
22 See Carluccio Bianchi, 'The Balance of Payments Constraint and the Growth of the Italian Economy', in Carluccio Bianchi e Carlo Casanova (eds) *The recent Performance of the Italian Economy. Market Outcomes and State Policy* (Milano: Franco Angeli, 1991), pp. 28 et seq.
23 See Pierre Secret, 'L'Activité Économique Française en 1974', Révue d'Économie Politique, 85 (1975), 1037 et seq.
24 Jean-François Eck, *Histoire de l'économie française depuis 1945* (Paris: Armand Colin Éditeur, 1990), p. 45.
25 Eighteen Annual Report of the President of the United States on the Trade Agreements Program–1973, Appendix A, p. 42; Twenty First Annual Report of the President of the United States on the Trade Agreements Program - 1976, Appendix A, Table 2.
26 I. M. Destler, *Making Foreign Economic Policy* (Washington, DC: The Brooking Institution, 1980), p. 193.
27 Gilbert Winham, *International Trade and the Tokyo Round*, p. 133.
28 See I. M. Destler, *American Trade Politics* (Washington, DC: Institute of International Economics; New York: Twentieth Century Fund, 1995), pp. 142–5.
29 US Code Congressional and Administrative News. 93rd Congress-Second Session, 1974. Legislative History. *Trade Act of 1974 (P.L. 93–618). Senate Report n. 93–1298*, p. 7197.
30 Ibid., p. 7228.
31 Ibid., p. 7227.
32 The International Trade Commission (formerly Tariff Commission) is the US agency especially charged with establishing the impact of imports on the domestic industry.
33 U.S. Code Congressional and Administrative News. *Trade Act*, pp. 7306 et seq.
34 Hans Mueller et al., 'Perils in the in the Brussels–Washington Steel Pact of 1982', *The World Economy*, 5 (1982), p. 263.
35 US Code Congressional and Administrative News. *Trade Act*, pp. 7318 et seq.
36 Council of the European Communities. *Directives for the GATT multilateral trade negotiations (final version)*. Brussels, 24 April 1975, I/40/1/75 (Cos 4) rev. 1.
37 Gilbert Winham, *International Trade and the Tokyo Round*, p. 101.
38 The Grand Father Clause was a GATT provision that allowed the parties to the General Agreement not to implement some of its articles if they addressed issues already regulated in a different manner by their domestic rules.
39 Saul L. Sherman, 'Reflections on the New Customs Valuation Code', *Law and Policy in International Business*, 12 (1980), 121.
40 GATT. *United States Statement at Meeting of Group 3 (e), 2 April 1974.* MTN 3E/W/12, 2 April 1974.
41 Commission of the European Communities, EC Directorate General For External

Relations. Brussels 3 January 1974. *Note for Information: Meeting of Special Committee (Article 113) on Friday 21 December 1973.*

42 Twenty-First Annual Report of the President of the United States on the Trade Agreements Program 1977, p. 23.

43 See Chapter 1, p. 13.

44 See Chapter 2, p. 36.

45 BISD 23rd Suppl., *United States Tax legislation (DISC).Report of the Panel presented to the Council of Representatives on 12 November 1976* (L/4422).

46 BISD 23rd Suppl,. *Income Tax Practices Maintained by France* (L/4423); BISD 23rd Suppl., *Income Tax Practices Maintained by Belgium* (L/4424); BISD 23rd Suppl., *Income Tax Practices Maintained by the Netherlands* (L/4425).

47 See Robert E. Hudec, 'Legal Issues in US–EC Trade Policy: GATT Litigation 1960–1985', in Robert E. Baldwin, Carl B. Hamilton, André Sapir (eds) *Issues in US–EC Relations* (Chicago and London: The University of Chicago Press, 1988), p. 29.

48 BISD 27th Suppl.,*Tax Legislation* (L/5271), p. 114.

Chapter 4

1 R. D. Putnam, 'Diplomacy and Domestic Policy: the Logic of Two Level Games', *International Organization*, 43 (1988), 427.

2 Bull. EC 4, 1978, point 1.3.2.

3 Peter H. Lindert, 'U.S. Foreign Trade Policy in the Twentieth Century', p. 444.

4 Bull. EC, Supplement 7/1977, p. 5

5 Ibid, p. 6

6 Bull. EC, Supplement 7/1979, p. 9.

7 Ibid, p. 11.

8 David G. Tarr, 'The Steel Crisis in the United States and the EC: Causes and Adjustments', in Robert Baldwin, Carl B. Hamilton, André Sapir (eds) *Issues in US–EC Relations*, p. 177, Table 7.4.

9 The data on the international position of the US, EC and Japan steel industry are taken from Walter Adams et al., 'The Steel Industry', in Walter Adams (ed.) *The Structure of American Industry*, 6th Edition (New York: MacMillan Publishing Co. Inc., 1982), p. 74. Table 1.

10 Peter H. Lindert, 'U.S. Foreign Trade Policy in the Twentieth Century', pp. 424 et seq.

11 Twenty-Second Annual Report of the President of the United States on the Trade Agreements Program 1977, p. 74.

12 Bull. EC 11, 1977, point 1.3.2.

13 Bull. EC 12, 1977, point 1.1.2.
14 Commission of the European Communities, *État d'Avancement des Travaux Concernant les Objectifs Généraux Acier et la Restructuration de la Sidérurgie Communautaire. Eléments d'Information pour la Préparation du Conseil du 27 Juin 1978*. Com. (78) 290 final, 21 June 1978.
15 Bull. EC 12, 1977, point 2.2.46.
16 Twenty-Third Annual Report of the President of the United States on the Trade Agreements Program 1977, p. 103.
17 Joseph Pelzman, 'The Multifiber Arrangement and Its Effect on the Profit Performance of the U.S. Textile Industry', p. 115.
18 Bull. EC 7/8, 1977, points 1.5.1. et seq.
19 Ibid.
20 Bull. EC, Supplement 11/75, p. 15
21 Ibid, p. 20, Table 9.
22 D. Gale Johnson, 'The Food and Agriculture Act of 1977: Implications for Farmers, Consumers, and Taxpayers', in William Felner (Project Director) *Contemporary Economic Problems, 1978* (Washington, DC: American Enterprise Institute for Public Policy Research, 1988), p. 206.
23 François Houillier, 'L'Agriculture et son Évolution depuis 1960 (La Situation en 1977)', *Revue d'Économie Politique*, 88 (1978), pp. 894 et seq.
24 See Takashi Shirahishi, *Japan Trade Policy 1945 to the Present Day* (London and Atlantic Highlands, NJ: The Athlone Press, 1989), pp. 179, 191.
25 David Flath, *The Japanese Economy* (Oxford and New York: Oxford University Press, 200), p. 173.
26 James C. Abegglen et al., 'Facing up to the Trade Gap with Japan', *Foreign Affairs*, 57 (1978–9), 159.
27 Ibid., 157
28 Twenty-Third Annual Report, Appendix H.
29 Bull. EC 3–1978, points 1.1.4–1.1.9.
30 See John Jackson et al., *Legal Problems of International Economic Relations. Cases Material and Text* (St. Paul, MN: West Group, 1995), Chapter 13.
31 Twenty-Third Annual Report, pp. 68 et seq.
32 See Enzo Grilli, *Italian Commercial Policies in the 1970* (World Bank Staff Working Paper, n. 428, October 1980), p. 28, Table IV.1.
33 Ibid.
34 See Chapter 3, p. 76.
35 J. M. Finger et al., 'The Political Economy of Administered Protection', *The American Economic Review*', 72 (1982), p. 455.
36 Takatoshi Ito, *The Japanese Economy* (Cambridge, MA: The MIT Press, 1992), p. 236.

37 Ivo Van Bael, 'Ten Years of EEC Anti-Dumping Enforcement', *Journal of World Trade* Law, 13 (1979), 408.

38 Twenty-Second Annual Report, p. 30.

39 Data provided by Joseph M. Grieco, *Cooperation among Nations. Europe, America, and Non-Tariff Barriers to Trade* (Ithaca and London: Cornell University Press), p. 178, Table 7.5.

40 Ibid.

41 Herbert Giersch et al., *The Fading Miracle. Four decades of market economy in Germany* (Cambridge: Cambridge University Press, 1992) p. 217; Also Eric Owen Smith, *The West German Economy* (London and Canberra: Croom Helm, 1983) pp. 93 et seq.

42 H. H. Glismann et al., *The Political Economy of Protection in Germany* (World Bank Staff Working Paper n. 427, 1980), p. 22.

43 Bela Balassa, 'The New Protectionism and the International Economy', *Journal of World Trade Law*, 12 (1978), 419.

Chapter 5

1 An in-depth analysis of the results of the Tokyo Round is provided by General Agreement on Tariff and Trade, *The Tokyo Round of Multilateral Trade Negotiations. Report of the Director General of GATT* (Geneva: General Agreement on Tariffs and Trade, April 1979).

2 Victoria Curzon Price, 'Surplus Capacity and What the Tokyo Round Failed to Settle', *The World Economy*, 2 (1979), 306.

3 Bull. EC 11–1979, point 1.3.5.

4 Twenty-Fourth Annual Report of the President of the United States on the Trade Agreements Program 1979, p. 76.

5 Bob Bergland, 'Preface – Agriculture', *Law and Policy in International Business*, 12 (1980), 257.

6 FAO Trade Yearbook Vol. 30, 1976: Table 5; FAO Trade Yearbook Vol. 35, 1981: Table 6.

7 James P. Houck, 'US Agricultural Trade and the Tokyo Round', *Law and Policy in International Business*, 12 (1980), 266, 268

8 GATT. Multilateral Trade Negotiations – Group 'Agriculture'– Meeting of July 1977. *Chairman's Summing up and Record of Decisions*. MTN/AG/7, 28 July 1977.

9 GATT. Multilateral Trade Negotiations – Group 'Agriculture' – *Statement by Australia on 20 July 1977*. MTN/AG/W/27, 22 July 1977.

10 Ibid.

11 Timothy E. Josling et al., *Agriculture in the GATT* (Basingstoke: MacMillan, 1996), p. 90.

12 Ibid.; also Theodore Cohn, 'The 1978–9 negotiations for an international wheat agreement: an opportunity lost?', *International Journal*, 35 (1979–80), 136; Twenty-Third Annual Report of the President of the United States on the Trade Agreements Program 1978, p. 57.

13 Theodore Cohn, 'The 1978–79 Negotiations', 136.

14 GATT. Multilateral Trade Negotiations – Group 'Tariffs' – *Statement made by the United States Delegation at the Group 'Tariffs' Meeting, March 1976*. MTN/TAR/W/15, 23 March 1976.

15 GATT. Multilateral Trade Negotiations – Group 'Tariffs' – *Statement made by the Delegation of the Commission of the European Communities at the Group 'Tariffs' Meeting, March 1976*. MTN/TAR/W/20, 26 March 1976.

16 Ibid., p. 4.

17 GATT. Multilateral Trade Negotiations – Group 'Tariffs'– *Tariff Cutting Formula, Proposal by Switzerland*. MTN/TAR/W/34, 12 October 1976.

18 Saul L. Sherman 'Reflections', 130.

19 GATT. Multilateral Trade Negotiations – Group 'Non-Tariff Measures' – Sub-Group 'Customs Matters' – *Value of Goods for the Purposes of Levying ad Valorem Duties on Customs GATT – MTN – Draft Valuation Code*. MTN/NTM/W/122, 8 November 1977. GATT. Multilateral Trade Negotiations – Group 'Non-Tariff Measures' – Sub-Group 'Customs Matters' – *Statement Made by the Commission of the European Communities at the Meeting of the Sub-Group of 15 November 1977*. MTN/NTM/W/126, 21 November 1977.

20 GATT. Multilateral Trade Negotiations Group 'Non-Tariff Measures' – Sub-Group 'Customs Matters'. *Meeting of November 1977. Summing-up by the Chairman*. MTN/NTM/38, 18 November 1977.

21 Gilbert R. Winham, *International Trade and the Tokyo Round*, p. 189.

22 Ibid.

23 Morton Pomeranz, 'Toward a New International Order in Government Procurement', *Law and Policy in International Business*, 11 (1979), 1278.

24 Ibid., 1277.

25 Ibid.

26 GATT. Multilateral Trade Negotiations – Group 'Non-Tariff Measures '– Subgroup 'Government Procurement'. – *Government Procurement Draft Integrated Text*. MTN/NTM/W/174, 17 July 1978.

27 GATT. Multilateral Trade Negotiations – *Subsidies/Countervailing Duties – Outline of an Approach*. MTN/INF/13, 23 December 1977.

28 Richard R. Rivers et al., 'The Negotiation of a Code on Subsidies and

Countervailing Measures: Bridging Fundamental Policy Differences', *Law and Policy in International Business*, 11 (1979), 1471 et seq.

29 GATT. Multilateral Trade Negotiations - Group 'Non-Tariff Measures' - Subgroup 'Subsidies and Countervailing Duties' - *Subsidies/Countervailing Duties Outline of an Arrangement*. MTN/NTM/W/168, 10 July 1978.

30 GATT. Multilateral Trade Negotiations - Group 'Safeguards' - *Draft Integrated Text on Safeguards*. MTN/SG/W/39, 22 June 1978.

31 GATT. Multilateral Trade Negotiations - *Statement by several delegations on Current Status of Tokyo Round Negotiations* - Geneva 13 July 1978. MTN/INF/33, 14 July 1978.

32 Bull. EC 9–1978, point 2.2.11.

33 Bull. EC 10–1978, point 2.2.10.

34 Commission of the European Communities. *Multilateral Trade Negotiations. Communication from the Commission to the Council*. COM (78) 750 final, 17 December 1978.

35 Commission of the European Communities. *Multilateral Trade Negotiations*. Com (79)99, 23 February 1979.

36 See Chapter 3, p. 74.

37 GATT Activities in 1979 and Conclusion of the Tokyo Round of Multilateral Trade Negotiations (1973–79): Tariffs (Geneva: General Agreement on Tariffs and Trade, 1980).

38 Twenty-Fourth Annual Report, p. 52.

39 Bull. EC 4–1979, point 1.2.7.

40 House of Lords - Select Committee on the European Communities. Session 1979–80, 41st report. Final Report on the GATT Multilateral Trade Negotiations (The Tokyo Round). Minutes of Evidence Taken Before the European Communities Commission, 23 May 1979. Submission by the Department of Trade, p. 12.

41 Bull. EC 11–1979, point 1.3.7.

42 House of Lords - Select Committee, p. x.

43 Twenty-Fourth Annual, p. 42; Bull. EC 4–1979, point. 1.2.6.

44 Hugh Corbet, 'Importance of Being Earnest about Further GATT Negotiations', *The World Economy*, 2 (1979), 324.

45 Twenty-Fourth Annual Report, p. 46.

46 Ibid.

47 For an in-depth analysis of the wine gallon method issue see Gilbert R. Winham, *International Trade and the Tokyo Round*, pp. 280–302.

48 General Agreement on Tariff and Trade, *The Tokyo Round*, p. 129.

49 Bull. EC 4–1979, point 1.2.4.

50 Victoria Curzon Price, 'Surplus Capacity', p. 312.

51 Robert S. Strauss, 'Forward', *Law and Policy in International Business*, 11 (1979), 1258.
52 Joseph M. Grieco, *Cooperation among Nations*, pp. 65, 102.
53 Ibid., p. 177.
54 BISD 31st Suppl., *Panel on Value Added-Tax and Threshold, adopted by the Committee on Government Procurement* (GPR/21).
55 BISD 27th Suppl., *Report of the Committee on Anti-Dumping Practices presented to the Contracting Parties at the Thirty-fifth Session* (L/5052).
56 BISD 31th Suppl., *Report of the Committee on Anti-Dumping Practices. Report (1984) presented to the Contracting Parties at their Fortieth Session* (L/5724).

Chapter 6

1 Michel Pébereau, *La Politique Économique de la France. Les Objectifs* (Paris: Armand Colin, 1988), p. 302, Table VIII.
2 Anthony S. Campagna, *U.S. National Economic Policy*, p. 435.
3 Economic Report of the President Transmitted to the Congress January 1980, p. 54; Federal Reserve Bulletin, 66 (1980), p. 40.
4 PPPUS – Jimmy Carter, 1980. *Remarks and a Question-and-Answer Session with Local Residents.* Lansdowne Pennsylvania, 1 October 1980.
5 Commission of the European Communities, *European Economy, Annual Economic Report, 1980–81* (Luxembourg: Office for Official Publication of the European Communities, 1981), p. 35
6 Ibid., p. 36.
7 Régis Platel, 'L'Environnement International en 1980,' *Révue d'Économie Politique*, 91 (1981), 852.
8 Michel Volle, 'Synthèse de l'Évolution de l'Économie Française en 1980 et 1981,' *Révue d'Économie Politique*, 91 (1981), 813.
9 See C. D'Adda et al., 'The Italian economy in the seventies and eighties,' in Carluccio Bianchi and Carlo Casarosa (eds) *The Recent Performance of the Italian Economy. Market Outcomes and State Policy* (Milano: Franco Angeli, 1991), p. 47.
10 N. W. C. Woodward, 'Inflation,' in N. F. R. Crafts and N. W. C. Woodward (eds) *The British Economy since 1945* (Oxford: Clarendon Press, 1990), pp. 191 et seq.
11 Margaret Thatcher, *The Downing Street Years 1979–1990*, (New York: HarperPerennial, 1995), p. 33.
12 See J. Foremann-Peck, 'Trade and the Balance of Payments,' in N. F. R. Crafts and N. W. C. Woodward (eds) *The British Economy*, p. 148, Fig. 5.5.
13 Twenty-Fifth Annual Report of the President of the United States on the Trade Agreements Program 1980–81, Table 5.1.
14 Ibid., Table 5.2.

15 Ibid., Table 5.4.
16 Bull. EC, 11–1980, point 1.2.1.
17 Gilbert R. Winham, 'Robert Strauss, the MTN, and the Control of Factions,' *Journal of World Trade Law*, 14 (1980), 386.
18 This brief critical outline of the main points of the Trade Agreements Act is based on U.S. Code Congressional and Administrative News. 96th Congress First Session 1979. Legislative History. *Trade Agreements Act of 1979 (P.L. 96–39).*
19 Ibid., p. 418.
20 Ibid., p. 471.
21 Hans Mueller et al., 'Perils in the Brussels–WashingtonSteel Pact of 1982,' *The World Economy*, 5 (1982), 264.
22 'Massive Trade Bill Sails Through Congress' *Congressional Quarterly Almanac*, 1979, p. 287.
23 J. M. Finger et al, 'The Political Economy', 455.
24 Steve Jefferys, *Management and Managed. Fifty Years of Crisis at Chrysler* (Cambridge: Cambridge University Press, 1986), pp. 206 et seq.
25 Lee Iacocca, *An Autobiography* (New York: Bantam Books, 1984), p. 239.
26 Twenty-Fifth Annual Report, Table 4.1.
27 Ibid., p. 50.
28 Ibid.
29 See Peter Dicken, *Global Shift. The Internationalization of Economic Activity.* Second Edition (London: Paul Chapman Publishing Ltd., 1992), p. 275.
30 Ibid., p. 67.
31 See Chapter 4, p. 93.
32 Commission of the European Communities. *Steel. Request for the Council's assent to the establishment of a system of production quotas for the steel industry.* Com(80) 586 Final, 6 October 1980.
33 'Agriculture'. *Congressional Quarterly Almanac*, 1980, p. 270.
34 Mark Newman et al., *A Comparison of Agriculture in the United States and the EC* (Washington, DC: United States Department of Agriculture- Economic Research Service, 1987).
35 Robert L. Paarlberg, 'Lesson of the Grain Embargo,' *Foreign Affairs*, 59 (1980–1), 161.
36 EC Commission, *Reflection on Common Agriculture Policy*. Bull. EC-Supplement 1980.
37 Ibid.
38 Ibid.
39 Barry Eichengreen et al., 'International Competition in the Products of U.S. Basic Industries,' in Martin Feldstein (ed.) *The United States in the World Economy* (Chicago and London: The University of Chicago Press, 1988), p. 284, Table 5.3.

40 Ibid., pp. 321 et seq.

41 Twenty-Fifth Annual Report, p. 71.

42 Twenty-Sixth Annual Report of the President of the United States on the Trade Agreements Program 1981–2, p. 48.

43 Ibid.

44 Robert E. Lipsey et al., 'Changing Patterns of International Investments in the United States', in Martin Feldstein (ed.) *The United States*, pp. 493 et seq.

45 A detailed analysis of the objectives and strategies of both US MNCs and EC MNCs in the automobile and electronics sectors, also with regard to the 1970s, is provided by Peter Dicken, *Global Shift*, Chapter 9 and Chapter 10.

46 Ronald W. Cox et al., *US Politics and the Global Economy. Corporate Power, Conservative Shift* (Boulder and London: Lynne Rienner Publishers, 1999), p. 191.

47 Ibid.

48 See Chapter 4, p. 106.

Bibliography

Main documentary sources

Commission of the European Communities. *General Report on the Activities of the Communities*, Brussels and Luxembourg: Office for Official Publications of the European Communities.

—*Bulletin of the European Communities*. Brussels: Secretariat of the Commission of the European Community.

Council of the European Communities. *Draft Minutes of the Meetings of the Council* (1971–9). *Unpublished*.

General Agreement on Tariffs and Trade. *The Tokyo Round of Multilateral Trade Negotiations. Report by the Director General of GATT*: Geneva: General Agreement on Tariffs and Trade.

—*GATT Activities*. Geneva: General Agreement on Tariffs and Trade.

—*Basic Instruments and Selected Documents Supplement* . Geneva: The Contracting Parties to the General Agreement on Tariffs and Trade .

—*International Trade*. Geneva: General Agreement on Tariffs and Trade.

United States Congress. *U.S. Code Congressional and Administrative News. Legislative History*. Saint Paul, MN. West Publishing Co.

United States Department of State. Foreign Relations of the United States, 1969–1976. Vol. 3, *Foreign Economic Policy, 1969–1972; International Monetary Policy, 1969–1972*. Washington, DC: Government Printing Office.

—Foreign Relations of the United States, 1969–1976. Vol. 31, *Foreign Economic Policy, 1973–1976*. Washington, DC: US Government Printing Office.

United States Government. *Economic Report of the President Transmitted to the Congress* Washington, DC: US Government Printing Office.

—*Annual Report of the President of the United States on the Trade Agreements Program*. Washington, DC: US Government Printing Office.

—*Public Papers of the President of the United States: John F. Kennedy*. Washington, DC: US Government Printing Office.

—*Public Papers of the President of the United States: Richard M. Nixon*. Washington, DC: US Government Printing Office.

—*Public Papers of the President of the United States: Jimmy Carter*. Washington, DC: US Government Printing Office.

US Census Bureau. *Statistical Abstract of the United States*. Washington, DC: US Government Printing Office.

World Trade Organization. *GATT documents*. Available at: www.wto.org/English/docs_e/gattdocs_e.htm [Accessed 12/10/2010].

Books

Aldcroft, Derek H. *The European Economy 1914–2000*, 4th edn. London and New York: Routledge, 2002.

Bergsten, C. Fred. *Toward a New International Economic Order. Selected Papers of C. Fred Bergsten*. Toronto: Lexington Books, 1985.

Braun, Hans-Joachim. *The German Economy in the Twentieth Century, The German Reich and the Federal Republic*. London and New York: Routledge, 1990.

Bromley, Simon. *American Hegemony and World Oil: The Industry, the State System and the World Economy*. Cambridge: Polity Press, 1991.

Buckley, Peter and Mark Casson. *The Future of the Multinational Enterprise*. London: MacMillan, 1976.

Cairncross, Alec. *The British Economy since 1945: Economic Policy and Performance, 1945–1995*, 2nd edn. Oxford: Blackwell Publishers, 1995.

Campagna, Anthony S. *U.S. National Economic Policy, 1917–1985*. New York and London: Praeger, 1987.

Coombs, Charles A. *The Arena of International Finance*. New York: John Wiley & Sons, 1976.

Cooper, Richard N. *The Economics of Interdependence. Economic Policy in the Atlantic Community*. London: McGraw Hill, 1968.

Cox, Ronald W. and Daniel Skidmore-Hess, *US Politics and the Global Economy. Corporate Power, Conservative Shift*. Boulder and London: Lynne Rienner Publisher Inc., 1999.

Curzon, Gerard and Victoria Curzon. *After the Kennedy Round. What Trade Policies Now?* London: The Atlantic Trade Study, 1967.

Destler, I. M. *Making Foreign Economic Policy*. Washington, DC: The Brooking Institution, 1980.

—*American Trade Politics*, 3rd edn. Washington, DC: Institute for International Economics; New York: Twentieth Century Fund, 1995.

Dicken, Peter. Global Shift. The Internationalization of Economic Activity, 2nd edn. London: Paul Chapman Publishing Ltd, 1992.

Duchêne, François, Edward Szczepanik and Wilffied Legg. *New Limits on European Agriculture. Politics and the New Agricultural Policy*. London: Croon Helm Ltd, 1985.

Dunning, John, *International Production and the Multinational Enterprise*. London: George Allen Unwin, 1981

Eck, Jean-François. *Histoire de l'économie française dépuis 1945*. Paris: Armand Colin Éditeur, 1990.

Farrer, T. H. *Free Trade versus Fair Trade*. London: Cassell & Company Limited, 1885.

Giersch, Herbert, Karl-Heinz Paqué and Holger Schneding. *The Fading Miracle. Four decades of market economy in Germany.* Cambridge: Cambridge University Pres, 1992.

Gilpin, Robert. *U.S. Power and the Multinational Corporation. The Political Economy of Foreign Direct Investment*. New York: Basic Books Inc. Publishers, 1975.

Glismann, H. H. and F. D. Weiss. *The Political Economy of Protection in Germany.* World Bank Staff Working Paper n. 427, 1980.

Grieco, Joseph M. *Cooperation among Nations: Europe, America, and Non-Tariff Barriers to Trade*. Ithaca and London: Cornell University Press, 1990

Grilli, Enzo. *Italian Commercial Policies in the 1970s*. World Bank Staff Working Paper n. 428, 1980.

Hau, Michel. *Histoire Économique de l'Allemagne XIXe-XXe siècles*. Paris: ECONOMICA, 1994.

Hudec, Robert E. *Enforcing International Trade Law. The Evolution of he Modern GATT Legal System*. Salem, NH: Butterworth Legal Publishers, 1993.

Iacocca, Lee. *An Autobiography*. New York: Bantam Books, 1984.

Ito, Takatoshi. *The Japanese Economy*. Cambridge, MA: The MIT Press, 1992.

Jefferys, Steeve. *Management and managed. Fifty years of crisis at Chrysler*. Cambridge: Cambridge University Press, 1986.

Johnson, D. Gale. *World Agriculture in Disarray*. London: Fontana The Trade Policy Research Centre, 1973.

Josling, T. E. *Agriculture in the Tokyo Round Negotiations*. Ashford: Headley Brothers Ltd., 1970.

Josling, Timothy E. and Stefan Tangermann T. K. Warley. *Agriculture in the GATT*. Basingstoke: MacMillan, 1996.

Kindleberger, Charles. *American Business Abroad. Six Lectures on Direct Investment*. New Haven: Yale University Press, 1969.

Kissinger, Henry A. *White House Years*. Boston: Little, Brown and Company, 1979.

—*Years of Upheaval*. Boston: Little, Brown and Company, 1982.

Maddison, Angus. *Dynamic Forces in Capitalist Development. A Long-Run Comparative View.* Oxford and New York: Oxford University Press, 1991.

McGovern, Edmond. *International Trade Regulation*. Exeter: Exeter Globefield Press, 1986.

Mandel, Ernest. *Europe versus America?: Contradiction of Imperialism*. London: N.L.B., 1970.

—*The Second Slump: A Marxist Analysis of Recession in the Seventies*. London: N.L.B, 1978.

Nagle, J. C. *Agricultural Trade Policies* .Westhead: Saxon House, 1976.

Newman, Mark, Tom Fulton and Lewrene Glaser. *A Comparison of Agriculture in the United States and the European Community*. Washington, DC: United States Department of Agriculture - Economic Research Service, 1987.

Owen Smith, Eric, *The West German Economy*. London and Canberra: Croom Helm, 1983.

—*The German Economy*. London and New York: Routledge, 1994.

Péberau, Michel. *La Politique Économique de la France. Les Objectifs*. Paris: Armand Colin, 1988.

Preeg, Ernest H. *Traders and Diplomats. An Analysis of the Kennedy Round of Negotiations under the General Agreement on Tariffs and Trade*. Washington, DC: The Brooking Institute, 1970.

Rosemberg, Samuel. *American Economic Development since 1945: Growth, Decline and Rejuvenation*. Houndmills: Palgrave MacMillan, 2003.

Rostow, W. W. *Getting from Here to There*. London: The MacMillan Press Ltd, 1979.

Servan-Schreiber, J. J. *The American Challenge*. London: Hamish Hamilton, 1968.

Shiraishi, Takashi. *Japan's Trade Policies 1945 to the Present Day*. London: The Athlone Press, 1989.

Skeet, Ian. *Opec Twenty-Five Years of Prices and Politics*. Cambridge: Cambridge University Press, 1988.

Tew, Brian. *The Evolution of the International Monetary System 1945–1981*, 2nd edn. London: Hutchinson, 1986.

Thatcher, Margaret. *The Downing Street Years 1979–1990*. New York: HarperPerennial, 1993.

Tracy, Michael. *Agriculture in Western Europe. Challenges and Responses 1880–1980*. London: Granada, 1982.

Vatter, Harold G. The U.S. Economy in the 1950s. An Economic History. New York: W. Norton & Company Inc., 1963.

Venn, Fiona. *Oil Diplomacy in the Twentieth Century*. London: MacMillan, 1986.

—*The Oil Crisis*. London and New York: Longman, 2002.

Vernon, Raymond. *Sovereignty at Bay: The Multinational Spread of U.S. Enterprises*. London: Longman Group LtD, 1971.

Viner, Jacob. *The Customs Union Issue*. London: Stevens & Sons Limited, 1950.

Williamson, John. *The Failure of the World Monetary Reform*. Sunbury on Thames: Thomas Nelson and Son Ltd, 1977.

Winham, Gilbert R. *International Trade and the Tokyo Round Negotiation*. Princeton, NJ: Princeton University Press, 1986.

Wyant, Frank R. *The United States, OPEC and Multinational Oil*. Lexington: Lexington Books, 1977.

Chapters in Edited Books

Adams, Walter and Hans Mueller. 'The Steel Industry'. In Walter Adams (ed.) *The Structure of American Industry*, 6th edn, pp. 73–135. New York: MacMillan Publishing Co. Inc., 1982.

Bianchi, Carluccio. 'The Balance of Payments Constraint and the Growth of the Italian Economy'. In Carluccio Bianchi and Carlo Casanova (eds) *The recent Performance of the Italian Economy. Market Outcomes and State Policy*, pp. 27–45. Milano: Franco Angeli, 1991.

Bordo, Michael D. 'The Bretton Woods International Monetary System: A Historical Overview'. In Michael D. Bordo and Barry Eichengree (eds) *A Retrospective of the Bretton Woods System*, pp. 3–98. Chicago and London: University of Chicago Press, 1993.

Branson, William H. 'Trends in United States International Trade and Investment since World War II'. In Martin Feldstein (ed.) *The American Economy in Transition*, pp. 182–257. Chicago and London: University of Chicago Press, 1980.

D'Adda, C. and B. Salituro. 'The Recent Performance of the Italian Economy. Market Outcomes and State Policy'. In Carluccio Bianchi e Carlo Casanova (eds) *The recent Performance of the Italian Economy. Market Outcomes and State Policy*, pp. 46–66. Milano: Franco Angeli, 1991

Eichengreen Barry, Charles W. Parry and Caldwell Philip. 'International Competition in the Products of U.S. Basic Industries'. In Martin Feldstein (ed.) *The United States in the World Economy*, pp. 279–366. Chicago and London: University of Chicago Press, 1988.

Fauvel, Luc. 'The Common Agricultural Policy of the European Economic Community and North American Exports'. In Charles P. Kindleberger and Andrew Shonfield (eds) *North American and Western European Economic Policies. Proceedings of a Conference Held by the International Economic Association*, pp. 299–336. London: MacMillan and Co. Ltd., 1971.

Foreman-Peck, James. 'Trade and the Balance of Payments'. In N. F. R. Crafts and N. W. C. Woodward (eds) *The British Economy since 1945*, pp.140–79. Oxford: Clarendon Press, 1991.

Hennings, Klaus Hinrich. 'West Germany'. In Andrea Boltho (ed.) *The European Economy: Growth and Crisis*, pp. 472–501. Oxford: Oxford University Press, 1982.

Hudec, Rober E. 'Legal Issues in US–EC Trade Policy: GATT Litigation 1960–1985'. In Robert E. Baldwin, Carl B. Hamilton and André Sapir (eds) *Issues in US–EC Relations*, pp. 17–58. Chicago and London: The University of Chicago Press, 1988.

Johnson, Gale D. 'The Food and Agriculture Act of 1977. Implications for Farmers, Consumers and Taxpayers'. In William Felner (project director) *Contemporary Economic Problems 1978*, pp. 167–209. Washington, DC: American Enterprise Institute for Public Policy Research, 1979.

Lindert, Peter H. 'U.S. Foreign Trade and Trade Policy in the Twentieth Century'. In Stanley Engerman and Robert E. Galman (eds) *The Cambridge Economic History of the United States*, pp. 407–62. Cambridge and New York: Cambridge University Press, 2000.

Lipsey, Robert E., Mario Schimberni and Robert V. Lindsay, 'Changing Patterns of International Investment in and by the United States'. In Martin Feldstein (ed.) *The*

United States in the World Economy, pp. 475–558. Chicago and London: University of Chicago Press, 1988.

Llewellin, John and Stephen Polter. 'Competitiveness and the Current Account'. In Andrea Boltho (ed.) *The European Economy: Growth and Crisis*, pp. 132–58. Oxford: Oxford University Press, 1982.

Maunder, Peter. 'International Trade'. In W. P. J. Maunder (ed.) *The British Economy in the 1970s*, pp. 247–78. London: Heinemann Educational Books, 1980.

Morgan, A. D. 'Commercial Policy'. In F. T. Blackaby (ed.) British Economic Policy 1960–74, pp. 515–63. Cambridge: Cambridge University Press, 1978.

Pelzman, Joseph, 'The Multifiber Arrangement and Its Effect on the Profit Performance of the U.S. Textile Industry'. In Robert E. Baldwin and Anne O. Kruger (eds) *The Structure and Evolution of Recent U.S. Trade Policy*, pp. 111–40. Chicago and London: The University of Chicago Press, 1984.

Rey, Guido. 'Italy'. In Andrea Boltho (ed.) *The European Economy: Growth and Crisis*, pp. 502–27. Oxford: Oxford University Press, 1982.

Sautter, Christian. 'France'. In Andrea Boltho (ed.) *The European Economy: Growth and Crisis*, pp. 450–71. Oxford: Oxford University Press, 1982.

Schenk, Catherine R.' Foreign Trade and Payments in Western Union'. In Max-Stephan Schulze (ed.) *Western Europe Economic and Social Change since 1945*, pp. 105–21. London and New York: Longman, 1999.

Tarr, David G. 'The Steel Crisis in the United States and the European Communities: Causes and Adjustments'. In Robert E. Baldwin, Carl B. Hamilton and André Sapir (eds) *Issues in US-EC Relations*, pp. 173–98. Chicago and London: The University of Chicago Press, 1988.

Tew, J. H. B. 'Policies Aimed at Improving the Balance of Payments'. In F. T. Blackaby (ed.) British Economic Policy 1960–74, pp. 304–53. Cambridge: Cambridge University Press, 1978.

Woodward, N. W. C. 'Inflation'. In N. F. R. Crafts and N. W. C. Woodward (eds) *The British Economy since 1945*, pp. 180–211. Oxford: Clarendon Press, 1991.

Articles

Abegglen, James C. and Thomas M. Hout. 'Facing up the Trade Gap with Japan'. *Foreign Affairs*, 57 (1978–79), pp. 146–69.

Balassa, Bela. 'The New Protectionism and the International Economy'. *Journal of World Trade Law* 12 (1978), pp. 409–36.

Bardan, Benyamin. 'The Cotton Textile Agreement 1962–1972'. *Journal of World Trade Law*, 7 (1973), pp. 8–35.

Bergland, Bob, 'Agriculture'. *Law and Policy in International Business*'. 12 (1980), pp. 257–65.

Cleveland, Harold Van B. and Ramachandra Bhagavatula. 'The Continuing World Economic Crisis'. *Foreign Affairs*, 59 (1980–1), pp. 584–616.
Cohn, Theodore. 'The 1978–9 negotiations for an international wheat agreement: an opportunity lost?'. *International Journal*, 35 (1979–80), pp. 132–49.
Coret, Hugh. 'Importance of Being Earnest about Further GATT Negotiations'. *The World Economy*, 2 (1979), pp. 319–41.
Curzon Price, Victoria. 'Surplus Capacity and What the Tokyo Round Failed to Settle'. *The World Economy*, 2 (1979), pp. 305–18.
Danielsen, Albert L. 'Oil Price Regulations and the United States'. *Journal of World Trade Law*, 13 (1979), pp. 383–94.
Finger, J. M., H. K. Halland and D. R. Nelson. 'The Political Economy of Administered Protection'. *The American Economic Review*, 72 (1982), pp. 452–56.
Houch, James P. 'U.S. Agricultural Trade and the Tokyo Round Agriculture'. *Law and Policy in International Business*, 12 (1980), pp. 265–96.
Houillier, François. 'Agriculture et son Évolution Depuis 1960 (La situation en 1977)'. *Revue d'Économie Politique*, 88 (1978), pp. 894–918.
Lorenzen, Shelley A. 'Technical Analysis of the Anti-Dumping Agreement and the Trade Agreement Act'. *Law and Policy in International Business*, 11 (1979), pp. 1405–16.
McLeod, Alex N. 'The Fearsome Dilemma: Simultaneous Inflation and Unemployment'. *Banca Nazionale del Lavoro Quarterly Review*, 32 (1979), pp. 377–89.
Mueller, Hans and Hans Van der Ven. 'Perils in the Brussels–Washington Steel Pact of 1982'. *The World Economy*, 5 (1982), pp. 123–42.
Platel, Régis. 'L'Environnement International en 1980'. *Revue d'Économie Politique*, 91 (1981), pp. 836–56.
Pomeranz, Norton. 'Toward a New International Order in Government Procurement'. *Law and Policy in International Business*, 11 (1979), pp. 1263–300.
Rivers, Richard R. and Greenwald John D. 'The Negotiations of a Code on Subsidies and Countervailing Measures: Bridging Fundamental Policy Differences'. *Law and Policy in International Business*, 11 (1979), pp. 1447–96.
Secret, Pierre. 'L'Activité Économique Française En 1974'. Révue d'Économie Politique, 85 (1975), pp. 1035–55.
Sherman, Saul L. 'Reflections on the New Customs Valuation Code'. *Law and Policy in International Business*, 12 (1980), pp. 119–58.
Shonfield, Andrew. 'The World Economy 1979'. *Foreign Affairs*. 58 (1979–80), pp. 596–621.
Taake, Hans-Helmut and Dieter Weiss. 'The World Textile Agreement: The Exporter's Viewpoint'. *Journal of World Trade Law*, 8 (1974), pp. 624–54.
Thirlwall, A. P. 'The Balance of Payments Constraint as An Explanation of International Growth Rate Differences'. *Banca Nazionale del Lavoro Quarterly Review*, 32 (1979), pp. 45–53.
Van Bael Ivo. 'Ten Years of EEC Antidumping Enforcement'. *Journal of World Trade Law*, 13 (1979), pp. 395–408.

Volle, Michel. 'Synthèse de l'Évolution de l'Économie Française en 1980 et 1981'. *Revue d'Économie Politique*, 91 (1981), pp. 810–37.

Winham, Gilbert R. 'Robert Strauss, the MTN and the Control of Faction'. *Journal of World Trade Law*, 14 (1980), pp. 377–97.

Index

ACTN *see* Advisory Committee for Trade Negotiations
Ad Hoc Group on Steel 95
Advisory Committee for Trade Negotiations (ACTN) 74
Aérospatiale 98
Afghanistan, Soviet invasion 164
agricultural commodities 78
agricultural policy 13
agricultural subsidies 78
agricultural trade 45
agriculture 11, 13, 14–20, 27, 45, 79, 82–3, 90, 99–102, 116–20, 136–7, 141, 164–6
Agriculture Act (1955) 18
Agriculture and Consumer Protection Act (1973) 44
Agriculture, Department of 165
Airbus 98
Airbus Industrie 98
aircraft 126–7, 135–6
Aircraft Agreement 129, 135
aircraft industry 90
Algeria 61
American Iron and Steel Institute 96
American Selling Price (ASP) 28, 30, 32, 73, 81, 122, 129, 133, 157
American Television Industry 111
antidumping 107–8, 109, 112, 122, 124–6, 132, 134, 141, 156–7, 161–2, 174, 175
  duties 133–4
Antidumping Act 76, 93
antidumping rules, EC 109
Argentina 119, 165
Arusha Convention 13
ASP *see* American Selling Price
Association of West European Shipbuilders (AWES) 92
Australia 3, 101, 118, 119, 120, 141, 165, 166
Automobile Importers of America 157
AWES *see* Association of West European Shipbuilders

BAC *see* British Aircraft Corporation
Baghdad Conference 61
balance of payments 1, 11, 75, 106
Bank of England 41
Barre Plan 70
Belgium *see also* Benelux countries 23, 24, 60, 61, 94, 109, 170
Benelux countries 16, 40
Bergland, Bob 117
Boeing 98, 127
Bonn Summit 89, 125
Bovine Meat Arrangement 137
Brazil 3
Bremen European Council 147
'Bresciani firms' 94, 162
Bretton Woods 34–45, 68
British Aircraft Corporation (BAC) 98
Brussels Convention 81
Brussels Definition of Value (BVD) 81, 122
Bundesbank 9, 40, 68, 144
Butz, Earl L. 43
Buy American Act 82, 129–30, 135
  repeal 103
BVD *see* Brussels Definition of Value

Canada 40, 84, 101, 109, 119, 125, 126, 131, 141, 165, 166
CAP *see* Common Agricultural Policy
Carter, Jimmy 87, 89–90, 93, 96, 128, 146, 160, 164
Carter administration 116–27, 145, 154, 157, 165, 172
CASA 98
CCC *see* Commodity Credit Corporation
cereals 52
China 15, 44, 130–41, 165
Chrysler 170
  bail out 158–61, 165

CIF *see* cost, insurance, freight
civil transport aircraft 98–9
clothing industry 96–7, 163
coal 60, 144
Commerce, Department of 160
Commission on International Trade and Investments 33
Committee on Anti-Dumping Practices 141
Commodity Credit Corporation (CCC) 44, 100, 165
commodity tax 111
Common Agricultural Policy (CAP) 12, 13, 17–19, 20, 27, 33, 48, 52, 56, 57, 86, 100, 101, 116, 166, 175
Common Customs Tariff 131–2
Common Market 12, 23, 24, 132, 140
Commonwealth 11, 12, 15
  sugar agreement 13
Community Common Commercial Policy 54
Concorde 98
Connally, John 35
Consumer Price Index (CPI) 7
  Italy 66
  UK 66
  USA 66
cost of living 13
Cost of Living Council 63
Cost Stabilization Program 45
cost, insurance, freight (CIF) 19
Cotton Textile Arrangement 17
Council of Agricultural Ministers 19
Council of Economic Advisers 160
Council of the Community 129
countervailing duties 124–6, 132, 174, 175
countervailing measures 133–4, 155
Court of Customs and Patent Appeals 111
CPI *see* Consumer Price Index
currency convertibility 22
current account balance 143
customs duties 50
customs valuation 122–3, 133

d'Estaing, Giscard 41
Dahrendorf, Ralf 33
dairy products 52, 120
Denmark 12, 39, 84, 94, 151
Deutsche Airbus 98
Deutschmark 6, 8–9, 42, 68, 148, 153, 170
  revaluation 6, 9
developing countries 43, 119, 123, 137, 138
Dillon Round 46
DISCs *see* Domestic International Trade Corporations
dollar (US currency) 1, 2, 11, 34, 36–7, 41
  depreciation 61, 108, 164, 169
  devaluation 37–8, 39, 67, 108, 117
  overvaluation 34
Domestic International Sales Corporations (DISCs) 36, 85
domestic subsidies 134

EAGGF *see* European Agricultural Guidance and Guarantee Fund
Eastern Europe 44
Eberle, William 38
EC *see* European Community
Economic and Social Committee 27, 52
economic development 50
economy, internationalization 14
ECSC *see* European Coal and Steel Community
ECU *see* European Currency Unit
EEC *see* European Economic Community
EFTA *see* European Free Trade Association
electronics industry 170
Emergency Agricultural Act (1978) 100
employment 91
EMS *see* European Monetary System
Energy Coordination Group 62
Energy, Department of 160
Energy Policy and Conservation Act 63
energy prices 5
ENI 64
Ertl, Josef 101
ESCS *see* European Coal and Steel Community
European Agricultural Guidance and Guarantee Fund (EAGGF) 101
European Coal and Steel Community (ECSC) 3, 109
  Treaty 163
European Commission 46, 115, 121, 129, 165
  subsidies 80
European Common Market 101

European Community (EC) 8, 22, 28, 30, 39, 48, 50–2, 77, 85, 102–4, 115, 116, 119, 120–1, 122, 126, 131, 132, 136, 146–51, 166
agricultural policy 38
agricultural trade 45
agriculture 18
antidumping rules 109
Commission 97
Council 78–9, 84
crude steel production 94
currency system 147
Economic and Social Committee 27
enlargement 84
farmers 27
shipyards 91
steel industry 94, 162
textile industry 14–15
European Council 50, 55, 90, 94
European Court of Justice 101
European Currency Unit (ECU) 146–8
European Free Trade Association (EFTA) 12, 95, 131, 132
European Monetary System (EMS) 147
European Regional Development Fund 92
exchange rate 6, 8
realignments 2
excise tax 136
export practices 52
export subsidies 20

fair trade 30
Fair Trade and Investment Bill 47
farms 99
Farrer, T. H. 29
FDI *see* Foreign Direct Investment
Federal Reserve (FED) 7, 10, 34, 145–6
Federal Reserve Bank of New York 39
FIAT 171
Final List products 133
Finance Committee 32, 74
floating exchange rate regime 39–41
Fokker-VFW 98
Food and Agriculture Act (1977) 99–100
food prices 45
food production 44
Ford, Gerald 67–8, 71–2
Ford Motor Company 160, 170
Foreign Direct Investment (FDI) 21–2, 23–4, 25, 146, 169, 171
foreign investment 21
franc 8, 41
devaluation 8, 9
France 2, 4, 6, 16, 18, 23, 40, 41, 42, 55, 62, 69, 70, 92, 97, 101, 109, 111, 123, 127, 148, 165, 168, 172
agriculture 52
devaluation 6, 8, 9
economy 9
farmers 18
GDP 70, 148–9
growth rate 9
inflation 149
petroleum consumption 63
Fukuda, Takeo 89, 104

G7 88–90
G7 Declaration 144
G10 38
gasoline 66
GATT *see* General Agreement on Tariffs and Trade
GDP *see* gross domestic product
General Agreement on Tariffs and Trade (GATT) 16, 20, 25, 29, 31, 45, 53–4, 55, 56, 76, 77, 78–9, 80–1, 82, 84, 85–6, 95, 101, 102, 105, 107, 110, 111, 113, 116, 117, 118, 119, 123, 124, 125, 126, 127, 129, 130, 131, 133, 135, 137–8, 140, 156, 163, 164, 168, 171, 173, 174, 175, 177
trade negotiations 46–57
General Motors 170
Generalized System of Preferences 52, 77
German Mark *see* Deutschmark
Germany 2, 4, 5, 6, 8, 16, 18, 23, 40, 41, 42, 60, 61, 68, 70, 88, 89, 92, 94, 101, 109, 112, 127, 148, 152, 163, 168, 170, 172
exports 42
GDP 148
petroleum consumption 63
revaluation 6
gold 37, 38, 40
Government Procurement (GPR) 123–4, 135, 139
Government Procurement Agreement 130

government-owned companies 140
GPR *see* Government Procurement
gross domestic product (GDP) 2, 4, 8–9, 30, 42, 65, 69, 147
  growth rate 5
Group of Ten 38
growth 5, 42, 67–8, 89, 90–104
Gundelach, Olav 117, 137

Haferkamp, Wilhelm 104, 117, 128
Hawker Siddeley 98
heating oil 66
Hegel, Georg Wilhelm Friedrich 105
high-technology sector 168–9
Hong Kong 15, 17, 97, 138
House of Representative
  Ways and Means Committee 32

Iacocca, Lee 158
IBM *see* International Business Machines
IDA *see* International Dairy Agreement
IEA *see* International Energy Agency
imports 7, 11, 31
  quotas 19–20, 32
industrial tariffs 120–1, 131–2
industry 14–20
inflation 1, 9, 11, 36, 42–5, 59, 64, 65, 67, 69, 88, 89, 143, 145–6
Interest Equalization Tax 35
interest rates 9
internal subsidies 134
International Business Machines (IBM) 33
International Dairy Agreement (IDA) 136
International Energy Agency (IEA) 62, 143
International Monetary Fund (IMF) 22–3, 41, 46
international monetary system 144
International Trade Commission (ITC) 75, 160
International Wheat Agreement (IWA) 118–19, 137
  Conference 137
International Wheat Council (IWC) 44, 118–19
internationalization 14
Iraq 61
Ireland 12, 23, 39, 84, 87, 94
Italy 2, 4, 6, 8, 10, 16, 23, 64, 69, 92, 109, 111
  consumer price index 66
  economy 69
  GDP 10, 69, 149
  inflation 149
  manufacturing industry 10
  trade deficit 149–50
ITC *see* International Trade Commission
IWA *see* International Wheat Agreement
IWC *see* International Wheat Council

Japan 1, 6, 15, 17, 40, 42, 48, 56, 59, 61, 62, 85, 87, 88, 89, 91, 92–3, 95, 102–4, 106, 109, 119, 123–4, 125, 126, 128, 129, 131, 153, 162, 166, 168, 171, 172
  agricultural trade 45
  exports 48
  surplus 103
  tariff rates 102
  trade policy 102
Jewish emigration 72
Johnson, Lyndon B. 6

Kennedy, John F. 20, 24
Kennedy administration 15, 29–30
Kennedy Agreement 28
Kennedy Round 11, 27–9, 47, 73, 80, 119, 156, 173
Kissinger, Henry 62
Kohl, Helmut 113
Korea 97, 172

labour costs 5, 68
Latin America 170
Libya 61
livestock feed 101
Lockheed 98
Loi d'Orientation Agricole 101
London Gold Pool 34
Long Term Arrangement (LTA) 15–16, 175
LTA *see* Long Term Arrangement
Luxembourg *see also* Benelux countries 23, 87, 94

Mark *see* Deutschmark
McDonnell Douglas 98

medium term note (MTN)
agreements 130
code 155
MFA *see* Multifibre Arrangement
MFN *see* Most-Favored Nation
Michelin S.A. 110
Middle East 143
Mill, Wilbur D. 32
minimum import prices (MIP) 101–2
MIP *see* minimum import prices
MNCs see multinational corporations
monetary policy 40
monetary system 55
money supply 9, 42
Most-Favored Nation (MFN) 49–51, 78, 105, 131, 138
MTN *see* medium term note
Multifibre Arrangement (MFA) 17, 96–7, 106
multinational corporations (MNCs) 21–5, 34, 43, 48, 170–1

national product 42–5
National Railways 103
National Union of Miners 60
Netherlands *see also* Benelux countries 18, 23, 24, 60, 61, 70, 101
New Deal Agricultural Adjustment Act 19
New Orderly Marketing Agreements 163
New Zealand 13
Newly Industrialized Countries (NICs) 91, 92–3, 138, 153
NFDM *see* non-fat dairy milk
NICs *see* Newly Industrialized Countries
Nixon, Richard 31, 36–8, 48–9, 53, 62
Nixon administration 30, 35
non-fat dairy milk (NDFM) 101
non-tariff barriers (NTBs) 73–5, 77, 78, 118, 129, 138–9, 141, 155
North Sea oil 64, 69, 150–1
Norway 12, 39, 40
NTBs *see* non-tariff barriers
nuclear power 144

OAPEC *see* Organization of Arab Petroleum Exporting Countries
OECD *see* Organisation for Economic Co-operation and Development
oil consumption 144
oil crisis 59, 60–4, 91, 92, 96, 97, 106, 143, 149–50
oil, North Sea 64, 69
oil price 61, 64–6, 143–4, 145, 149
oil supply 60
OMAs *see* Orderly Market Agreements
OPEC *see* Organization of Petroleum Exporting Countries
Orderly Market Agreements (OMAs) 106, 175
Organisation for Economic Co-operation and Development 42, 64, 66, 82, 87, 92, 95, 96, 123, 136, 143, 151, 162, 173, 176
inflation 71
Organization of Arab Petroleum Exporting Countries (OAPEC) 61–2
Organization of Petroleum Exporting Countries (OPEC) 60–1, 62, 63, 66, 77, 143, 144, 151, 153

Paris European Summit 54
petrochemical sector 164
Philips 171
Poland 15
Pompidou, Georges 38, 41
Portugal 14, 61
pound (UK currency) 10, 37, 41
devaluation 11
productivity 5, 59
profit margins 108
protectionism 14–20, 31, 33, 109, 115–16, 122, 173–4, 176
public procurement 135

quota restrictions 106

raw materials 43
Reagan, Ronald 159, 160
recession 7, 64–71, 72, 85, 90–104, 125, 161, 176
Reciprocal Tariff Act (1934) 53
Rehm, John 157
restitution payments 19
Revenue Act (1962) 25
Revenue Act (1964) 6
Ricardo's paradox 14

Rome Treaty 23, 54
Roosa Bonds 34

Saudi Arabia 62
Scandinavian countries 56, 131
Schelling, Frederic 105
Schmidt, Helmut 89
SCM *see* Subsidies and Countervailing Measures
SDRs *see* Special Drawing Rights
Securities Investor Protection Act 7
'Seven Sisters' 61
shipbuilding 90–2
  Japan 91
  UK 90–1
  USA 90–1
shipyards 91
  EC 91
Shultz, George 40
Siemens 171
SME 148
Smithsonian Agreement 34–8, 39, 46
'snake in the tunnel' 39, 41, 147
social agriculture 18
Solomon, Anthony 93
South Africa 61
South Korea 17, 106–7, 138
Soviet Union *see* Union of Soviet Socialist Republics
Special Drawing Rights (SDRs) 135
Special Trade Representative 74–5
stagflation 7
steel 90
Steel Committee 95
steel industry 17, 27, 92–6, 130
  EC 94
Strauss, Robert Schwarz 103, 116–17, 121, 128, 138–9
subsidies 19, 80, 110, 124–6, 133–4, 136, 155, 156
  domestic 134
  farm export 137
  internal 134
Subsidies and Countervailing Measures (SCM) 133, 139–40
subsidization 14–20, 111–12, 118, 119, 124, 134, 162
sugar 52
Supplementary Understanding on Internal Subsidies 125
Sweden 23, 39, 40, 109, 126
Switzerland 40
synthetic fibres industry 96–7

Taiwan 17, 97, 106–7, 138, 172
Tariff Act (1897) 110
Tariff Act (1922) 110
tariff barriers 105
tariff compensation 84
tariff protection 112
tariff rates 139
tariffs 27–9, 31, 49, 50–1, 118, 126, 131, 174
  reductions 132
Tax Reduction and Simplification Act 1977 87
Telephone and Telegraph Public Corporation 103
textile industry 14–15, 16, 27, 32, 90, 96–7, 130, 163
Thatcher, Margaret 113, 150
Thatcher administration 150–1
  monetarist policy 150–1
Thomson 171
TNC *see* Trade Negotiations Committee
Tokyo Conference 57
Tokyo Declaration 56, 79, 144
Tokyo Round 30, 53, 55, 79–83, 103, 115, 117, 118, 123, 127, 128, 130–41, 154–8, 159, 164, 169, 171, 172, 177
Tokyo Summit 144
TPM *see* Trigger Price Mechanism
Trade Act (1974) 71–7, 85–6, 103, 105, 110, 120, 128, 130, 131, 154, 160, 175
Trade Act proposals 29–33
Trade Agreements Act (1979) 154–7
trade balance 14, 143, 151–3
trade barriers 168, 176
Trade Expansion Act (1962) 14, 31, 72, 105, 175
Trade Facilitation Committee 103
trade growth 42–5
Trade Negotiations Committee (TNC) 56, 79, 82–3
trade policies 85–6
Trade Reform Act 48, 53
trade relations 59

Trades Union Congress (TUC) 150
Transportation, Department of 160
Treasury Department 76–7, 111
Treaty of Rome 101, 111
Trigger Price Mechanism (TPM) 93, 94, 161–2
TUC *see* Trades Union Congress

UAW *see* United Automobile Workers
UNCTAD *see* United Nations Conference on Trade and Development
unemployment 6, 10–11, 72, 89, 125, 143, 147, 176
Union of Soviet Socialist Republics (USSR) 44, 50, 72, 164–5
  invasion of Afghanistan 164
United Automobile Workers (UAW) 158, 160
United Kingdom (UK) 2, 4, 6, 10, 15, 23, 39, 42, 60, 69, 84, 92, 97, 109, 111, 150, 166, 170
  Conservative government 13, 150
  consumer price index 66
  devaluation 6, 11
  GDP 150
  imports 10, 11
  inflation 69, 150
  Labour government 10, 37, 127, 150
  petroleum consumption 63
  recession 69
  steel industry 112
United Nations Conference on Trade and Development (UNCTAD) 77
United States (US) 1–8, 47–50, 61, 78, 80, 84, 85, 102–4, 115, 119, 120, 123, 125, 126, 127, 131, 132, 135, 136, 140, 145–6, 166
  agricultural exports 100
  agriculture 43, 44, 117
  aircraft industry 4
  automotive industry 30, 158–61
  balance of payments 6, 25, 34–5, 46
  balance of payments deficit 8
  car industry 2–3
  chemical industry 4
  consumer price index 66
  current account 152
  deficit 1
  Department of Commerce 1
  discount rate 7
  economic policy 34–8
  economy 3, 7
  exports 7, 23, 42
  farm exports 117
  farm industry 99
  Federal Reserve 145–6
  GDP 6, 68, 152
  GNP 145–6
  growth 67–8
  imports 1, 7, 14, 17
  inflation 7, 67–8, 152
  interest rates 161
  Japanese exports 3
  oil consumption 63
  productivity 4
  recovery 88
  steel industry 3, 161–3
  Tariff Commission 28, 32
  tax policy 68
  tax system 25
  taxation 36
  textile industry 3, 15, 30
  trade balance 2–3, 25, 37, 67, 152
  trade deficit 1
  Treasury 34, 36
  utility industries 4
  war in Vietnam 6
Uruguay Round 115–41, 157
US Steel Corporation 161–2
US Trade Representative (USTR) 157, 160, 161
USA *see* United States of America
USSR *see* Union of Soviet Socialist Republics
USTR *see* US Trade Representative

value added tax (VAT) 111, 140, 150
Vanik Amendment 50
VAT *see* value added tax
VER *see* voluntary export restriction
Vietnam 6, 35
Volcker, Paul 40, 145
Volkswagen 3
voluntary export restraint (VER) 17, 95, 106, 175

wages 5
Washington Energy Conference 62
Watergate scandal 49
Ways and Means Committee 32, 74–5

Werner Report 39
West Germany *see* Germany
Western Europe 4, 5, 22
Wheat Trade Convention 119
Wholesale Price Index (WPI) 7
Williams, Albert 33
Williams Commission 33, 46
Wine Gallon Assessment 129
world economy 72
WPI *see* Wholesale Price Index

Yaoundé Convention 13
yen 108, 153
Yom Kippur War 61, 64

Zenith Radio Corporation 111